THE 7:47 CONNECTION

CALLED TO A HIGHER ALTITUDE

Don't Miss Your Connection!

NONYE AKUBA

Although the publisher and the author have made every effort to ensure that the information in this book was correct at press time and while this publication is designed to provide accurate information in regard to the subject matter covered, the publisher and the author assume no responsibility for errors, inaccuracies, omissions, or any other inconsistencies herein and hereby disclaim any liability to any party for any loss, damage, or disruption caused by errors or omissions, whether such errors or omissions result from negligence, accident, or any other cause.

The publisher and the author make no guarantees concerning the level of success you may experience by following the advice and strategies contained in this book, and you accept the risk that results will differ for each individual. The testimonials and examples provided in this book show exceptional results, which may not apply to the average reader, and are not intended to represent or guarantee that you will achieve the same or similar results.

The content of this book is for informational purposes only and is not intended to diagnose, treat, cure, or prevent any condition or disease. You understand that this book is not intended as a substitute for consultation with a licensed practitioner. Please consult with your own physician or healthcare specialist regarding the suggestions and recommendations made in this book. The use of this book implies your acceptance of this disclaimer.

Copyright @ 2022 by Nonye Akuba

All rights reserved. No part of this publication may be reproduced, distributed, or transmitted in any form or by any means, including photocopying, recording, or other electronic or mechanical methods, without the prior written permission of the author, except in the case of brief quotations embodied in critical reviews and certain other noncommercial uses permitted by copyright.

Unless otherwise noted, all Scripture quotations are
taken from the King James Version of the Bible

Abbrievation Legion

AMP- The Amplified Bible	KJV- King James Version
NAS – New American Standard	NLV – New Life Bible
NKJV – New King James Version	NLT – New Living Translation

Anointed Hustle Books/The House of Noa Media Trade Paperback
ISBN: 978-1-7334793-0-1
eBook ISBN: 978-1-7334793-5-6
Book Cover design by Semnitz™
Published in the United States of America

ACKNOWLEDGEMENTS

First and foremost I must thank Elohim Chayim for choosing me as the vessel to bring this idea and concept to fruition. It has been a reality-shifting and life-altering experience, as well as a remarkably awakening, humbling and empowering journey. I wish I could thank each of you that have touched my life and soul specifically, yet there are far too many names to mention. It is my desire that you know I am forever grateful as you are inextricably included in the host of sisters and brothers in Christ that have poured into me and/ or have prayed for me over the years. I would also like to thank all of you that have participated in teaching me many of life's lessons, both palatable and difficult, but all necessary for my growth. A special thanks to my divine destiny helpers, burden bearers, my dear sister friend, Kim Barnes, and my daughter, Xiaoli Naira-Iman. You are all loved and appreciated.

Isaiah 43:19

"Behold, I will do a new thing; now it shall spring forth; shall ye not know it? I will even make a way in the wilderness, and rivers in the desert."

King James Version (KJV)

Table of Contents

INTRODUCTION 1

PART I: IDENTIFICATION CHECKPOINT 5
   EARLY SIGNS THERE IS A FIRST-CLASS TICKET WITH YOUR NAME ON IT 6
      HIDDEN IDENTITY 6
      THE OUTSIDER 11
      HYPER-SHIFTING CAREERS/PURPOSE 14
      YOU'VE BEEN MARKED 15
      HIGHWAY ROBBERY/DEMONIC HIJACKING 20
      DISCARDED CLUES AND HINTS 21
      PROPHETIC HERITAGE 24
      INEXPLICABLY LONG WILDERNESS SEASON 25
      SPIRITUAL WARFARE 27
      JOSEPH'S BLUNDER 31
      WORDLY FORFEITURE 32

PART II: NOW BOARDING 36
   SIGNS IT'S TIME TO CATCH YOUR 747 CONNECTION 37
      POSITIVE ID 37
      HE'S CLEANING YOU UP 41
      ACQUIESENCE TO DESTINY DESTRUCTION 42
      DESTINY DESTROYERS 44

PART III: FASTEN YOUR SEATBELTS 51
   YOUR HOLY PAUSE EXPERIENCE 52
   ILLEGAL PAUSE 55
   SLEEPING BEAUTY 58
   ONSLAUGHT BY THE COUNTERFEIT: 61

> CONFRONTATION WITH WITCHCRAFT: 63
> A CLOSER LOOK: ENEMY SPIRITS 68
> POSTURE WHEN CONFRONTING THE DEMONIC......... 87

PART IV: EMERGENCY EXIT 92
> EXPOSURE OF THE ENEMY 93
> BATTLE IN THE NATURAL/PHYSICAL REALM 93
> BATTLE IN THE SPIRITUAL REALM 95

PART V: FULL UPRIGHT POSITION 100
> HOW TO DEFEAT THE ENEMY 101
>> ARSENAL FOR SPIRITUAL WARFARE 101
>> THE AWAKENING 105
>> PROPHETIC REVELATION (POSITION/OFFICE) 106

PART VI: PREPARE FOR TAKEOFF 119
> HOW TO ADVANCE TO YOUR PROMISE 120

PART VII: TAKE OFF AND CLIMB 128
> POTENTIAL FLIGHT HAZARDS 129

PART VIII: CRUISE CONTROL 155
> LIFT VS. WEIGHT 156
> TURBULENCE 157
> PUSHING PAST THE PAIN 159
> PRESS FORWARD 165
> YOU WILL BE VICTORIOUS 168

PART IX: CLEARED TO LAND 171
> YOU ARE ANOINTED 172

PART X: PREPARE FOR LANDING: YOUR FINAL
DESTINATION 177
> THE 747 ANOINTING 178

THE ABIDING ANOINTING 178
FIRE ANOINTING 180
PROVISION ANOINTING (MANNA) 182
OVERCOMER'S ANOINTING 185
ROYALTY ANOINTING 190
DOMINION ANOINTING 194
WEALTH ANOINTING 199
THE ACCELARATION ANOINTING 206
THE ANOINTING OF GOD'S FIERCE RETRIBUTION .. 210
HEALING ANOINTING 218
THE EAGLE AND THE LIONNESS ANOINTINGS 227
THE EAGLE ANOINTING 228
THE EAGLE ANOINTING: A CLOSER LOOK 232
THE LION ANOINTING 237
THE LIONESS ANOINTING: A CLOSER LOOK 241
THE BATTLE, THE ENEMY AND ITS VENOM 245
AFTERWORD 248

Introduction

I have always felt deep inside that my life had a calling. My earliest memory of this is at some point during high school. It was a thought that passed one day as I lay on my mother's living room carpet and watched television. I recall the thought being somewhere along the lines of, "What if God wanted me to preach?" I seriously pondered the thought and felt this knowing, a resonance in my spirit that I was somehow on the mark. But I quickly brushed it off. "Nah, can't be. Not me, not the kid!" The thought of it as I came back to myself was so ludicrous, so unwelcomed, and quickly rejected because I knew for sure that life was not meant for me. I had no desire to live anywhere near the straight and narrow road. I wasn't as bad as I could be, but I definitely had no desire to be any better.

And unfortunately, or fortunately, depending on how much you believe that everything that happened to me was His plan, it took me forty-seven (yes, forty-seven) years to get here. Is it a coincidence that God led me to name my ministry The 747 Connection? Probably not. Though I do not believe in coincidences. I do, however, believe in God, winks, as explained by Squire D. Rushnell. And I believe God, the Most High, Elohim, Yeshua Hamashiach, the Holy Spirit, whatever name that you are most comfortable calling the God of Israel, called me to write this book at this particular time, for a particular purpose and a particular woman having a particular experience. If you are currently turning the pages of this book, that woman may indeed be you, and I believe God is calling you to a higher level of intimacy, purpose, and understanding of Him and His plan for your life.

In the pages of this book that follow, I will do my best to reveal how God unfolded this level of increased partnership with Him in my life. I do believe that this book is God-inspired. I had no idea how to start it, how to organize it, word it, or what purpose He had for it. But I do know that the Holy Spirit has held my hand the entire way—whispering new ideas, concepts, and relationships in my ear or nudging me to pay attention to patterns as I looked back over the life I've had up until this point. It is my sincere desire that this book serves as a kind of honing device to lead my sisters in Christ to a deeper sense of knowing who they are in Christ and why He has made you exactly how you are with the specific experiences you have endured. My prayer is that you can use many of the signposts enumerated in the book to determine where you currently are in the process and to identify and then execute the steps necessary to elevate to a higher plane and remain victorious.

WHY 747?

The 747 Connection is a specific and unique calling from God which He placed on my heart and revealed to me in April 2022. During my morning prayer time and while in a posture of pouring out my heart to the Lord, the Holy Spirit led me to Luke 7:47. The pages of my bible literally opened to the page, and as I laid my eyes on the verse, I began to cry uncontrollably although I had read the verse many times before this moment. If you are not familiar with the passage, it references the woman who approached Jesus with an Alabaster box and then broke the box to release the fresh, poignant, expensive scent of spikenard, which she utilized to anoint Jesus's head in oil. The men surrounding Jesus at the time looked on in horror, for she was thought to be an unclean woman of ill repute. They regarded her as a woman with too many sins to be afforded the privilege of touching their Lord and who was wasting

Introduction

expensive oil that could be sold for profit. When I revealed the purposes for which God has called me, many people who knew me at different stages of my life felt the same way. Just as old friends, colleagues, and lovers felt it inconceivable, unbelievable, and deemed it totally unreasonable, so did the men surrounding Jesus during this account recorded by Luke. Jesus, however, perceives the indignation, repulsion, and nonbelief in their hearts and shares a parable with the men to describe why the woman's actions, sacrifice, and reverence of him were welcomed, accepted, ranked high, and deeply touching.

I invite you to read the story for yourself in Luke 7:36-50, so you can bear witness to the clear point Jesus makes by sharing the parable and then posing this question which I have paraphrased, "Who is more thankful to the creditor that forgives a debt, a person whose debts are few, or the person whose debt is great?" In the same manner, who is more thankful for salvation and the forgiveness of their sins? The person whose sins are few that expects to some degree to enjoy the inheritance of eternal life, or the woman who knows she has sinned so much that the mere thought of him being loving enough to allow her share in his kingdom brings her to tears each time she thinks about it? This is the scripture on which this body of anointing is hinged. It is a crown that is placed on the women who have suffered due to rash or immature decisions, who have been rejected, exiled, ostracized, abandoned, mocked, and yet still chose each time to praise Him, trust Him, remain on the straight and arrow, and to give of what they had even when they were hungry themselves. No matter how many times they may have backslid, they return with a contrite heart and humble spirit until they realize there is no greater love than God and continuously choose Him time and time again. We must always remember that God calls people we personally would never choose. And let me be totally transparent here and share: if I were God, I would not be my top choice.

After reading the verse, I turned to the internet's Hebrew strong search engine to type in 747, and there it stated, "Beacon of Light." I knew

Christ was sharing how he saw me no matter what I had been through; the detours, the missteps, the outright insolent disobedience. He still saw me as a beacon of light, someone who could share my experiences with others and be trustworthy enough to lead them to Him. After this encounter, the Holy Spirit began to reveal my full identity in Christ, my position in the kingdom, who He called me to be, and what He called me to do.

Shortly after the Lord revealed the scripture to me and my position in the kingdom, a prophetic word was released over me that spoke of a gold plane soaring to higher and higher heights. Bells went off in my head with an alarm—747, a gold plane. Could this prophecy be specifically for me? Could it have anything to do with the earlier revelation of how Jesus saw me? Again, I do not believe in coincidences.

I began to research the history of the 747. I needed to understand what God wanted me to know about myself and my identity. It was then that I discovered that the 747 was not only the first of its kind but is nicknamed "Queen of the skies." What was even more interesting is that it was created to fly more passengers over longer distances without stopping. Whoa…If this was indeed a ministry for me, wouldn't it mean that I, or more specifically if I wrote a book, would be flying believers over the long distance of their lives' journey nonstop until they reached a new level of understanding of their identity in Christ? I will not get into all the fun facts I have learned about the jumbo jet since then, but I will say that the significance of its name and purpose leads me to believe that Christ has called me to a specific position in the Body of Christ—to fly more women, those who may feel most separated from God. Women who, because of their experiences, feel they have a longer distance to travel to get to the love of God and the revelation of His grace. I can make this a little quicker by sharing my story, experiences, and some of the wisdom I have learned along my journey.

Part I

Identification Checkpoint

The 7:47 Connection

EARLY SIGNS THERE IS A FIRST-CLASS TICKET WITH YOUR NAME ON IT

HIDDEN IDENTITY

Hidden is defined in the Biblical Dictionary, Index, and Concordance in The Holy Bible Authorized King James Version and published by Bible House in Charlotte, North Carolina, as concealed. When considering the unspoken and fundamentally silent identity struggle I suffered through during my childhood and adolescence, part of the reason I had such a hard time is because I lacked integral information that I believe would have been anchoring. When I use the word identity here, I am referring to one's unique and distinguishing spiritual, lineage-affirming, cultural blueprint, which could very well contribute to, steer, or influence one's career choice or life's work. I am speaking of identity as the essence of a person that makes them who they are and proud of it. When one is firmly planted in and connected to their identity, one feels a sense of grounding. It's an inner honing device of sorts that will always guide you home—not in a tangible sense per se, but in a spiritual sense that spurs an unshakeable feeling of alignment with one's true, authentic self.

My mother did an excellent job of raising me—simply excellent—no qualms there and no doubt about it. As a single-parent mother raising a daughter in the Bronx, she still managed to imprint/burn her value system into a rigidly attitudinal, rebellious, and stubborn child. Part of the rebellion was simply being named Nonye Olukame Akuba. It didn't take me long to discover that my name immediately made me other,

Identification Checkpoint

questioned, suspicious, and set me apart as not being the same. Many women and men may have African or African-inspired names, but the last name and middle name too? It's a bit more acceptable and commonplace today with so many first and second-generation Africans born here today, but back then, not so much. And then, when friends and acquaintances entered my household and realized my mother spoke the Queen's English, African accent free, it was even more confusing for them, for my mother was a Black American born and bred in the United States. I would feel I had to explain that my mother was born in Montgomery, Alabama, to Ruby Lee and Washington McCants and raised on 112th street in Harlem. She attended Morgan College and Columbia University and was bacillus of her AKA chapter. Her second marriage was to a Nigerian Igbo student named Ugo Akwuba. And although she was not African and had never visited the continent, she felt compelled to name her daughter Nonye Olukame Akuba.

Truthfully speaking, the name has grown on me. I believe it is beautiful, yet at the time of my rearing, totally problematic for me because she could not remember what it meant. She had written it down but had misplaced it. To make matters worse, my parents divorced when I was three years old. The man I grew up with in my household that was as close to a father that I would ever know was not my father, and he was not Nigerian. And he didn't live with us for very long. So here you have this child, being raised in a single-parent household carrying a name that set me apart and up for ridicule—immediately—with no idea how to defend the name I was carrying because I did not have the slightest idea what the name meant, what it meant to be Nigerian, Igbo, or whatever else my mom told me because my father had decided he would not take part in my rearing. When it was time to defend my identity, I could not because I honestly did not know what I was defending. The most she could offer was that my last name was really spelled Akwuba, but my dad changed it to Akuba to make it easier for people to pronounce, but that she believed it meant "Lion and wealth," but she was not sure. I know now that this was problematic on a spiritual level. As Akuba in Ghanian means *welcome*, but Akwuba in Igbo means an *abundance of wealth*. The Holy Spirit would reveal that a lot of the contention I have experienced in my life is due to the mismanaging of my name.

All of us must journey to find our rightful place and identity in this world. When you come into the game lacking important information, it can make life very difficult. Your name, whatever it may be, matters, and it is important. In many cultures, it is believed that your name speaks to who you will become and your destiny. Think about the many names of God. If you have ever wondered why He has so many names, it is because each name speaks to a specific aspect of His character that He desires to reveal and demonstrate to His children. Yet we still cannot begin to understand the entire breadth of who He is. The key point I would like for you to remember is that the meaning of your name or what you decide to name your children is not only an insight into your and their character but your destinies.

And this is indeed biblical. Consider the story in Genesis of Abraham and Sarah. The Holy Spirit pointed out Abraham and Sarah as an example, for God could not bless them as long as their names were Abram and Sarai. While Abram means *exalted father* and Sarai means *princess/woman of strength*, their names did not allow for the full breadth of the blessing God desired to bestow upon them and required change. God changed Abram's name to Abraham, which means *father of many nations,* and Sarai's name to Sarah, the possessive form of Sarai, which may indicate an expansion in Sarai's identity from a local princess to one of global stature. The name changes allowed the blessing and promises of God to activate and flow. And so, I have recently commenced the process to legally change my last name to Akwuba. Even today, I recall my father's eldest sister being very upset to find that the spelling of my last name was incorrect. I did not see the big deal. But for her, it meant my correct lineage. Now I understand her stance, yet I also understand the spiritual implications of my name not being accurate. Yet, if the biblical reference I have provided is not sufficient to understand this premise, sit for a minute and recall the Floyd Mayweather interview when the world's highest-paid boxer speaks of the financial transformation that occurred in his life once he changed his name to *Money Mayweather*. Names matter.

Genesis 17:4-6
As for me, behold, my covenant is with thee, and thou shalt be a father of many nations. Neither shall thy name any more be called Abram, but thy name shall be Abraham; for a father of many nations have I made thee. And I will make thee exceeding fruitful, and I will make nations of thee, and kings shall come out of thee.

Genesis 17:15-16
And God said unto Abraham, As for Sarai thy wife, thou shalt not call her name Sarai, but Sarah shall her name be. And I will bless her, and give thee a son also of her: yea, I will bless her, and she shall be a mother of nations; kings of people shall be of her.

Even with these crises of lost identity, my mom fought to ensure that my self-esteem was strong and unwavering. She constantly and repetitively reminded me of my attractiveness, intelligence, gifts, and uniqueness, and it was an amazing feat considering a lot of what I was feeling secretly. I do not believe I am alone in this. I believe all critically thinking, conscious beings have an innate desire to find themselves, belong to the right people, the right tribe, and carry out their purpose. I also believe that many of us have lost or forgotten our true identity in the spiritual sense. Yet, the bible asserts that before we were in the womb, God knew us. And it is His desire for us to remember.

Jeremiah 1:5
Before I formed thee in the belly I knew thee; and before thou camest forth out of the womb I sanctified thee, and I ordained thee a prophet unto the nations.

I interpret this to mean that before we entered the earthly realm or natural plane, we were given a purpose and a mission to carry out on this earth, yet once we are born into this world or take our material form, it is forgotten. If we are lucky, or more specifically, if we are determined to do the work and seek to find our purpose, we will eventually discover who we were meant to be and carry out what we were meant to carry out.

I am just now making this discovery for myself. Today I stand totally and wholeheartedly in the full breadth of who I am; my name, my purpose, my beliefs, my failures, and my successes. I stand on it and in it with ten toes down—and without apology. When I think of my name—the first, middle and last, it totally makes sense. It speaks to my unique experience and journey, my identity, and my path. The meaning of my name was hidden for many years. I had to literally search it out. And the more I discovered what it meant, the more my identity and purpose came into focus. I believe the 747 woman will relate to this pursuit of truth. It may not be the meaning of your name that was hidden. It may be the identity of a parent, hidden truth, an event, or all of the above. Maybe you never knew you were adopted or never knew you were actually your aunt's daughter and not the child of whom you were taught to call your mother. Whatever your unique case may be, there will be a missing piece of your puzzle or link that you have had to put together, and it will be a fundamental component of your experience and journey.

Luke 8:17
For nothing is hidden that will not become evident, nor anything secret that will not be known and come to light

Luke 12:2-3
But there is nothing covered up that will not be revealed, and hidden that will not be known

Daniel 2:22
It is He who reveals the profound and hidden things; He knows what is in the darkness, And the light dwells with Him

Proverbs 25:2

It is the glory of God to conceal a matter, But the glory of kings is to search out a matter

THE OUTSIDER

During my pursuit of a Master's Degree at New York University's School of Continuing Education, I had the honor of being a student of Helio Garcia, a Marketing and Public Relations Associate Adjunct Professor who also serves as an adjunct professor of management at NYU's Stern Executive MBA program, and is a contract lecturer at Wharton School/UPenn. During his captivating class, he shared the importance of framing. How a public relations nightmare—if caught early enough, could be framed in a way to avoid debilitatingly negative impact, a career-ending public debacle entirely, or at least lessen the blow. The key to being able to sink, swim and or successfully navigate the incident rests solely on how the event is framed—as in what is the controlling narrative or lens through which the public needs to view what happened. Proper and timely framing of an event, corporation, or person is critical to their survival.

One of my favorite writers is Julia Cameron, the renowned author of *The Artist's Way*—a self-help, introspective journey for artists that have lost their way and need support recovering healthy creative lifestyles. Through insightful, and what you may assume are sometimes silly tools and exercises, she guides you on a path of healing that unblocks and inspires writers, artists, musicians, and the like to conjure the faith, trust, and strength to free their creative voices and give their creativity a place in the world. In her book *Walking in This World*, Julia introduces what she calls healthy believing mirrors as well as their importance in the artist's life. Believing mirrors are people that accurately mirror back to you who you are—your talents, potential, capabilities, and uniqueness. They can celebrate you and speak of your bigness without feeling small. Yet what is most important is that they mirror what you believe and want to believe about yourself, not what they think or want you to be. Julia goes further to state that when you do not surround yourself with appropriate believing mirrors capable of providing accurate perceptions of who you are, you can wind up with a very distorted, small, and even powerless view of yourself that will undoubtedly lead you astray, or cause you not to try to succeed. The problem with negative, misaligned, or toxic believing mirrors is that if you are not careful, a relationship with them can kill your dreams as they may not allow space and time for you to grow into your vision or for the vision to grow into its fullness. And unfortunately, many times, they may not even know how to do so, for it is challenging to do what was never done for you.

It is unfortunate that the vast majority of friends, lovers, and acquaintances that have crossed my path did not have the proper lens for me, and neither were they people I would consider believing mirrors. What is more tragic than that is through most of my childhood years, adolescence, and early twenties, I continuously tried to locate positive images of myself through the eyes of others. Now, at forty-seven years of age, I am clear that the framing of my story was very off. My highlight reel is not of a stuck-up, arrogant, mean, or aloof misfit. What I did have was a very different set of values, opinions, thoughts, and sense of style, as well as my own way of responding to situations. I went left when others went right. I answered in French, while others answered in Portuguese. Yet because I did not fit into their definition of what was acceptable or how they believed I should have acted, many times, I felt wrong-headed and intrinsically flawed. Consequently, I have always felt like an outsider. Even during my "coolest" seasons, I felt different; I knew I walked to the beat of a different drum, knew my conscience and value system were hewn together differently—not better or worse, just different. And because of this, I was easily labeled the odd one, the stuck-up one, the one this person or that person did not like for whatever reason, the one that just did not fit in, or who thought she was better and was easily marginalized, stigmatized and minimalized for whatever reason. Over time, I began to frame myself in this way—the loner, the black sheep, the rebel, the renegade, the misidentified, misjudged, misunderstood misfit, and before I knew it, I morphed into an unspoken

Identification Checkpoint

enemy to the community, clique, organization, or whatever body that governed the territory. Yet when I look back on it from my current perspective, it makes sense as I am purposed to go head to head with and against wherever there is a large body operating in cliquish group think.

747 woman, I am certain you relate. As whatever the social construct is where people are literally afraid to stand by you or hide their penchant for your friendship for fear of losing approval from powers that be, is a familiar experience for you. Very often, you are relegated to the periphery of the group—yet over the years, you have become so strong, so unbothered, so in your own world, and so dedicated to running your own race that you have learned not to care. What I have come to understand is this experience is something to relish and celebrate, for it is exactly how God created me and you to be. God has called you to be unconcerned and unbothered by the group or the consensus of the group, so when He calls you to speak the truth, you can and will do so without question or hesitation as you do not feel the repercussion of being deemed an outcast. Even more insightful is the understanding that that thing which people do not like about you, the thing that most of them cannot rationally explain or put their hands on, which rubs them the wrong way or causes them to label you strange, is your anointing. Not only is it a gift to you from God, but it is designed to protect you and keep you away from groups that operate under a hedge of falsehood, phoniness, backbiting, backstabbing, gossip, slander, ridicule, and judgment. God's desire to protect you from fitting in these groups and situations prevents you from learning to prey on the weak, ensures that you do not learn to discourage and mock but rather to give genuine support and upliftment, and teaches you how to disengage and feel uncomfortable with gossip and slander. The distance has allowed you to value biblical knowledge, wisdom, and righteousness over the pursuit of worldly things or a place in worldly circles where His true spirit is neither understood nor welcomed. Your rejection is always God's protection and a sign that he has a bigger stage, purpose, and ending for you in store.

Exodus 23:2 (NLT)
You must not follow the crowd in doing wrong. When you are called to testify in a dispute, do not be swayed by the crowd to twist justice.

Romans 12:2 (NIV)
Do not conform to the pattern of this world…

John 1:11 (NIV)
He came to that which was his own, but his own did not receive him

Luke 6:22 (NLT)
What blessings await you when people hate you and exclude you and mock you and curse you as evil because you follow the Son of Man

1 Peter 2:4 (NLT)
You are coming to Christ, who is the living cornerstone of God's temple. He was rejected by people, but he was chosen by God for great honor.

HYPER-SHIFTING CAREERS/PURPOSE

The 747 woman, in many cases, is extremely talented and gifted. It is clear to everyone that knows her that she has a strong creative anointing. However, to the unsuspecting eye, to the natural eye that lacks spiritual insight, she appears to be flaky and flits from career to career. She may announce different purposes from time to time, different entrepreneurial undertakings and initiatives, and may even venture into the non-profit area. She will be misjudged as unstable when it comes to her life's path. Someone to not be taken seriously for mockery and jest. Yet even in these times, there is one gift or talent that stands out. It is the one for which she gets the most compliments. Therefore, she may begin to take it seriously. However, she is confused, and so are others around her, as to why it still has not blossomed into a fully successful career like the career paths of many of her counterparts.

Interestingly enough, the 747 woman is not completely misguided, for she may have some idea of the life she deeply desires or the goals she wants to attain. She may even be able to create a jaw-droppingly robust vision board, but her fundamental purpose—what she should be specifically doing right now, how she should be using her talents, alludes her. And as it pertains to kingdom matters, she has no clue of her spiritual identity, ranking, or position beyond feeling that she is unusually favored by God and possibly an intercessor. The 747 woman has struggled with a shifting purpose throughout her life. She may very well have a job or career that she is lukewarmly proud of, but in her heart, she knows she was meant for more, even if she has not discovered what that more is yet. Although she may be more aware of God's love and grace than others around her, as far as being very clear on her sins, transgressions, and mistakes, she has no real idea of her identity in the kingdom in terms of her position, rank, mission, or purpose.

Jeremiah 29:11
"For I know the plans I have for you," declares the LORD, "plans to prosper you and not to harm you, plans to give you hope and a future."

YOU'VE BEEN MARKED

I don't know how common these experiences I am about to share, but I believe they are integral to anyone that may indeed be a 747 woman. When I state that you have been marked, I mean exactly that. You have been set apart before the womb. And just as Satan used Herod in an attempt to locate and kill our Lord and Savior, Satan has used many people you have encountered in an attempt to locate and derail you—and in rare cases, even kill you.

I have had many strangely peculiar experiences that, when looking through the lens of a possessor of the 747 inheritance, are considered near-death experiences or experiences that were designed to derail, deter, prevent and estrange me from my purpose. My older sister, Mikko Andrea Grant-Carter, is fourteen years my senior. Recently she shared a story with me that occurred during her childhood that was disheartening but not at all surprising. She recalled being asleep in bed when she was awakened by my father, who was pleading with her to convince my mother not to go forward with her pregnancy with me. Lord forgive him. Can you imagine? A grown man (your one and only father) pleading with his fourteen-year-old bonus child to confront her mother about aborting the sibling in her mother's stomach. Before I even entered the world, the enemy was tracking me and fully aware of what it might mean to the kingdom if I ever walked in my purpose. Afraid of my possible impact, he tried to erase me from the annals of history—early.

When I was a young child, about three years old, my mother worked at a Treatment facility for troubled teen girls. My mother was a gifted educator and social worker, and I believe she had an anointing for healing teenagers and women. She was loved dearly by many, and I would remember people getting off the street, out of street life, pulling themselves all the way together, and coming to our home to thank my mom for her kindness, generosity, support, and wisdom as they travailed to a new life. One of these young ladies loved her dearly, so much so that when my mom brought me to work one day and left me on the stage in the facility's auditorium, the young lady lit the curtains on fire. The love and attention my mother was showing me were a bit too much for her to bear. My mother said she rushed to get me off the stage, and thankfully, the fire was put out.

When I was four or five, I attended a swimming pool party. My mom sat in the bleachers as I paddled around on a floating device. She believed I was safe as my god sisters and godmother were in the water. I remember paddling and enjoying every bit of the time I was having until a rambunctious, stout boy knocked me off the float. Immediately I went under. I could not swim. I remember the feeling. I remember grasping for air and finding myself near a pipe that I tried to climb up to get my head above water. It did not work. The kids around were having fun, and many had not noticed that I had gone over. I remember my eldest god sister tugging at me, but I was not a small child. I was built solid, and she was not strong enough to bring me out of the water. There was a moment when my head rose out of the water, and I saw my mother standing in the bleachers and screaming for someone to assist me. She must have been horrified. Eventually, my godmother was able to come to my rescue and pull me up and out of the water. Strike three, devil.

I wish that were the last time, but it was not. I recall an outing with a childhood friend in the summer of 1995. We decided to leave a birthday party for an acquaintance early, and since we were on New York City's West Side, we decided to go to the Tunnel. Yes, that Tunnel. If you are a Hip-Hop baby by any chance and are familiar with rap music in the 1990s and early 2000s, yep, that is the one. I was dressed in a sparkling, sequence bodycon dress, with at least two-inch heels that were murdering my feet. Whatever pain I was feeling, I decided to ignore it because I just knew I was looking cute-cute. As a matter of fact, both of us looked summer bunny beautiful. Although I had driven my mother's car to the event, we decided walking to the club would be quicker and less time-consuming as we were pretty close and were too thirsty to waste time finding a parking spot. We set out to cross over to the club, and the moment we did, a truck came careening down the street. The driver, a female, looked me straight in the face, pressed down on the gas pedal, and drove straight toward me. My friend screeched in horror, and we took off for the curb. My friend was pretty shaken up. Needless to say, we decided not to go to the Tunnel. She continued to ask me all night, "Who was that? Who was that? She tried to kill you! Why did she do that?" To this day, I have no idea who it was or why it happened. Every now and that same friend would bring it up and ask, "Do you remember that?" "Who was she?" and I still have no idea. Yet, I do know if we had not moved as quickly as we did, or if I had tripped, stumbled, or succumbed to the pain I felt wearing those heels, I would not be here to share this story. That is just how close that truck came to mowing me down.

In the summer of 2020, I had grown accustomed to going for long two-hour walks that would lead me far away from my home. I was in between jobs and was doing my best not to gain the infamous Covid 19. The walks were long and quiet as the roads were virtually empty, and I enjoyed the solace that was afforded me—the peace of mind that allowed me to work out issues, take time to be grateful, strategize and just grab a quiet moment for myself. On this day, I noticed the street was particularly empty. No one else was walking, and there was no construction going on—just a quiet morning. It was not long before I realized there was a gentleman some ways off walking toward me. I felt an extremely uneasy feeling. It was not a typical feeling. I had seen men on the path many times before, but something was different. I immediately stopped walking on the sidewalk and began to walk up the middle of the street to ensure I would be fully visible to anyone looking out their window from either side of the street in case he tried to attack me. At once, the man picked up his pace and started making these weird calling noises. It was as if he was making noise deliberately to confirm that no one was on the street or alert in the homes lining the sidewalks. And his suspicion was right, for nothing came of his attempts to elicit a response. Nothing and no one moved—not even a slight wrestling of a curtained window. He began to walk even faster. I looked up and saw a pickup truck coming down the road. I literally jumped before the truck in an attempt to wave him down. He had to slam on his brakes to prevent hitting me. I asked him to roll down his window and begged him if he could take me up the road. He was nervous as he should have been because he saw the man standing on the nearby corner perpendicular to where we were, and I believe he thought we were together, and it was a setup attempt. He was suspicious and may have even been afraid. Rightly so, since the man was one block away and had his eyes on me. When he saw us look in his direction, he began doing stretches—randomly on the street corner, yet watching to see if the man would allow me in his truck. Thankfully the man allowed me to enter his vehicle, which was dangerous in itself, but I could think of no other way to get to safety. When I finally made it home, I called a prophet that I had known some years ago—a seer. I had hardly said hello before he said, "He would have killed you."

Identification Checkpoint

If I am honest, I would have to say that I have had a host of abusive relationships—some mentally abusive, some emotionally abusive, some physically abusive, and some a combination of all three with a dose of cruelty to boot. Not all of my relationships, but more than any one woman should ever experience, as one is one too many. In hindsight, it is clear that the goal of many of these broken souls was to somehow make me feel small, to control me, or punish me for having the audacity to be true to who I am—not who they wanted me to be, or who they thought I was based on how I looked. And so, although in the majority of these relationships, there was not an explicit and deliberate attempt to take my life, there was a slow, methodical and intentional attempt to batter my self-esteem, self-worth, essence, and identity. Do I deem any one of them a monster? I do not. I do not know who they are now. Back then, they were broken souls on a journey toward their own healing, and I can only pray that they have done the work necessary to evolve into the God-fearing, loving, uplifting, successful, protective, and powerful men God purposed them to be. Yet, the Bible teaches us God's anointed, prophets and messengers, are always targeted—sometimes early.

Exodus 1:15-16
And the king of Egypt spake to the Hebrew midwives, of which the name of the one was Shiphrah, and the name of the other Puah: And he said, When ye do the office of a midwife to the Hebrew women, and see them upon the stools; if it be a son, then ye shall kill him

1 Samuel 19:1
And Saul spake to Jonathan his son, and to all his servants, that they should kill David.

Acts 12:1
Now about that time Herod the kind stretched forth is hands to vex certain of the church. And he killed James the brother of John with the sword. And because he saw it pleased the Jews, he proceeded further to take Peter also

Acts 23:12

And when it was day, certain of the Jews banded together, and bound themselves under a curse, saying that they would neither eat nor drink till they had killed Paul."

2 Kings 6:31 (NIV)

[The king of Aram] said, "May God deal with me, be it ever so severely, if the head of Elisha son of Shaphat remains on his shoulders today!"

Galatians 6:17

From henceforth let no man trouble me: for I bear in my body the marks of the Lord Jesus

HIGHWAY ROBBERY/DEMONIC HIJACKING

If you take the time to reflect on your experience, there are several instances or incidents in your life that, if you are honest, should have been a rock-solid opportunity for you to excel, succeed or walk through a door purposed to take you to the next level. Yet, for whatever reason, right before your hand turned the knob, the opportunity was cut off in some way. Even more familiar may be the instances where you suffered a loss or theft that took something from you that was irretrievable. Be certain that I am not stating that every opportunity is meant to materialize. There are times when our rejection is for our protection. However, the instances I would like you to consider are the ones where the door was shut in such a way that you cannot deny it was the enemy's attempt to steal your innocence or destiny. The incidents demonstrate a blatant rejection or unprovoked attack. When I look over my life, several incidents come to mind. One is the theft or the demonic hijacking of my innocence. At the age of six, I was molested by a man who accompanied one of my mom's girlfriends to our home to visit. He asked to come to the bathroom and made his way to my bedroom. At the age of nine, I was molested by a distant relative—an adolescent male that later would be outed as having touched several young girls in the family and his neighborhood.

Identification Checkpoint

Other instances include intentional efforts by certain individuals to block me out of opportunities. I cannot state what their driving motives were—whether they desired to curtail my light, to cause pain, or if they somehow believed the decisions they made were harmless. For instance, an example of one of the situations in which I spoke transpired in my twenties and involved my performance of a hook/chorus on a song that managed to climb to number one on the rap billboards in the early 2000s. There was a video. I was an aspiring rapper, and having the opportunity to be included in it may have opened some doors. Yet, I was not given the opportunity to do so—the opportunity to rap along with my own voice. Was I upset? Not necessarily, as by this time, I had learned to brush a lot of things off. But it was duly noted. I cannot say much about that specific decision. However, there were many instances and incidents in my past that ring similar. And many of them were pre-mediated and deliberate. I need to state here that I have no ill will toward anyone. I share my experiences to serve as a signpost for others to find their way.

Matthew 24:43
But know this that if the good man of the house had known in what watch the thief would come, he would have watched and would not have suffered his house to be broken up

DISCARDED CLUES AND HINTS

Before my announcement that I was a prophet, or more specifically "a recovering Jonah," is how I believe I introduced myself, I had been told by one of my closest friend's spiritual mentors that I was a prophet some years prior. I was not even on the phone with him very long before he asserted with what seemed like one hundred percent certainty that I was a prophet. He then requested that I purchase a book entitled *Prophet Arise* by John Eckhardt. I thought his assertion was interesting, even amusing, and I went ahead and purchased the book for I had heard of the author and utilized a book of his to win several spiritual battles. Upon its arrival, I thumbed through it and believed the list that John Eckhardt shared as attributes of the prophet's experiences resonated with my own life, but "eh, moving on." I purchased that book back in 2015.

Jonah 1:1-3
Now the word of the lord came unto Jonah the son of Amittai, saying, Arise, go to Nineveh, that great city, and cry against it, for their wickedness is come up before me. But Jonah rose up to flee unto Tarshish from the presence of the LORD, and went down to Joppa

Another prophet (seer) had a conversation with me once and stated, "you will eventually come to a fork in the road and will have to decide whether you will walk in your prophetic gifting." "Huh? What? Um, okay…But what did you say about the guy I'm dating again?" A total rebuff and dismissal of the idea that I would in any way walk in it. A few years before that, the same prophet would say to me plainly, "God wants you to walk with Him." I believe I responded, "Yeah, I know." Yet again, I went ahead with my own plans for my life, my daughter, and my desire to remarry and stake my claim on this world by accomplishing MY vision.

Many years later, a friend of mine informed me how she would join a certain gifted prophetess's/seer's live sermons and sessions (I believe it was on Periscope) and how the word she gave her blessed her life. Without hesitation, I joined the next session, and when I finally mustered up the nerve to ask the prophetess a question (I have no idea what the question was specifically, but I am certain it was about a romantic relationship), she referred to me as "Jeremiah, the weeping prophet." Okay…I knew I cried a lot during prayer for myself and others, but… A prophet? A weeping one at that? I was convinced that she had made a mistake, was speaking to someone else, or maybe she was talking about the guy I was dating. After all, he was pretty spiritual. It must be him. No chance under heaven she was referring to me as I had conveniently forgotten previous encounters of the same.

During the summer of 2020, as I returned from a trip to the country with my daughter, a trip I had no business taking or having her accompany me on, I stopped to fill up on gas. I want to state that the chances of me stopping at this particular gas station were slim as there were at least two other stations located at this very exit. As I pumped gas, a woman that I greeted before paying for gas at the register approached me and, you guessed it, stated she was a prophet named Micah. I had not shared my life experience or what I was currently experiencing before she asked if she could share something with me. She then went on to state with certainty, "Stop doubting yourself…He said to tell you that you hear Him. You are a hearer. He is with you. Don't be sad. Great things are going to happen for you." I stood at that pump with that woman and cried uncontrollably while hiding the breakdown from my daughter, who sat in the car unaware. I have tried to find Prophetess Micah several times but have been unsuccessful. I hope our paths cross again soon.

I've had a host of friends say teasingly in moments where I made some assertion with lucid accuracy, diagnosed some spiritual issue in their life, or when sharing wisdom and encouragement, "Okay, prophet!" or, "You sound like a preacher," or even more common, "That conversation really blessed me." I even recall an ex of mine asking, "Are you a prophet?" after telling him he had a physical anointing to excel in sports and needed to walk in it in order to be instrumental in the lives of wounded young men. I have had strange spiritual experiences and dreams, and I have received information I would not have known if it were not for the revelation I received in a dream. You may have had a few prophetic experiences where you have given a timely word of encouragement based on what you heard or saw during prayer, yet it is something you have minimized, turned into a conversational piece, a quick fun fact about yourself, but nothing more.

Isaiah 43:1
But now thus saith the Lord that created thee, O Jacob, and he that formed thee, O Israel, fear not: for I have redeemed thee, I have called thee by thy name; thou art mine

John 15:16
Ye have not chosen me, but I have chosen you, and ordained you, that ye should go and bring forth fruit, and that your fruit should remain...

PROPHETIC HERITAGE

Possessing or not having a prophetic heritage is not a deal breaker to identifying yourself as a 747 woman, but it may be a qualifying aspect. My maternal grandmother was said to have a prophetic gift. She had prophetic dreams about members of our family and was said to announce that her eldest son was dead moments before service men knocked on her front door to inform her that he had been killed in a car accident. Her prophetic gift revealed itself to me, the second eldest of five grandchildren, each time she would ask me some seemingly random question about a young man I was dating. The answer to which I would never know, but in just a few days or weeks after, would be revealed.

Before my grandmother's youngest son, Washington "Love" McCants, whom I affectionately called Uncle Love as a child, passed away, I told him of a vision I had of my grandmother in a wheelchair with her hair braided in cornrows. I had not seen my grandmother in the years prior to her passing (that is another story), but I asked him if what I saw made any sense to him. He eagerly confirmed during the time he cared for her that he would braid her hair and that she had been taken to a wheelchair prior to her passing. He then said, "Oh, you're the one that has her gift," as he was the child that was standing beside her when she announced the vision of her dead son just moments before the servicemen knocked on their front door to confirm it.

Acts 3:25
Ye are the children of the prophets, and of the covenant which God made with our fathers, saying unto Abraham, And in thy seed shall all the kindreds of the earth be blessed

Deuteronomy 18:18
I will raise them up a prophet from among their brethren, like unto thee, and will put my words in his mouth; and he shall speak unto them all that I shall command him

INEXPLICABLY LONG WILDERNESS SEASON

I am undoubtedly, without reservation, convinced that my wilderness season is coming to an end. I am only days, hours—maybe even moments away from walking out of this season. If I am honest with myself, I would have to say that I have been in my wilderness season since birth. If indeed your wilderness season ends when you reach the promised land, or let me state more accurately, when you take possession of the Promise land, then I was born in the wilderness, reared in the wilderness, became educated, pursued dreams, changed dreams, started businesses, ended businesses, entered various relationships, got married, gave birth to my daughter, got divorced and entered new relationships all while in my wilderness experience.

During my wilderness experience, I have doubted God, trusted God, felt abandoned by God, heard God, disobeyed God, praised God, worshipped God, thanked God…I have been befriended, unfriended, abused, misused, misjudged, falsely accused, mocked, smeared, abandoned, blessed, promoted, disrespectful, disrespected, demoted, targeted, saved from calamity by angels—heavenly and earthly, prayed, fasted, grown up, womaned up, faced up to my transgressions, pride, arrogance, mistakes, missteps, misjudgments, negligence and have begged for forgiveness. I have had seasons of fur coats and fine cars, seasons of walking with holes in my shoes and driving unleveled due to the spare tire that was much smaller than the remaining three. I have had seasons of hoopties with no air condition in over ninety degree weather and food scarcity aided by church pantries. I learned to tithe during seasons of rich and overflowing increase, during seasons of just enough and seasons of deficit. I have tithed my food stamps during seasons of abject lack and poverty and have learned a thousand times that people will judge you, discount you and dismiss you, especially when they have no idea what you are doing or what God is doing in your life. I have learned that most people are more like Job's three friends who will assign blame to you rather than counting you as righteous and under spiritual attack, but while people chided me, mocked me, gossiped about me, laughed at me, slandered me, judged me as unfaithful, unfavored, unwise, unfocused, unprotected, unworthy, unimportant, unrighteous and downright stupid, God was writing my story and had a plan for me. If this sounds even vaguely familiar, 747 woman, please do not despise small beginnings, do not despise the years in the wilderness, for it is during this time that you may feel the farthest away from your loved ones, but I assure you it is when you will feel and be the closest to God. Though the season may be inexplicably long, he is leading you, directing you, molding you, and refining you to be exactly who you need to be, to accomplish exactly what He has always planned for you to accomplish.

Zechariah 4:10 (NLT)
Do not despise these small beginnings, for the LORD rejoices to see the work begin…

Deuteronomy 32:10 (NKJV)
He found him in a desert land and in the wasteland, a howling wilderness; He encircled him, He instructed him, He kept him as the apple of His eye

Genesis 16:7
Now the angel of the Lord found her by a spring of water in the wilderness, by the spring on the way to Shur

Hosea 2:14
Therefore, behold, I will allure her, and bring her into the wilderness, and speak comfortably to her

Isaiah 43:19
I will even make a way in the wilderness, and rivers in the desert

Identification Checkpoint

1 Peter 1:6-9 (NLT)
So be truly glad. There is wonderful joy ahead, even though you must endure many trials for a little while. These trials will show that your faith is genuine. It is being tested as fire tests and purifies gold—though your faith is far more precious than mere gold. So when your faith remains strong through many trials, it will bring you much praise and glory and honor on the day when Jesus Christ is revealed to the whole world.

SPIRITUAL WARFARE

Inexplicably long wilderness seasons build undeniably strong, resolute warriors for the kingdom. The wilderness does not mean spiritual attacks are on hold, as the truth is quite the opposite. During the forty years the Israelites were in the wilderness, they were confronted with enemies and entered several battles. And it is no different from us in our wilderness season. However, those around us who have not experienced demonic attacks, or at least are not spiritually astute enough to identify them as such, have no idea what it is like to fight spiritually. We appear spooky, cooky, weird, foolish, or disillusioned. And I get it; if you have not been exposed to this level of spiritual enlightenment, if you have not been born again, you cannot see. Many are even tempted to believe we are doing something wrong. We must be doing or not doing something to be experiencing such a level of chaos and underachievement at times. I have felt the judgmental glare of friends and sensed the unspoken judgments in the silences during conversations where I am asked what I am up to or if I followed through on some suggestion they believe will make my life better, having no idea that they may be operating more like Job's three friends, than an individual with wise counsel. If we recall, Job's friends were rebuked for believing Job's suffering was solely due to his transgressions or him having angered God. They were rebuked by God for the judgmental and accusatory error in their thinking.

Job 42:7

…the Lord said to Eliphaz the Temanite: "My anger burns against you and your two friends, for you have not spoken of me what is right, as my servant Job has."

Job's friends had no knowledge or understanding that God was initially pleased with Job and found him blameless. Yet the devil asked God if he could test Job citing he was only upright due to the hedge of protection God had around him.

Job 1:6-12

Now there was a day when the sons of God came to present themselves before the LORD, and Satan came also among them. And the LORD said unto Satan, Whence comest thou? Then Satan answered the LORD, and said, From going to and fro in the earth, and from walking up and down in it. And the LORD said unto Satan, Hast thou considered my servant Job, that there is none like him in the earth, a perfect and an upright man, one that feareth God, and escheweth evil? Then Satan answered the LORD, and said, Doth Job fear God for nought? Hast not thou made an hedge about him, and about his house, and about all that he hath on every side? thou hast blessed the work of his hands, and his substance is increased in the land. But put forth thine hand now, and touch all that he hath, and he will curse thee to thy face. And the LORD said unto Satan, Behold, all that he hath is in thy power; only upon himself put not forth thine hand. So Satan went forth from the presence of the LORD.

Other acquaintances, friends, and family members with no knowledge of the word beyond the Lord's Prayer, if that, may believe you are lazy and complacent and that they pegged you wrong, finding you incapable of thriving in the real world as they assume everything was handed to you. They are totally blinded to things of the spirit, and it would never occur to them that what you are experiencing is spiritual warfare and only for a season.

Identification Checkpoint

1 Corinthians 2:14
But the natural man receiveth not the things of the Spirit of God: for they are foolishness unto him: neither can he know them, because they are spiritually discerned.

John 3:3
"Jesus answered and said unto him, Verily, verily, I say unto thee, Except a man be born again, he cannot see the kingdom of God.

Most people who have known me since childhood are aware that I have been in some form of parochial school for my entire life. I had a fiercely religious, praying grandmother and a mother, who, while she was not a holy roller, forced me to attend Sunday School as a child and teen, and to do a stint in the church's youth choir for a year or two. Yet, spiritual warfare was never discussed or mentioned. My mother was a firm believer in prayer, but spiritual warfare and demonic attacks? Other than Jesus being tempted by Satan during his forty-day fast, I was completely unaware.

My own spiritual path had led me to read the *Power of Positive Thinking* by Norman Vincent Peale, the *Battlefield of the Mind* by Joyce Meyer, and *The Wisdom of Florence Scovel Shinn* published by Simon & Schuster in my twenties, and I believed I walked in some level of spiritual authority because of the knowledge and understanding I had ascertained because of them. But my understanding did not go beyond that. During hard times, my understanding of changing things included praying, praying really, really hard, and praying with the word. I believed that if I prayed hard enough and had faith the size of a mustard seed that things would work out. If I kept my peace, the calm in me would be reflected externally and would put an end to whatever conflict and chaos I was experiencing—or God would just simply answer my prayers and remove the situation under grace in a perfect way. Yet, when the inexplicable downturns, obstacles, and mishaps intensified, and there seemed to be no end in sight, I believe God sent assistance from three different friends that would take my prayer life to another level.

While fighting for custody of my daughter, one friend slipped me Apostle John Eckhardt's book entitled *Prayers that Rout out Demons* (This is the reason I was familiar with the author when I was told to purchase his book, *Prophet Arise*). Without question, I immediately started meditating on and reciting prayers and bible verses for victory and protection. When my car was to be repossessed, another friend mentioned a fast led by her Pastor in which she had participated. She could not contain her excitement regarding her answered prayer. At once, I began to research biblical fasting and implemented it in my life. A gentle nudge from yet another friend led me to join Word of Faith Cathedral in Austell, Georgia, headed by Bishop Dale C. Bronner. These three kind gestures, or testimonies, ushered me into a new level of spiritual understanding, authority, and power. And the more battles I faced, the more adept and aware I became in terms of what I needed to do to keep myself, my daughter, and my loved ones safe. The more I trusted and had faith that God was with me, the quicker the obstacles were obliterated.

Psalm 144:1 KJV
"Blessed be the Lord my strength which teacheth my hands to war, and my fingers to fight: My goodness, and my fortress my high tower, and my deliverer; my shield, and he in whom I trust; who subdueth my people under me."

Psaslm 144:1 (NIV)
"Praise be to the LORD my Rock, who trains my hands for war, my fingers for battle. He is my loving God and my fortress, my stronghold an my deliverer, my shield, in whom I take refuge, who subdues peoples under me."

I say this to say at this juncture, the 747 should be extremely adept at spiritual warfare. You are not new to warring in the spirit, and demons are well aware of who you are and the level of damage you are capable of inflicting when it is time for a showdown. You are most probably an intercessor. You may even be a healer or have a gift of deliverance. One thing for sure is you know, even if you do not believe you have elevated to the heights for which you were destined, that when you pray for yourself, but more so when you pray for other people, things undoubtedly happen for them—and quickly.

JOSEPH'S BLUNDER

If you are indeed a woman of God, you have heard the story of Joseph and the cloak of many colors a thousand times. We have all felt empathy and compassion for Joseph's treatment at the beginning of the story when his jealous and envious brothers callously plan his demise due to the inadequacy, neglect, and envy they felt in the face of their father, Jacob, for favoring their younger brother. As we become older, the perspective of the story expands a bit, and we are able to clearly see that Joseph's boasting of his vision, albeit innocent, courted the harsh treatment he received. By Joseph's ill-timed sharing of his vision, we are taught lessons about the magic of containment or the importance of hiding and protecting visions, dreams, and plans while they are in the embryonic stages. I learned this lesson very late in life.

During my adolescence, I remember a particular conversation I had with my late mother. We were in her bedroom chatting about life when I mentioned to her how different I feel at times. My mother responded by sharing she felt the same. She stated even while she was pregnant with me, she was aware that I would be different. She was clear that she did not know what I would do exactly, but she stated my name would be in lights. I felt the same. I was excited. I felt vindicated in a sense and was happy to feel that what I had sensed about my destiny wasn't crazy. My mom had never said anything even remotely similar to me about that before. Yet, at that moment, I felt my most secret feelings about my future were confirmed.

During my freshmen year at Spelman College, I worked for a few months in the Bursar's office. I hated it. But I did my best to show up, and when I did show, I was only a little more than lackluster at best. Probably not my brightest or smartest moment, but at that time in my life, the importance of work ethic, reputation, and networking were far from me. Yet I was respectful and pleasant—at least, I hope I was…I remember clearly that one of the administrators in the office was particularly kind. He had a robust personality, a distinctive yet small patch of white hair on his head, and always had a smile on his face and something cheerful to say. Although daily banter with him made the job less mundane, I quit the job as soon as I could. I would see him from time to time as I walked across the campus, and I would always wave emphatically. One day as I walked across campus, I spotted him standing outside on the steps of the Bursar's office. I waved as always, and he yelled to me in passing, "Hey Nonye, I know you are going to make us proud one day! I know you are going to be famous!" I can't lie. I was shocked to hear the words, and they sent an electric wave of excitement through my body. To many of you, it may not be a big deal, but for me, it was confirmation of a destiny that awaited me. Both experiences left me feeling exhilarated, so much so that I blurted the statements to anyone who would listen. And just as Joseph's boasting rubbed his brothers the wrong way, my excitement did equal harm to the relationships I held with many at this time. That is not to say that what I shared caused the deterioration of the friendships, but I am sure my excitement with what I believed to be God's confirmation of the huge destiny before me did not make me their most favored person.

Genesis 37:5
And Joseph dreamed a dream, and he told it to his brethren: and they hated him yet the more

WORDLY FORFEITURE

I am a Hip-Hop baby—tried and true. Since I was a little girl, as many of my friends crooned along with R&B hits, I was patiently waiting for the premiere New York deejay of whatever era to get on the air, so I could blast my stereo as loud as the speakers would allow. As I have grown spiritually, that love has been tested. When you are faithful to your purpose, certain languages, values, belief systems, and concepts grieve

Identification Checkpoint

the Holy Spirit. I cannot listen to secular Hip-Hop like I used to and want to, yet there are times when I succumb. When I do, I try hard to find clean versions of the songs I love. This is now. In my twenties, I worked very hard to learn how to rap, structure songs, develop cadence, a stage presence, pay for studio time, network... You name it, I did it. Yet, when the time came to own the moment, it never seemed pressing.

There are three specific instances that come to mind. The first is when I rhymed for Mase. The R&B group 112 had just released their single on which he had been featured along with the Notorious B.I.G. It hit the streets with meteoric success. At the time, I knew of him through a childhood friend of mine, but I was not quite ready to reveal to that friend how serious I was about a rap career. A work acquaintance of mine named Nadine knew him as well and had attended college with him. During one of their conversations, she quipped that her colleague rapped. He told her to put me on the phone, and I rapped for him. Without hesitation, he asked me to come to Harlem that evening with Nadine so I could meet up with him and rap some more. I asked a couple of friends if I should go. "Mase? Nah, don't even waste your time. He's not going anywhere." So I didn't. How absolutely wrong they were and how silly of me to have listened to them. Strike one.

A few years later, I was working as a receptionist at a marketing firm on Fifth Avenue. A few of the guys in the mailroom knew I rapped. They excitedly informed me that we shared the same building as Roc-a-fella, and they had seen Jay Z a few times. Really? Nah, get out of here. I did not pay the information or their excitement much mind. Until... the day I accompanied them to lunch. Upon our return to our office building, as we awaited the elevator, none other than Jay Z himself walked into the lobby and preceded to wait for the elevator with us. I was never one to be star-struck, but I was definitely staring at him. I just could not believe he was standing there, and when we got on the elevator, he was clearly concerned or at least off-put by the intensity of my stare and gestured in a way to state, "You okay? Is something wrong?" I stated, "No, I'm just surprised to see you." He asked, "Why? My office is in this building. Stop by and say hello," and he exited the elevator. Neither I nor the mailroom guys could believe it. They asked me when I was going and volunteered to accompany me. I replied, "Nah, he was just trying to be nice because I was staring at him..." They incredulously rebutted, "Are you serious? He would not play like that!" But I never went. Do I even have to explain the magnitude of the foolery behind this fumble? Good. Strike two.

And the third? A combination of several opportunities with notable individuals in the music industry, although the most prominent would be attending an audition amongst a few other females to rap the hook (chorus), which landed me a billboard plaque that made it to number one on the Billboard Hip Hop chart that I mentioned in a previous section. Yet after some time, I began to feel that the path was not for me and then one day, I finally asked God in prayer (for I had never asked before that moment), "God, if this is not the path you have for me, take the desire in me to go this route from me," as I always believed the music would be the springboard to catapult in all the things I *really* wanted to do. I promise you after that prayer, the desire to be a rapper was gone. I never felt the desire for a music career again. I was totally disconnected from the desire and removed from visions of that life as if it had never existed.

I honestly believe that God utilized those times to demonstrate to me an open door to take that path. I believe He was demonstrating that the path is here for you and can be made available, yet there is a preferred path He would rather me take. I either missed or forfeited that connection. Depends on how you look at it. I will not miss this one.

Psalm 32:8
I will instruct thee and teach thee in the way which thou shalt go: I will guide thee with mine eye

Identification Checkpoint

Psalm 86:11

Teach me your way, LORD, that I may rely on your faithfulness; give me an undivided heart, that I may fear your name

Part II

Now Boarding

SIGNS IT'S TIME TO CATCH YOUR 747 CONNECTION

POSITIVE ID

In law enforcement, positive id refers to the identification or proof of identity of an assailant or perpetrator by an eyewitness. I use the definition here to demonstrate what occurs when it is your time to move forward and answer your calling. I do not believe it always happens in this manner. I believe, as stated by the Apostle John Eckhardt that many prophets are appointed directly by God, as in the case of Jonah and Moses. No man or woman spoke over their lives and declared them a prophet. Jonah was sent to Nineveh by God Himself, and Moses was declared a prophet by God Himself.

Exodus 4:12
"Now therefore go, and I will be with thy mouth, and teach thee what thou shalt say."

Exodus 7:1-2
And the LORD said unto Moses, See, I have made thee a god to Pharaoh: and Aaron thy brother shall be thy prophet. Thou shalt speak all that I command thee: and Aaron thy brother shall speak unto Pharaoh, that he send the children of Israel out of his land.

However, in many cases, God will use man to identify the beginning of another's ministry, as in the case of John the Baptist and his identification of Jesus the Messiah.

John 1:29-36

The next day John seeth Jesus coming unto him, and saith, Behold the Lamb of God, which taketh away the sin of the world. This is he of whom I said, After me cometh a man which is preferred before me: for he was before me. And I knew him not: but that he should be made manifest to Israel, therefore am I come baptizing with water. And John bare record, saying, I saw the Spirit descending from heaven like a dove, and it abode upon him. And I knew him not: but he that sent me to baptize with water, the same said unto me, Upon whom thou shalt see the Spirit descending, and remaining on him, the same is he which baptizeth with the Holy Ghost. And I saw, and bare record that this is the Son of God. Again the next day after John stood, and two of his disciples; And looking upon Jesus as he walked, he saith, Behold the Lamb of God!

The Bible recounts that John even recognized and identified Jesus when they were in the womb.

Luke 1:41-44

And it came to pass, that, when Elisabeth heard the salutation of Mary, the babe leaped in her womb; and Elisabeth was filled with the Holy Ghost: And she spake out with a loud voice, and said, Blessed art thou among women, and blessed is the fruit of thy womb. And whence is this to me, that the mother of my Lord should come to me? For, lo, as soon as the voice of thy salutation sounded in mine ears, the babe leaped in my womb for joy.

I believe I was positively identified in April of 2021, although I did not see the experience with as much gravity as I do now or through the same lens. In April 2022, right smack in the middle of the spiritual war in which I was entrenched, a friend of mine forwarded a Facebook live recorded by a prophet she follows on the social media platform. The ministry is led by Prophetess Cheryl and is entitled Iamawife-Proverbs 31. I recall not wanting to listen as I had become fatigued praying for my romantic relationship, and by this point, I had surmised it was ending forever and ever, with no hope of ever rekindling, Amen. Yet something told me I needed to listen. Surprisingly, sister Cheryl was not focusing on marriage at all but instead talked of lineage, bloodline, and the rising of the Noahs of this generation to break generational curses.

It would not have been a big deal if she had not stated specifically that the Holy Spirit was saying, "You will not be like everyone else. You will not look like everyone else." She continued, "Tell them that their name is Noah." She goes on to state, "That's why you're so different. That's why people can't pinpoint you. That's why people look at you strangely. That's why people don't understand the relationship that you have with God. That's why you look different from your relatives. That's why you look different from your peers…That's why you look different—because you are a Noah."

Now to someone else, this has no real meaning, but for me, it has profound meaning as the initials of my name are N.O.A, which I pronounce phonetically as "Noah." If you know me in any capacity as an adult, you know that in corporate circles and even when penning books, I often state that my name is "Noa" to prevent people from saying Nonye incorrectly. As such, it made it difficult to brush off the prophetess's message. She then went on to say because I look different, act different and speak differently, God is changing my family's lineage through me. That's heavy. Some people may think it's nonsensical, crazy, and some kind of delusion of grandiosity. I do not. I am an intercessor for many and the intercessor for my family. Period. There is no doubt about it. I pray for many, some I know personally and many I do not. But I definitely pray and fast for my grandmother's grandchildren and great-grandchildren, whether I have a relationship with them or not. And she states clearly, that as a Noah, as one identified as a Noah, we are not perfect, but we alone God has found righteous, and because of that, everyone connected to us is blessed. And it is His plan and intention to remove everything disruptive and distorted from our bloodlines.

Whoever wants to refute this may do so. As Sister Cheryl states, we have haters, just as Noah did, that do not believe. But it is true. She states that our instructions have come from God, and because we are doing what God has said, and because we are trusting Him no matter what man may tell us if we are doing what God told us to do, then we are doing what is right before Him. She goes on to state that when we are doing what is right in God's eyes, it is going to look crazy to the world. And boy, is she right!

I circled back to my girlfriend and said, "Wow, thank you for sharing. You know those are my initials and my pen name, right?" She responded, "Yes, I know. That's why I sent it."

And so in April 2022, I was identified as a Noah, the changer of the destiny of my ancestral line, the transformer of my bloodline, the resetter of my lineage, the one that does what everyone else does not, and will not do, and that is why we look crazy to everyone else. We are building something that has never been built before. We believe in God the way he has not been believed in past generations. Even when we have to drag and fight ourselves into obedience, we serve the Lord. Even when we sin, we know to repent. Noahs change the lineage. Be extremely clear that this is not done in, by, or through our own power, but by the power of the Holy Spirit within us, in partnership, or better yet, in servitude to our Lord and Savior Jesus Christ, and by pleading His blood, and walking in the Holy Spirit every single day.

Isaiah 58:12
And they that shall be of thee shall build the old waste places: thou shalt raise up the foundations of many generations; and thou shalt be called, The repairer of the breach, The restorer of paths to dwell in.

Hebrews 11:7
By faith Noah, being warned of God of things not seen as yet, moved with fear, prepared an ark to the saving of his house; by which he condemned the world, and became heir of the righteousness which is by faith.

HE'S CLEANING YOU UP

One of the signs or precursors to your 747 moment is your decision to heed the nudging from the Holy Spirit to clean up your life. This period involves a conscious decision to disavow, disengage, and disconnect from many of the things you were doing that was unclean or polluting your walk with Christ. What it is for you is specific to your situation. For me, it was a struggle with lust and finally standing firm in my decision to refrain from pre-marital sex. And if it came down to it, being willing to accept the desire of the man I was living with to leave and not enter into marriage once I stated my shacking-up days were over. More importantly, I had made the decision to recommit to God because my worship, prayer, and fasting life had waned, and I was no longer keeping God as my top priority. Your case may be different. It may be refraining from using illicit or illegal drugs, getting intoxicated, gambling, or scamming (stealing), I don't know what it is for you specifically, but you have made a recent decision and have begun to set new, firm boundaries for yourself and those around you regarding your walk with Christ.

This decision has set events in motion that will initially leave you shocked and even bewildered. After which, your emotions may run the gamut from anger to disappointment, to regret to compassion. I am not certain why you have picked up this book, how you came across it, who may have purchased it for you, or if it will even resonate. However, the Holy Spirit saw fit for you to come into possession of this knowledge right now. My prayer is that you will be able to assess your current situation and use what I have gleaned from my personal journey as well as what has been revealed to me by the Holy Spirit to be successful on whatever journey you have currently embarked on, and victorious in whatever spiritual battle you are facing.

The next section of this book will be particularly useful if you find yourself in a current spiritual battle quite unlike any that you have experienced previously. In the pages that follow, I will illustrate the desolate places you may have recently exited or may be in right now. I have described each place with the degree of spiritual acuity that will assist you in identifying exactly where you are and attune you to what is transpiring spiritually. After which, I have listed several spiritual enemies that may be in your midst at this particular time before defining them clearly before the section's close.

Matthew 23:25-26
Woe unto you, scribes and Pharisees, hypocrites! for ye make clean the outside of the cup and of the platter, but within they are full of extortion and excess. Thou blind Pharisee, cleanse first that which is within the cup and platter, that the outside of them may be clean also.

Psalm 51:10
Create in me a clean heart, O God; and renew a right spirit within me.

ACQUIESENCE TO DESTINY DESTRUCTION

Doris Jakelloh of Elashib Ministries, an online Youtube ministry, did an excellent segment where she warned us about and expounded on the dangers of destiny destroyers. I would surmise that destiny destroyers may be the hugest enemy obstructing the children of God on the path to discovering their kingdom purpose and staying committed to the path once they find it. Destiny destroyers, as insidious as they are in nature, can fool us into believing they are harmless. As overtly and blaring obvious as they may be to those around us, many times, they are stealthy to those they are plaguing. Unfortunately, we have a tendency to discount them, downplay them, or be in total denial about them as we barrel ahead into deeper levels of destruction. What starts as an innocent choice to entertain an itsy-bitsy bit of destruction or waiving—be it temporarily or otherwise, of our values, morals, and commitment to walk a righteous path—will always lead to dire consequences. Let me clearly state that none of us walk a righteous path in our own power. We all do our best to walk righteously after we have confessed Jesus as our Lord and Savior, entered into his grace, and allowed his precious blood to wash us clean of sin so that we may walk with and be led by the Holy Spirit. Yet there are decisions we can make and certain lifestyles we can lead that can grieve the Holy Spirit and cause him to turn away from us—even if that was not our intention. Bishop Dale C. Bronner states, "When you play with the devil, you always stay longer than you want to stay, and pay more than you want to pay." I even recall an ad on a train I used to ride in New York that showcased poetry to give people something to lay their eyes on during their trip, stating something along the lines of "When dining with the devil, one always desires a handle with a long spoon, but when the opportunity arises, only a short handle spoon is available." When we make decisions that can lead us toward destruction and death, we usually have to make a conscious decision and conscious effort to do the work necessary to turn back, as the price to pay, the burden to carry, and collateral damage are more than we ever imagined. Sometimes the work consists of confession and repentance—a complete turning away and renouncing of what we were entertaining, and God will see fit to forgive us. Other times we can go so far that we not only forfeit our destiny but our very own lives and salvation.

Just as our internal forays with destiny destroyers can be deadly for us, so can the decisions we make to engage, entertain and turn a blind eye to individuals dabbling in a bit of destiny destruction of their own due to their habits and addictions to ill-considered behaviors. Our proximity to them can undoubtedly cause us physical, mental, and spiritual harm. If you find yourself here, currently fighting or indulging in sinful behaviors that are working to kill your destiny, or you continue to surround yourself with individuals that you know are living in agreement with spirits and behaviors (sins) whose effects are negatively impacting your ability to access your blessings or spiritual inheritance, then you are on dangerous ground. To do so is a portal to the demonic, a crack in your foundation, and an open invitation for Satan to steal territory, deceive you, oppress you and build strongholds in your life according to his pleasure. Playing with poisonous playmates is extremely dangerous for the child of God, for if these individuals refuse to raise to your spiritual level, you will sink to theirs. Below I have enumerated the destiny destroyers that you are most probably dealing with at this time and examples of many biblical characters that either succumbed to or were seduced by their wilds.

DESTINY DESTROYERS

Disobedience – Disobedience can be defined as failure or refusal to obey the rules or someone in authority. Biblical disobedience is a direct affront to God's authority, sovereignty, omniscience, and omnipotence. For if the Lord is all-knowing, all-seeing, all-powerful, and all-sufficient when He gives you instructions to follow, would it not be in your best interest to do so? Does He not see everything you cannot see—what is ahead and what is to come? When you are obedient, you demonstrate your love and trust for Him and your desire to keep safe the precious gem He has entrusted you with and given you stewardship over by following Him. That precious gem is you! Yet, when we are disobedient, we demonstrate our lack of trust, respect, and reverence for the Lord, which undoubtedly grieves Him and puts us in harm's way. Our disobedience will always depress, suppress, repress and sabotage God's purpose in our lives. It is a destiny destroyer, indeed.

Luke 6:46 KJV
Why do you call me "Lord, Lord, and not do what I tell you to do?

James 1:22 KJV
But be doers of the word, and not hearers only, deceiving yourselves.

1 Samuel 12:15 KJV
But if you will not obey the voice of the Lord, but reel against the commandment of the Lord, then the hand of the Lord will be against you and your king.

If the previous verses regarding disobedience are true, than the opposite must be true when you choose obedience and to fulfill his purpose for your life:

Luke 11:28 KJV
But he said, "Blessed rather are those who hear the word of God and keep it!"

Romans 5:19 KJV
"For as by the one man's disobedience the many were made sinners, so by the one man's obedience the many will be made righteous."

Rebellion – Rebellion is open defiance toward authority, established convention, or constituted government. For our purposes, it can be further described as willfully flagrant resistance or opposition to God's established kingdom. It is a hostile posture against God, his kingdom, its constitution (the bible and its applicable laws, principles, and guidelines), and its system of operation. It is a poor and costly choice for any believer that hopes to reach their mandated kingdom-purposed destiny. To be a believer and surround oneself with the rebellious threatens your future, as a commitment to a path of rebellion can cause God to turn from you, or worse, consider you as an enemy.

Psalm 107:1
Because they rebelled against the words of God and contemned the counsel of the Most High, therefore he brought down their heart with labour; they fell down, and there was none to help.

Proverbs 17;11
An evil man seeketh only rebellion: therefore a cruel messenger shall be sent against him.

Isaiah 63:10 KJV
But they rebelled, and vexed his Holy Spirit: therefore he was turned to be their enemy, and he fought against them

Proverbs 28:9
The one who turns away his ear from hearing the law, even his prayer is an abomination.

Greed – An intensely selfish and excessive desire for more of something than is needed, sufficient or necessary. Greed will always have you single-mindedly focused on the object of your pursuit but to your own detriment. Greed causes you to quickly burn through the blessings of God and to be blinded to God's generosity, favor, grace, and mercy. Greed ensures that you praise the gift and abandon the giver. Greed can cause you to lose your freedom, your provision, and your most prized relationships. It is a destiny destroyer that will quickly remove your heart, mind, and soul from the purposes of God.

Luke 12:15
"Then he said to them, "Watch out! Be on your guard against all kinds of greed; life does not consist in an abundance of possessions.""

Job 20:20
"Because his appetite is never satisfied, he does not let anything he desires escape."

Ephesians 5:3
"But among you there must not be even a hint of sexual immorality, or of any kind of impurity or of greed, because these are improper for God's holy people

Ecclesiastes 5:10
"Whoever loves money never has enough; whoever loves wealth is never satisfied with their income…"

Proverbs 21:26
"All day long he craves for more, but the righteous give without sparing."

Mark 8:36
What good is it for someone to gain the whole word, yet forfeit his soul?

Selfish Ambition - Selfish ambition can be defined as the illegitimate and brazen, oftentimes covert, unethical, and/or violent desire to elevate beyond or move ahead of others with no concern for their welfare or safety.

Psalm 119:36
Turn my heart toward your statues and not toward selfish gain.

Jeremiah 17:11 KJV
"As a partridge that broods but does not hatch, so is he who gets riches, but not by right; It will leave him in the midst of his days, and at his end he will be a fool."

NLV
"Like a partridge that hatches eggs it did not lay are those who gain riches by unjust means. When their lives are half gone, their riches will desert them, and in the end they will prove to be fools"

Isaiah 56:11
Meanwhile, the dogs have a mighty appetite they can never get enough. And as for them, they are the shepherds who lack understanding; they have all turned to their own way, each one to his gain, each and every one.

Philippians 2:3-4(NIV)
Do nothing out of selfish ambition or vain conceit. Rather, in humility value others above yourselves, not looking to your own interests but each of you to the interests of the others.

Proverbs 13:11
Dishonest money dwindles away, but whoever gathers money little by little makes it grow

1 Timothy 6:10 (NIV)
For the love of money is a root of all kinds of evil. Some people, eager for money, have wandered from the faith and pierced themselves with many griefs.

1 Timothy 6:9 (NIV)
Those who want to get rich fall into temptation and a trap and into many foolish and harmful desires that plunge people into ruin and destruction

Evil Company - Adding a positive to a negative will always result in a negative. That is a mathematical law, and it cannot be disputed. As such, if you are the lone person in your circle walking with God or doing your best to live in accordance with a life God would find pleasing, you will eventually be led to depart from your circle. If you refuse, *your allegiance to bad company will compromise your commitment to walk with God*. Whatever or whomever you surround yourself with, you will invariably become. If you surround yourself with thieves, the adulterous, idolatrous, slanderous, mean-spirited, or non-believers, then it is only a matter of time before you become the same and allow their values and morals, or lack thereof, to govern you. We all know, many of us firsthand, that the penal system is overrun with individuals that were unable to depart from the wrong crowd, negative friends, acquaintances, and associates.

1 Corinthians 15:33
"Be not deceived: evil communications corrupt good manners" KJV
"Do not be misled: "Bad company corrupts good character." (NLV)

Proverbs 25:26
"Like a muddied spring or a polluted well are the righteous who give way to the wicked"

2 Corinthians 6:14
"Do not be yoked together with unbelievers. For what do righteousness and wickedness have in common? Or what fellowship can light have with darkness?"

1 Corinthians 5:11 (NIV)
"But now I am writing to you that you must not associate with anyone who claims to be a brother or sister but is sexually immoral or greedy, an idolater or slanderer, a drunkard or swindler. Do not even eat with such people."

Proverbs 13:20
"Walk with the wise and become wise, for a companion of fools suffers harm."

Generational sin/Bloodline issues – General sin and bloodline issues are those issues, or more specifically, those patterns or sins that are passed down from generation to generation in your genealogy. It is a dominant pathology or condition that plays out in every generation of your family. For some of us, it is divorce and single parenthood, while for others, it is sexual abuse. For many, it is alcoholism, drug abuse, parental abandonment, murder, adultery, etc. It can even be the presence of certain diseases in your family or pathology in your lineage where every woman in your family dies by the age of fifty-five. It is not foolishness or malarkey. It is a very real thing whose effects can be detrimental when ignored, dismissed, and not deliberately averted or spiritually confronted. It is a common destiny destroyer.

Deuteronomy 5:9
"…for I, the LORD your God, am a jealous God, punishing the children for the sin of the parents to the third and fourth generation of those that hate me."

Exodus 34:7
"And the LORD passed before him and proclaimed, "The LORD, the LORD God, merciful and gracious, longsuffering and abounding in goodness and truth, keeping mercy for thousands, forgiving iniquity and transgression and sin, and that will by no means clear the guilty; *visiting the iniquity of the fathers upon the children, and upon the children's children, unto the third and to the fourth generation.*"

Pride – Pride is the deep pleasure or excitement aroused when one considers a personal accomplishment or accomplishment of a loved one. Pride, as referenced in the bible, refers to excessive consciousness of one's own dignity, pedigree, and importance. It speaks to one's profound and obstinately high opinion of oneself. In many cases, it is coupled with off-putting arrogance and self-aggrandizement that blinds a person's ability to see situations clearly and objectively or accept good counsel. It ensures the individual never or begrudgingly gives God credit for their success as they believe they are the sole source of their good. They boastfully believe that they do not depend on anyone except themselves, and neither do they owe anyone anything. Pride is a poison that skews a person's view, understanding, and receptiveness as they are unable to hear what a person is stating to them. It leads to self-righteous delusion and undoubtedly ensures the individual walks in their flesh. Refusal to be spirit-led due to pride sidelines you and separates you from your destiny.

Psalm 10:4
In his pride the wicked man does not seek him; in all his thoughts there is no room for God.

Proverbs 16:5
"The LORD detests all the proud of heart. Be sure of this: They will not go unpunished."

Galatians 6:1-3
Brothers and sisters, if someone is caught in a sin, you who live by the Spirit should restore that person gently. But watch yourselves, or you also may be tempted. Carry each other's burdens, and in this way you will fulfill the law of Christ. If anyone thinks they are something when they are not, they deceive themselves.

Proverbs 29:23
Pride brings a person low, but the lowly in spirit gain honor.

Proverbs 21:24
The proud and arrogant person—"Mocker" is his name— behaves with insolent fury.

Proverbs 21:4
Haughty eyes and a proud heart— the unplowed field of the wicked— produce sin.

Proverbs 18:12
Before a downfall the heart is haughty, but humility comes before honor.

Part III

Fasten Your Seatbelts

YOUR HOLY PAUSE EXPERIENCE

When utilizing the term Holy Pause, I am referring to an edict sent directly from the throne of heaven, placing a halt on any and all purpose-related activity, productivity, and progress due to the enemy in your midst.

Psalm 27:5
For in the time of trouble he shall hide me in his pavilion: in the secret of His tabernacle shall he hide me;

Psalm 31:20 NKJV
You hide them in the secret place of Your presence from the plots of man; You shall keep them secretly in a shelter from the strife of tongues

Psalm 17:8
Keep me as the apple of the eye; Hide me in the shadow of Your wings

Psalm 64:2 NKJV
Hide me from the secret counsel of the wicked, From the rebellion of the workers of iniquity

There are several instances in the bible when God conceals his prophets or chosen, but I would like to bring your attention to the time I associate most with the Holy Pause definition. This instance denotes that all activity associated with an anointed one or prophet's callings ceased as God hid them from their enemies. The Holy Pause is most exemplified in the story of Obadiah.

I Kings 18:3-4
And Ahab called Obadiah, which was the governor of his house. (Now Obadiah feared the Lord greatly for it was so, when Jezebel cut off the

prophets of the LORD, that Obadiah took a hundred prophets, and hid them by fifty in a cave, an fed them with bread and water.)

I utilize this instance as an example of a Holy Pause, for I am sure one hundred prophets of the Lord were not able to operate in their normal capacity as mouths of the Lord to the people whilst held up in a cave for their protection.

As for your experience of a Holy Pause, it may even be more treacherous than in the case of the one hundred prophets because the enemy has taken up residence in your life, your inner circle, and many times, more often than not, your home is an enemy of God. You are in clear and present danger, but because of the proximity and masterful guile of this person and the spirit within them, you are completely oblivious. The spirit to which I am referring I have identified as the hyena spirit. This spirit, characterized by its deceptive, manipulative, controlling, lull-inducing opportunistic characteristics, is a thief that sees you as a meal or as their meal ticket. It is extremely skilled at wearing his/her mask that you are completely unaware of their true intentions and motives. Although you have been unable to identify their intentions, they have easily identified you. Whether it be due to your tendency to be a loner or due to a season of separation in your life, you have been targeted. You are unaware, yet I assure you that everyone else around this person is not, and they are completely aware of this person's campaign of deception, lies, and false accusations against you. To add insult to injury, they are collectively mocking you—all of them—as that is exactly what the laughing, opportunistic hyena spirit does. Thankfully, God has disengaged all progress and upward movement for your safety and the safety of the destiny he has purposefully hidden inside you. You may not know the potential for your greatness. You may suspect it, but may not be totally confident in that knowing, but the hyena sees it, and it enrages them because they have either not identified theirs, forfeited it, or may like yours better. Either way, your destiny—spiritual and financial is on their menu.

What is God's response to this enemy of your life and the enemy of His plan? Thanatosis or Tonic Immobility. Tonic immobility is a reflex many animals possess that allows them to minimize their struggle or the possibility of injury by ceasing to move. Most of us know the term as playing possum. Linda Roberts, the author of *"Discover Your True Worth: Becoming the Woman God Created You to Be,"* introduces the concept when discussing how Samson so easily submitted to Delilah's manipulation. In this case, Roberts asserts that Samson surrendered to his enemy's attack. Yet, in the case of the 747 believer, I believe it is a demonstration of God's protective hand on your life. It is a God-imposed, God-enforced move of God that brings all forward moving or upward mobility in your life to a screeching halt. Isn't our God awesome?! To think that he loves you enough and thinks that the calling on your life is so critical to the plans of His kingdom that when someone who can risk it all or steal it from under your nose has slipped past your defenses, he steps in to halt all movement. It is His way of saying, "Move on. There is nothing to see here. No reason to stay. No gold to strike with this one." How brilliant is our God? The God that can hide his sons and daughters in plain sight for their protection.

You may act like you cannot see what is going on in your current situation, but there are signs. You just refuse to see them. This person that God deems necessary for Him to protect you from has demonstrated that they are a liar, deceitful and concerned—wholeheartedly with unscrupulous self-advancement from your sweat, tears, and toil—be it spiritual, mental, physical, or monetary. They do not truly love you, support you, or believe in you, and most importantly, they are unconcerned with pleasing God or with how God sees them.

ENEMY SPIRITS IN YOUR MIDST
- ⚠ DELILAH
- ⚠ JEZEBEL
- ⚠ HEROD
- ⚠ THE HYENA SPIRIT
- ⚠ JUDAS
- ⚠ SERPENT
- ⚠ WANDERER/VAGABOND SPIRIT
- ⚠ SQUIRREL
- ⚠ FROG

ILLEGAL PAUSE

On the surface level, the illegal pause appears to be the same as the Holy Pause, yet it is not. During a Holy Pause, God has halted a degree, if not all, progress in your life to hide you from an enemy. During this time, you are experiencing a great level of discomfort as you cannot understand the level of lethargy and apathy that has beset you in regard to your purpose and very recent work.

In contrast, you will know that you are engaged in an illegal pause because you are not actively pursuing your life's purpose or goals, and you are pretty laissez-faire about it. You may even be intentionally avoiding all things God and all things even remotely associated with your calling.

There are two instances of the illegal pause in scripture. The first is found in the all too familiar story of Jonah. His spiritually illegal response to the Lord brought a host of problems for him and those around him.

Jonah 1:1-3

"Now the word of the LORD came unto Jonah the son of Amittai, saying, Arise, go to Nineveh, that great city, and cry against it; for their wickedness is come up before me. But Jonah rose up to flee unto Tarshish from the presence of the LORD, and went down to Joppa; and he found a ship going to Tarshish: so he paid the fare thereof, and went down into it, to go with them unto Tarshish from the presence of the LORD."

The second is quietly mentioned when we study the work of Apostle Paul. When Paul and Barnabas decide they should return to the towns to which they preached to check on their progress, Barnabas desired to bring John, called Mark. Paul did not because of an illegal pause taken by Mark at some time prior. Paul was so displeased with Mark's illegal pause that the disagreement caused him to part ways with Barnabas.

Acts 15:36-39

"And some days after Paul said unto Barnabas, Let us go again and visit our brethren in every city where we have preached the word of the Lord, and see how they do. And Barnabas determined to take with them John, whose surname was Mark. But Paul thought not good to take him with them, *who departed from them from Pamphylia, and went not with them to the work.* And the contention was so sharp between them, that they departed asunder one from the other: and so Barnabas took Mark, and sailed unto Cyprus;

Although the illegal pause which I speak of may be even more deliberate and longer than that of Jonah's and Mark's, I offer those instances for scriptural context. The illegal pause of which I speak is a total dismissal of the idea of being sold out for God, finding your purpose, or being committed to it. Instead, there is a very real effort to slay your ambitions and quiet any resistance to your new existence. You have become quite fine with the relinquishing of your purpose. You are complacent and are slowly morphing into a person you have never been, almost entering an agreement with the malevolent being in your life to be their life force and ultimate undergirding. This is not the decision to be a supportive life mate who is actively pursuing their kingdom purpose while remaining helpful and supportive to that of their kingdom mate, or who is partnering with their mate to manifest their kingdom purpose assignment. This is a total relinquishing of yourself and all of the excavation work you have done to figure out who God created you to be and what he has called you to do. You may not know what he has called you to do in its entirety, but whatever you do know, you have jettisoned without remorse. The unholy pause has not been placed on you by God or another person. It is a rebellious demonstration of free will. Although quite similar to the Sleeping Beauty state in which we will delve next, in terms of the lack of unproductiveness, the Sleeping Beauty state is different because there is a willful attempt of someone around you to lull you into a false sense of security which is threatening your spiritual identity, resources, and destiny.

ENEMY SPIRITS IN YOUR MIDST
- ⚠ DELILAH
- ⚠ JEZEBEL
- ⚠ WITCHES, WARLOCKS, AGENTS OF DARKNESS
- ⚠ HEROD
- ⚠ PHAROAH
- ⚠ LEVIATHAN
- ⚠ RACCOON
- ⚠ ARMIDILLO
- ⚠ FROG
- ⚠ SERPENT
- ⚠ SQUIRREL
- ⚠ HYENA
- ⚠ WANDERER/VAGABOND SPIRIT
- ⚠ HAMAN

SLEEPING BEAUTY

Millicent Jackson, leader of a ministry movement named, The Kingdom of God Matters, released an extremely timely and alarmingly accurate, informative, and empowering segment on the Sleeping Beauty archetype on which I will expound. If you have recently escaped this sleeping beauty-like experience, congratulations are in order as you have successfully evaded spiritual death, a hollow, zombie-like existence, or a very real and tangible demise. If this experience is not even vaguely familiar, be very, very thankful. While you may not have experienced a recent threat of this magnitude, you may have experienced a tangible effort by those around you to either deceive you, separate you from your resources, or derail your destiny. Please read the following scenario as a cautionary tale or bleeping alarm imploring you to stay alert to a very real and potentially life-jeopardizing peril. For those of you that believe this moniker may describe a very recent experience, I pray that you are no longer in this place. I pray the nightmarish-pseudo-fairy tale is now over.

I believe most healthy relationships—business, platonic and romantic have a honeymoon or fairytale phase, which inevitably comes to an end. It is no fault of the parties involved but rather the natural progression of the healthy relationship and the process that begins as you discover your mutual imperfections. The end of the honeymoon phase signals the relationship's growth into a new phase of maturity and development which should ultimately usher the relationship into a place of unconditional love or at least as close as we can get to it. Yet, in this particular instance, I am not referencing the gradual blossoming of a relationship into a healthy, mature, loving relationship. But rather, a relationship that, over time, has deteriorated into a one-sided energy-sapping liaison that has hemorrhaged your joy, peace of mind, and financial and spiritual resources.

As such, the pain, confusion, and disillusionment you experience daily as you try to reconcile the barrage of deceit and lies geared to make you disbelieve what you know, see, and feel are draining. And although the

Holy Spirit and your intuition herald messages of light at a soprano-like octave to awaken you from the very nefarious and deliberate attempt to lull you to sleep, you ignore them. You are constantly on the offensive—fending off the daily barrage of deceit, lies, false promises, gestures of disloyalty, and all manner of abuse and cruelty. So you pray. Though it seems that the harder you pray for God's intervention, the more this person watches you pray to God, and the more hostile they get. Yet you are still unaware of this person's secret disdain for your desire to seek an authentic, intimate relationship with God. You are still unaware that you were targeted because of your trusting and forgiving nature. You are still unaware of this person's opportunistic and envy-fueled plot to level up by stripping you of your resources, life's direction, purpose, and relationship with God. And for many of you that find this to be eerily reminiscent of a recent romantic situation, you may have suspected an even more diabolical plan.

As Millicent Jackson warns, many of us are being used as a cover—the perfect cover for an individual who is living a double life. Therefore their deception is not only geared to keep you in a foggy, energy-draining, destiny-swallowing, demonic stupor, but for you to run interference and provide a clean image for this person's unquenchable sexual addiction, penchant for drug-fueled orgies, couples only swinger parties, undisclosed homosexual lifestyle, penchant for minors, incestuous and/or extra-marital affair, secret pregnancy, gambling habit, or criminal activities that may include the trafficking of young girls, illicit drugs or other nefarious activities. Only you know what you were helping this individual hide, willfully ignoring, or just in dangerous denial about. But your refusal to speak against the behavior, set boundaries, or RUN FOR YOUR LIFE kept you locked in a perpetual state of spiritual paralysis and immobility. You naively entered into an agreement to be misused, abused, controlled, and subjected to a noxious and toxic existence. You disengaged from family, loved ones, friends, and your purpose—and became a shell of your former self. You were in bondage—mental, emotional, spiritual, physical, financial, and sexual, and totally oblivious to the slow and methodical breakdown of your personage.

And consequently, you are dancing with the devil sleeping beauty, or more accurately, sleep-walking with an energy vampire. You are entertaining a narcissist who was happy to receive the attention and adulation that was once reserved for God. Whatever you believe this relationship to be, it is not. It is toxic, noxious, and blatantly idolatrous. The only thing reminiscent of your previous life is your ability to press forward in prayer—and thank God as it is your only saving grace. And as God graces you to avoid the snares and webbed nets, you discover an even more sinister campaign of lies, rumors, and false accusations beginning to take form. The entire experience is unreal—surreal even. You have an idea that the person is behaving surreptitiously and have even caught them in several lies, but you have no idea of the magnitude of the betrayal. Though the more layers unravel, the more piercing the devastation. I want to make clear that not every 747 woman will have this specific experience, and those that may, may not experience the degree of toxicity illustrated here. Yet, whoever the culprit is, and however they have shown up in your life, there is no denying that there is a very real, deliberate attempt to mislead, misuse, abuse, and dominate you into submission and, if that fails, a sinister campaign to destroy your reputation and leave you in total ruin quickly takes its place.

ENEMY SPIRITS IN YOUR MIDST
- ⚠ DELILAH
- ⚠ JEZEBEL
- ⚠ WITCHES, WARLOCKS, AGENTS OF DARKNESS
- ⚠ HEROD
- ⚠ PHAROAH
- ⚠ LEVIATHAN
- ⚠ RACCOON
- ⚠ ARMADILLO
- ⚠ FROG

⚠ SERPENT
⚠ SQUIRREL
⚠ WANDERER/VAGABOND SPIRIT

ONSLAUGHT BY THE COUNTERFEIT:

During this season, your experience of the counterfeit may be two-fold or multi-layered. You have come to the realization that the individual you were in a relationship with (romantic, business, mentor, etc.) is a counterfeit you were either unable or unwilling to discern as such. However, they presented themselves in the beginning, whatever they stated as their intention has now been outed as a total fabrication because this experience brings into focus a gross betrayal where you are either skipped over, overlooked, or replaced for another who is indeed your doppelgänger—albeit superficially. Whomever your initial betrayer is, their betrayal demonstrates their belief that this person that they have passed you over for is in better standing or more promising for them, their goals, vision, and future spiritually, mentally, emotionally, financially, or even physically. They believe that this person trumps your level of intelligence, the breadth of your experience, your network, your business savviness, and the essence of your personhood. Whatever your spiritual state when this information crystallizes—whether have been spiritually sidelined, are fast asleep, in the midst of an unauthorized spiritual pause, or engaging dangerous destiny destroyers by your hand or at the hands of others, if it has not already occurred, then you are moments away from a confrontation with this counterfeit. And they are indeed a counterfeit because as unknown as this person is to you, it is clear that they have opted to play the background and are very much aware of who you are, have gone to great lengths to research you and to manipulate situations to ensure constant comparison in order to sabotage your current relationship and prove to your betrayer that they are the better choice. This will be evident in their conversation, and the topics they steer the conversation toward, by words said and words left unsaid. Woman of God, this counterfeit has targeted your life and what they believe that you possess. Be clear, they have been studying you via information given to them by your betrayer and their own efforts. They have waited for a long time to get the opportunity to speak to "the one." And they are clear that you are the one and have done everything in their power to convince your betrayer(s) that you were not and are co-conspirators in the betrayal and, in many cases, are the inciting agent.

Isaiah 54:17 (NKJV)
No weapon that is formed against you shall prosper. And every tongue which rises against you in judgment You shall condemn. This is the heritage of the servants of the LORD, And their righteousness is from Me," says the LORD

ENEMY SPIRITS IN YOUR MIDST
- ⚠ JUDAS
- ⚠ JEZEBEL
- ⚠ DELILAH
- ⚠ WITCHES
- ⚠ WARLOCKS
- ⚠ AGENTS OF DARKNESS
- ⚠ FROG
- ⚠ VIPER

CONFRONTATION WITH WITCHCRAFT:

I am going to be very honest here. I have never been one to put much stock into stories of people I knew being hexed, or stories heard via the rumor mill concerning victims of someone putting roots on them - although I heard many growing up. Whenever a friend would tell me a story about a woman putting roots on her ex-boyfriend or new love interest, I always took it with a grain of salt. I am not too sure why I did not pay it much mind. Maybe it was a cultural thing, but whatever the case, I would listen to the story and, in my mind, cynically say, "Hmmm, that's interesting."

In hindsight, I was a bit more aware of it than I wished to believe or admit. I definitely visited a Wiccan shop located in New York City's village with a friend to purchase candles—specifically colored candles to assist me with focusing my intent on a certain desire. I am pretty sure I did not make the connection then that it was witchcraft or at least a portal leading to it, but I understand that fully now. As I span through my rolodex of memories, I remember a girlfriend stating her hairstylist suggested that she put a cinnamon stick in a jar of honey to keep her man sweet on her, "Hmmm." I thought nothing of it then, but now? Now I understand it to be a dangerous undertaking and a walk on a slippery slope to rebellion.

When I think of this premise further, I recall that I used to purchase a hair serum from a little shop in the Bronx that sold candles, many of them in honor of the Catholic saints. Back then, it was not a big deal to enter, but today, not a place I would frequent. And just as I mentioned in an earlier section, I most definitely came across a book of spells and chants in my high school's library. I am never able to think of that memory without asking myself why a Wiccan book would be in a Catholic High School library. There was even a hair salon I frequented in Harlem that was next door to a live chicken coup. I remember asking someone what they were doing with all of those chickens and was told they were for use in the Santeria religion. I knew then that was something for which I needed to steer clear. Thank the Lord that my naivety did not take me that far. Yet it has, in seasons and years past, led me to pay for palm readings, tea leaf readings, tarot card readings, psychic readings, read horoscopes, etc. I share my experience to inform you of how innocent the foray into the demonic is and the seemingly harmless deceptive ploys of the devil to lead believers to open and enter Satanic portals.

Hosea 4:6
My people perish for lack of knowledge

At these times in my life, I did not consider these things harmful at all. Let me state boldly that I have prayed and repented, profusely denouncing and renouncing any and all covenants, contracts, vows, agreements, exalting of demonic altars—anything that I have ever done—me, my child, my mother, father, grandparents, forefathers, and foremothers have been rebuked in the name of Yeshua the Christ—and cleansed by his blood! It has been renounced, denounced, rejected, ejected, dejected, and obliterated by Holy Ghost fire and the all-consuming, fiery hand of God the Father Almighty!

Some of you will say, "Dis tew much" and think I am going overboard with my assertion that it is a gateway to the demonic, believing all of my denunciations are unnecessary, or you may think the initial decision to even do it was woefully foolish. Please be mindful that the Holy Spirit convicts us at different levels according to our understanding, position, office, and purpose in the kingdom and at designated times during our lives. There are many things some of you will never do that I have, and there are many things that you have done or do that God would never allow me to get away with—and I mean never, as small as it might be for you. That is just how it is; it has always been that way for me, and most prophets will tell you the same.

Yet this is the full gamut of my interaction with what I now believe to be witchcraft and portals leading to particularly dark places, which would undoubtedly lead to the erecting of and agreement with wicked, satanic, unholy, unrighteous, and just plain evil altars and/or agreements, contracts, vows, covenants, and strongholds.

If indeed you are under attack, at this time, God will reveal it to you. The revelations will start out very small—things that you may chalk up as to being said in gist, but as this experience intensifies, so too will your revelations, truth, and dreams concerning what is transpiring and has been transpiring for some time. For me, an example of a small revelation occurred during a very casual conversation where someone that I did not think of as an enemy at the time mentioned someone we knew in common, that I was certain did not like me, had joined a new religion and was in town searching for a live chicken. "I'm sorry…pardon me, what?" That is exactly what I thought to myself. Yet my response was not one of fear, although I knew immediately whatever they were doing was targeted my way. How foolish for anyone on this earth to believe the blood of a chicken would frighten me when I am saturated and drenched in the blood of Yeshua, the Christ—the Lamb slain from the foundation of the world (Revelation 13:8).

I even recall being in the car with this person while noticing that they continued to play a certain rap song where the artist stated he sold his soul to the devil—continually playing that exact part and song. It was not accidental. It was not coincidental. It was intentional and geared to put me on notice that they had decided who they would worship. I would also like to add that on several occasions, the person stated they were "dealing with" or "fighting their demons." Sisters in Christ, this is not a phrase to take lightly. This is not a phrase you should ignore if someone in your proximity states it, nor is it a phrase for you to ever repeat, for I assure you it is a mirror into the soul and speaks to where you are spiritually. Am I stating that whoever says these words are demon-possessed? I cannot say that with one hundred percent certainty without having contact with the person, but if they say it a lot and often, especially if you have warned them about the power of their words and their ability to attract or repel experiences into their lives, it is highly likely. Often you are not able to tell just by looking at a person with your natural eyes. Discernment of spirits requires you to look through your spiritual eyes, or spiritual discernment, more specifically, biblical discernment.

Malachi 3:18
Then shall ye return, and discern between the righteous and the wicked, between him that serveth God and him that serveth him not

During another conversation with a person eventually revealed as an enemy and practicing witchcraft, I witnessed, in real time, her anger after discovering that someone had betrayed her. She immediately shared that she was contacting her roots/voodoo lady to take care of him. If you are anything like me, the logical thought that follows is if you put roots on someone that has angered you or against someone that did not give you what you want, you will undoubtedly put roots on that person to get what you want, and on me too. It was clear she was both envious of me and jealous and believed I had something she wanted that she was determined to get.

Unbeknownst to me—until it was revealed by the Holy Spirit, every single one of these individuals and a few others, including a relative, were attacking me spiritually—spell work, incantations, chants, witchcraft, hexes, ill-spoken words, or just plain praying to God for my harm, hurt, abandonment, embarrassment, removal and/or demotion. Let me state clearly, I do not fear witches, warlocks, voodoo priests, priestesses, sorcerers, sorceresses, enchantresses, etc. I will not be spiritually hunted, surveilled or surveyed, triggered or intimidated by telepathic threats and/or insults by individuals who use the blood of chickens or whatever else to interrogate me via my dreams, monitor my destiny, inflict curses and/or harm me… I am a child of the Most High God and I will not be moved. And please believe this for it is my wholehearted belief and assertion that I am indeed cloaked in the Lord's favor and surrounded by a hedge of His protection.

Galatians 3:26
For ye are all the children of God by faith in Christ Jesus

Proverbs 8:35
For whoso findeth me findeth life, and shall obtain favour of the LORD

Psalms 62:5-6
My soul, wait thou only upon God; for my expectation is from Him. He only is my rock and my salvation: He is my defence; I shall not be moved."

Proverbs 12:3
A man shall not be established by wickedness; but the root of the righteous shall not be moved

Job 1:10
Hast not thou made a hedge about him, and about his house, and about all that he hath on every side? Thou hast blessed the work of his hands, and his substance is increased in the land

As far as I am concerned the only blood that has any power is the blood of Jesus Christ, the Messiah, the Highest Priest, the Lord of Lords and King of Kings, the Resurrected King, the Warrior Prince, the propitiation of my sins, not just for my sins, but the sins of the entire world (1 John 2:1-2). And I believe in the depths of my soul that the God of Israel fights for me (Exodus 14:14). Now that that is settled, let me make this crystal clear, although I do not fear them or any power they may have, and know Elohim fights for me, if indeed I am called by my Father to enter battle, I will war against any demonic agent of darkness coming my way, or in the way of my loved ones, and send whomever they are, and whomever they war in the name of, back to the eternal fiery pit of hell from which they came. I am aware that what I am recounting is not your everyday experience and to the natural eye these incidents sound bizarre, weird, spooky and chock full of paranoia. You may not be a person that would be seduced into using these weapons, but you would be shocked to know the amount of people who are and use them regularly. When you have a call on your life and do you best to live a righteous, spirit led life, this is more commonplace than you think. For the 747 woman, this experience, as strange as it may sound is not only relatable but shockingly accurate.

Ephesians 6:12
For we wrestle not against flesh and blood, but against principalities, against powers, against the rulers of the darkness of this world, against spiritual wickedness in high places

I want to clearly state that at this point I am unaware if these individuals are still practicing witchcraft. For the sake of their souls, I hope not. Yet, their use of witchcraft during this season has placed a schism between us that will never allow the relationship we shared before this time to be restored—not as it was previously constituted, for that relationship is irretrievably broken. Even so, I have forgiven them. At this time, however, their energy should not be spent trying to restore a relationship with me, but rather on asking Yeshua for forgiveness, making Him the Lord of their lives and entering relationship with Him.

A CLOSER LOOK: ENEMY SPIRITS

For the purposes of the following section, I am defining spirit as the demonic hold, influence or presence of an unholy spiritual being or entity that is expressed through specific personality traits, characteristics, and behaviors.

Many of the spirits listed below will correlate to specific animals and their traits. Do not be alarmed or find it strange. Jesus our Lord and Savior is referred to as the Lamb of God (John 1:29), the Lion of the tribe of Judah (Revelation 5:5) and is our Divine Scapegoat (Leviticus 16). Time and time again Jesus refers to believers as his flock—his sheep. The parable of the sheep and the goats is yet another example of Jesus using animals or an earthly understanding to illustrate spiritual truths. Further, Jesus utilizes animal metaphors to prepare his disciples for their missions and as a way of highlighting the walk of the believer and the potential perils that can befall them.

Matthew 10:16

"Behold, I send you forth as sheep in the midst of wolves: be ye therefore wise as serpents, and harmless as doves."

As such, I have listed the revelations received from the Holy Spirit regarding the demonic entities and beings in my midst during this time. The Holy Spirit worked in wondrous ways to reveal to the animals to include, research, which characteristics to highlight, connect, etc.

Agents of Darkness (See witches and warlocks)

Armadillo – The Armadillo spirit is named after the placental mammal. Armadillo means "little armored one" yet when considering this spirit, the name is misleading as the *Armadillo spirit symbolizes one that rejects/refuses to utilize the armor of God and instead chooses worldly armor.* This spirit represents predators that are typically bullies, externally (individual vs. others), yet internally are cowards avoiding self-reflection, introspection or long honest looks at themselves (individual vs. personal demons/addictions/trauma). *This spirit is co-dependent and seeks a cadre of human sources of energy rather than building a sustaining, life giving relationship with God.* Its preference is to seek and attach to weak individuals that share weak attributes/that will not challenge them. Afraid to be out front, center stage, or to confront wrongs without the aid of narcotics or alcoholism, and they can be extremely withdrawn and quiet in a crowd. This spirit has poor judgement and decision-making skills utilizing chemical dependencies to mask low self-esteem, trauma, and depression. Yet fundamentally, it is what Emmalea Butler, contributor to the SundaySchoolNetwork.com asserts as being dead in Christ, unprepared for spiritual battle and unable to fight battles the way in which God has prepared us to engage.

Bondage – Unfathomable toil, hardship and oppression. Intense incoherence, bewilderment, and despondency. An arrest of freedom of thought, attitude, mental aptitude, emotions, action, physiology, finances, etc. *Bondage ushers in the grave risk of increasing hopelessness and apathy toward the purposes of God.*

Delilah – Linda Roberts, in her book entitled, *Discover Your True worth: Becoming the Woman God Created You to Be,"* deems the Delilah spirit a "God-opposing spirit…It is as a manipulating spirit by which they control people through seductive behavior designed to distract them and keep them from fulfilling God's purposes for their lives. She describes this spirit as very attractive—sometimes beautiful and even states, *"A Delilah is anything or anyone that takes a person away from God."*

Frog – Biblically, the frog is known as an unclean spirit. Unclean spirits are most readily identified by their idolatrous and sexually immoral nature. As such, the power of the frog spirit rests in its tongue as individuals possessing this spirit tend to be gifted with charismatic speech (when the audience is known), easily gain favor with others (popularity) when the audience is not perceived as intimidating or on a higher level, and are masterful in the art of sexual seduction—making love to their victim's ears and mind which lays the snare leading to sexual bondage. In addition, this spirit has the ability to cloak its intentions (spiritual invisibility), lull victims into a trance, engage multiple mates/sexual partners and is privy to incestuous breeding. Extremely influential, this spirit courts others to join their campaigns of attack (gang-stalking). Individuals attached to this spirit are mentally unstable, thrive in chaos, and suffer from severe insomnia. Further, the eyes of the frog are located on the top of its head, it has a large field of vision. Individuals with this spirit easily identify, monitor, track and hover their victims. *The frog spirit acts as a hypnotic pied piper enticing its victim to substitute their pursuit of God for the pursuit of carnal pleasures particularly sensual in nature.*

Goliath – Goliath is the dreadful, Philistine giant from Gath, which David slayed. David's battle with Goliath and impending victory is the entry point of David's ascent and end to his God ordained hidden season. History notes that Goliath dwarfs David in stature. When considering the enemy in your midst that is attached to this spirit, you may feel dwarfed by their physical stature, social or financial status, or even when taking into account the amount of people they have gathered to go up against you and you alone. It is important to state that although a confrontation of this type or magnitude may be new to you, this individual is accustomed to starting these types of fights and conflicts and has grown accustomed to winning them. But David is not threatened. He is incensed by Goliath's mockery of the God of Israel and their response to the Philistine's challenge of war. The Israelites were intimidated, dismayed, mocked and afraid. Individuals possessed by the spirit of Goliath are indeed bullies, targeting individuals they consider to be weaker, isolated and without what they believe is adequate support. They seek to intimidate their opponents, stalk fear in them and taunt them with a sense that going up against them is a losing battle in order to douse your faith in God. David identifies Goliath as an "uncircumcised Philistine" highlighting that he was not in covenant with God. As such, the *Goliath in your life stands outside true covenant with God*. They may recite a few bible verses, but they have not taken the time or effort to develop an intimate relationship with the Lord that would allow for the renewing of their minds, lasting transformation or true power.

Haman – Haman is central to Queen Esther's story. The spirit of Haman operates in individuals that want a glorious come up or promotion filled with bells, whistles and fanfare without the true work it takes do so. Individuals under the influence of the spirit of Haman seek to curry favor or gain approval from people seated in the high places of their lives. The individual's sense of self-value and worth is usually deeply intertwined in acceptance of these individuals as they follow how they are perceived by them more than they will ever value you. These key figures can be their employer, client, fraternity, sorority, neighborhood clique, etc. But there is an established pecking order/hierarchy in which they seek to ascend or maintain position. These individuals will even manufacture false allegations against if indeed they believe it will please those they are trying to impress. Yet, currying favor with those with social status is just a symptom of a deeper desire to relish in the worship that is reserved for those in high positions—not for the specific position but for the level of adoration they believe that position affords. If after their efforts this adulation and worship is not received, as in the case of Mordecai refusing to worship Haman, they are enraged and seek to humiliate, degrade, socially annihilate and harm the transgressor that rebuffed their quest to assert their power before an audience. In the 747 woman's case, these hollow people are usually the individual's fake friends, shallow acquaintances, toxic family members and many times overbearing, highly manipulative, possessive parents. This spirit desperately craves accolades and worship and will use underhanded, unscrupulous and at times violent measures to secure it—and if in the possession of a believer, even better. Just as Haman loathed the Israelites and Mordecai—to the point of seeking his death, *the spirit of Haman detests and seeks to harm those that place God first and pursue righteousness*—just like the spirit of King Saul.

Herod The Great – The spirit of Herod the Great (BC) is a spirit of fear. *It points to an individual's fear of God's will and plan for humankind.* This spirit goes to great measures to stop the plans of God. This spirit will materialize in your life as someone that is afraid you will abandon them once you are successful or someone who does not want you to become more successful than they are, so much so, they will do whatever they can to stop it. This spirit materializes as a saboteur and conspirator in your inner circle. The Herod spirit is zealous in its monitoring, detection, and hovering efforts - driven by extreme paranoia, insecurity and belief that those around him are disloyal and plotting to dupe, abuse or humiliate them.

Hyena – Similar to how hyenas in the wild form coalitions and weigh some relationships in their clan as more important than others, those individuals operating in the hyena spirit value social status above all. Just as their counterparts in the animal kingdom are oftentimes referred to as intelligent tricksters, so too are individuals walking in this spirit as they are masters of distraction, deception and conciliation (for the sake of appearances only). They tend to be raised in ultra-matriarchal environments which may explain their comfort with the rumor mill and tendency to utilize verbal expression as a weapon. The hyena spirit orchestrates smear campaigns, hurls false accusations and seeks to mock and jeer its enemy. The laughter associated with the Spotted Hyena is actually the animal's way of alerting others in their clan to a food source, which is akin to this spirit's mocking and jeering of a believer to alert others to a new victim in which to harass or in younger circles, gang-stalk. Not only are hyenas thieves of dignity and reputation but in the wild, they are known to shamelessly snatch a meal if they see an opportunity to do so. As such, when the hyena spirit is in operation, it will stealthy snatch money, jewelry, vehicles, sensitive data, etc. *The hyena spirit seeks to mock God and their victim's belief in His saving hand and will voraciously eat what is intended for the believer if and when given a chance.*

Jezebel – Many of us are used to hearing the name Jezebel thrown around and assume this spirit can only be carried by a female. The seasoned saint, however, knows that is far from the truth. The Jezebel spirit can be possessed by a male or female and is primarily interested with derailing and/or killing those in the kingdom deemed for leadership positions. The Jezebel spirit can enter any person that is not a professed, Christ-led child of God, but it is particularly relentless in its pursuit of prophets, messengers, preachers, reverends, pastors, bishops, apostles, evangelicals, teachers, etc., that currently hold the office or have been identified to be promoted to the office. The Jezebel around you is a puppet master solely interested in controlling, subjugating and dominating decisions governing your life and path. The spirit is predominant in its use of manipulation and mind control and is usually present wherever witchcraft is being practiced.

The Jezebel takes time to study your weaknesses and strengths in order to successfully identify how you can be tempted and/or kept in bondage. *Jezebels are masters of seduction utilizing money, association, influence, affluence, gifts, power, fame, prestige, and even food to snatch your attention away from spiritual things and purposes of the kingdom.* The spirit accomplishes this by seducing you with whatever it takes so that you focus on worldly things instead. The Jezebel spirit is oftentimes associated with a flashy lifestyle as it is a means to attract its victims. Often filled with pride and arrogance, the Jezebel spirit will claim that they know the Lord, yet manipulate the words of the bible. Without keen discernment their spiritual counseling may seem just, but true discerners of the spirit will know that the word they offer is convoluted and contaminated. The message offered by the Jezebel spirit will always seek to make the believer feel good at the expense of what is truly biblical, sound doctrine. This spirit is one of a counterfeit. It is not of God and the individual it possesses does not know God, or knows God in word, not practice. The Jezebel spirit is a boomerang spirit of sorts, meaning that the Jezebel manipulating and oppressing the believer is usually dealt a serving of their own medicine. Typically, they too are being manipulated by a Jezebel in their midst.

This observation is illustrated in Mark 6:17-28 as it corresponds to the case of Herod Antipas. John The Baptist preached publicly against Herod's marriage to his deceased brother's wife, Herodias, whom I believe had an even stronger Jezebelian spirit than Herod. Although Herod Antipas gave the order that ultimately killed John the Baptist, it was Herodias' cunning puppeteering that truly called for his death. Herodias was enraged by John the Baptist's zealous indictment and denunciation against their sinful, immoral and adulterous nature of her marriage to her husband's brother. Although Herod had John imprisoned, he did not wish John's blood on his hands for the Jews regarded John the Baptist as a prophet. Herodias, on the other hand, wanted his imminent death. She instructed her daughter, Josephine, the child she shared with her former husband, who was now both niece and stepdaughter to Herod, to dance for Herod during her birthday celebration. Herodias informed Josephine that once she danced for Herod before his court, he would grant her whatever she wished for her birthday gift. Herodias instructed Josephine to ask for the head of John the Baptist on a platter—and Herod obliged.

The spirit of Jezebel was not only active in Herod Antipas an adulterer and enemy of God's prophet, but also in Herodias due to her manipulation of Herod and her daughter. I would go further to say that the Jezebelian spirit was even present in Josephine because of her dance, which I am assuming was sensual in nature due to Herod's response to grant her whatever she desired for her birthday. We, as believers must be vigilant against the Jezebel spirit. It is sly, arrogant, cunning and delighted by what they believe is the slaying of the believer. The Jezebel spirit will cause divisiveness, part you from destiny helpers and burden bearers, speak ill of you without knowing you simply to oppress the plans of God and to keep you isolated, or from achieving your God given purpose. The Jezebel spirit will take you off path and if you are unable to identify and defeat it, it will surely delay or destroy your destiny or call for leadership.

Judas – The spirit of Judas Iscariot is a spirit of greed, surreptitious movement, covert operations and betrayal. The Judas kiss is infamous in Christian and secular circles, and it points to the fact that the Judas in your life is a trusted loved one or friend. It is an individual who is extremely affectionate (as demonstrated by Judas's kiss), smiles at you—calling you sister, friend, lover, or family" as they twist a knife in your back. You have given them a level of responsibility, role or office that should only be given to someone with pure intentions for you just as Judas held the trusted position of treasurer. The spirit will manifests in a friend, romantic relationship, mentor relationship, best friend, etc. There is indeed a bond of trust in the beginning which erodes over time due to the person's greed for money, status, or desire for accolades (clout chasing).

King Saul – When we first encounter Saul, we learn that Saul is the top of the line, head and shoulders above the rest—literally. The bible says in 1 Samuel 9 that there was not a more "goodlier person than he: from his shoulders and upward he was higher than any of the people." As Saul's journey as king progresses he grows in stature and prominence with the people, saving Israel from many of its enemies. Yet, when David comes on the scene exhibiting his prowess as a gifted warrior and man of battle, Saul is unable to contain his jealousy. He is disturbed when the women come out to meet David after another victory with joy playing instruments and singing "Saul hath slain his thousands, and David his ten thousands" (1 Samuel 18:7). The comparison enrages Saul and from then his envy of David grows as he begins to fear him and perceive him as a threat. Saul even determines to give his eldest daughter to David in marriage as long as he fights valiantly for him all the while expecting David to be slain if he goes up against the Philistines. From this point, matters get worse as David continues to gain favor with the Lord and Saul continues to be disobedient until God states he will be removed as king and David will be his successor. Once beloved by Saul, David is both stunned and disheartened as Saul's hatred and unfairly zealous pursuit of him intensifies. I am certain David loved, respected and admired Saul and could not make sense of Saul's change of heart.

I am certain you feel the same when you consider the individual(s) that have set you up as their enemy. Their jealousy and envy seems nonsensical as you have only been kind and loving to them. Yet any person attached to the King Saul spirit is indeed envious, jealous, laying snares, targeting you unfairly, allowing their deep seated feelings of inadequacy and insecurity to cause them to constantly compare themselves to you and hate the magnitude and prevalence of your blessings. This person ultimately becomes angry with you because of the favor God has placed on your life, your good fortune and blessings, and seeks to destroy you. This individual's desire to cause you harm ratchets daily and can eventually lead to all sorts of violence being committed against you, including but not limited to assault, violent ambushes, murder, or murder for hire plots. *The spirit of Saul disregards the goodness of God in one's own life by constantly comparing itself to others—specifically loved ones, and erroneously believes that blessings given to others are unattainable or achievable for them.*

Leviathan – The Leviathan spirit is described in the bible as a scaly serpent—more specifically a piercing, crooked serpent—a dragon that is in the sea (Isaiah27:1) with an exterior the Lord describes by stating, "the flakes of his flesh are joined together: they cannot be moved" (Job 41:23) as he asks Job whether or not he can save himself against him. The Biblical Dictionary, Index and Concordance in The Holy Bible Authorized King James Version published by Bible House in Charlotte, North Carolina regards leviathan as a serpent, sea monster, crocodile and dragon that symbolizes evil and is used to refer to Satan.

I believe Leviathan represents what John C. Maxwell calls "bad pride" as it epitomizes a sense of conceit, arrogance and superiority and is indicative of how the spirit might manifest in the life of today's Christian. Further, in the Bible Dictionary Leviathan is defined as a "writhing" animal. As the Oxford dictionary defines writhing as "twisting, squirming, movements or contortions of the body," and the literal definitions for Leviathan (Livyatan) in Hebrew mean "to twist, turn wind or coil," it is comprehensible why Leviathan is deemed the twisting and coiling spirit as individuals enmeshed in this spirit are masters at twisting people's words and twisting situations as to turn people against each other (triangulation) in order to manufacture varying levels of drama and chaos which they happily feed off.

When discussing pride as a destroyer of destiny, I mentioned that a telltale sign a person has an issue with pride is their inability to receive the words spoken to them. This spirit ensures they cannot hear, neither can they see opposing perspectives. If you recall, I made an effort to denote the serpent as having scales and an impenetrable exterior. Prophetess Tiphani Montgomery, Head of the Covered by God Ministry Movement, asks that we recall and then deduce that the scales described as covering Leviathan's exterior cover its entire body which undoubtedly would include its eyes and ears. *Therefore, the scales which extend to the individual's eyes and ears incapacitate their ability to see and hear spiritually.* This revelation compels us to pay attention to Tiphani's assertion which is amplified by the way in which Saul, whom Jesus revealed himself to on the road to Damascus as he sojourned to kill Ananias, a righteous man of God, was rendered blind and then cured of blindness. Acts 9:17 states that God sent Ananias to lay hands on Saul that he "mightiest receive thy sight, and be filled with the Holy Spirit. And immediately there fell from his eyes *as it had been scales*: and he received sight forthwith, and arose, and was baptized." The healing of Saul's blindness due to his persecution of God's people prior to his transformation and name change to Paul, required the falling of scales from his eyes, which exemplifies the deduction that he was indeed under the influence of the Leviathan spirit.

It is also just as important to note that Saul was healed by Ananias, the same person he intended to kill. As such, you may be called by the Holy Spirit and tangibly asked by the same person who has persecuted you to forgive, intercede, pray for and heal them after it is revealed that they attempted to annihilate you spiritually, mentally, emotionally, physically, socially, or financially.

Correspondingly, prior to Saul's conversion the bible describes him as a merciless persecutor of the church, violently dragging both women and men from their homes for persecution, calling for and consenting to the death of believers as well as cruel threats and slaughter against the disciples of the Lord. Simply put, Saul witnessed and authorized executions. Prior to his conversion, he was a man with a murderous spirit just as the spirit of Leviathan is a murderous spirit. Leviathan ensures any relationship where it is present will be murdered as the relationship will not experience growth or life. It eventually morphs into an artificial relationship that strangles authentic understanding and heart connection, stripes vitality and vigor, fosters negligence, and arrests development. The Leviathan spirit also manifests as excessive lying to ensure the individual possessed with the spirit always come out on top looking better than everyone else involved in the conflict. It emerges through secret competition as the person possessed with the spirit must always assert their superiority, and also as anger when they perceive that a blessing or honor the believer receives trumps their own. As such, there is an excessive constant striving to assert their dominance, and a desire for your embarrassment, harm, and persecution inflicted by them or by others. It is indeed a demonic spirit and one very close to Satan's heart as it written in Job 41:34 "[Satan] beholdeth all high things: he is a king over all the children of pride."

Pharoah – The spirit of Pharoah is one of oppression and ownership. It seeks to keep God's people in bondage and subservience. The individual operating in this spirit does not want to see you grow, walk in your purpose or attain any form of success as it would threaten what they believe to be their station in your life. It is an unreasonably obstinate and stubborn spirit with whom you cannot reason or compromise. Pharoah had to be confronted by ten plagues before he allowed the Israelites to depart. The Pharoah spirit is vehemently against your worship to God and prayer life as Moses pleaded with Pharoah to let God's people go so that they may worship him. TD Jakes in his *Revelation through Retrospect* sermon, asserts that the reason why Pharoah pursued the Israelites even as they escaped to the Red Sea was due to his desire to retrieve the treasure now in their possession. The treasure was the gold and silver God instructed them to borrow from the Egyptians prior to their departure which Bishop Jakes states represented the blessing/wealth transfer—wealth that Pharaoh desperately wanted back. Much like Pharoah, the individuals attached to this spirit find your relationship and level of intimacy with God time-wasting, trivial and powerless. Yet, they are aware that a blessing rests on your life, and although they do want to believe it, they sense that God just might make good on the promises for which you have been praying—or, more palatable for their level of understanding, one day you might just get lucky. Just in case you are the golden goose, they must ensure you are clear on whom you owe allegiance, who is calling the shots, and who ultimately owns you. *The Pharoah spirit doubts the power, sovereignty and authority of God, detests your reverence for God and seeks to claim your blessing.*

Raccoon – *The raccoon spirit represents an individual that has decided to turn away from God and the true light of Jesus Christ to abide in darkness.* Many animal scientists believe the darkened, masked eyes of the raccoon are believed to protect the raccoon's eyes from damaging light. Any person that is operating in the raccoon spirit perceives light, or more specifically, a life associated with light, righteousness and uprightness to be particularly damaging to who they are and their current lifestyle. Furthermore, the masked eyes represent masked intentions and their propensity due to a rejection of God to seek their sustenance in desolate places.

Serpent/Snake – The serpent spirit represents the spirit of ravenous ingestion, constriction and exacerbation. The objective of this spirit is to convince believers to doubt the faithfulness and deity of God. *This spirit seeks to challenge and ultimately corrupt your trust in God and belief that God is all powerful, all knowing, all seeing and all sufficient in your life.* Individuals walking in this spirit desire your allegiance and belief that they will be there for you—even when God is not because neither God nor His word can be trusted. Individuals led by this spirit are compulsive liars, speak with a forked tongue, are spiritually bipolar—professing love for God or you one day and hating God and/or you the next. The spirit revels in confusion and spiritual captivity—exhausting your love, kindness and peace while devouring your resources. Its python-like grasp causes financial suffocation and extreme weariness.

Anaconda: Individuals hosting the anaconda spirit submerge their victims in psychological games and warfare for which they are unfamiliar and unprepared to combat. Mentally exhausting verbal confrontations, exchanges and spats leave the believer drowning in feelings of disappointment, sorrow, despondency and spiritual apathy which is an attempt by the perpetrator to suffocate and drown the Holy Spirit residing within.

Cobra: The cobra spirit is a spirit that values brawn, muscle and excessive force over intellectual capacity and genuine tenderness. It is also unreasonably thin-skinned. When considering the cobra one must take into account the eight sets of muscles and their ability, in conjunction with its ribs, to reach its head by lengthening, rotating, expanding and contracting in such a way that both supports and agitates the snake's skin and allows it to flare and form its fierce protective hood. Specifically, it is the extending of ligament and rib that packs its head with a muscular system in preparation for attack. As such, individuals attached to this spirit, not only regard physical power (muscle) over intelligence, but they are particularly intimidating and easily puff up, (just as the cobra's hood) when their power, position or perspective is threatened. When seeing this spirit in action, the muscle-headed bully may come to mind.

Moreover, just as this reptile injects its prey with poisonous toxins that collapse its nervous system when in its natural habitat, the cobra spirit injects the believer's mindset, self-image, emotional capacity and environment with toxins that paralyze your ability to see, breathe, think, move and function at your usual capacity.

Moreover, the spirit has a duplicitous nature. It is a great pretender—pretending to love its victims, even going as far as feigning desire for marriage in romantic situations. This duplicitous nature is demonstrated by its fork tongue which utters loving sentiments and demeaning insults in the same breath. In addition, this spirit will pretend like they are interested in partnership, and collaboration but is more interested in what you can bring to the table for them, or more specifically, the bountiful fruit you bear and your approaching harvest season. This behavior is akin to the reptile's preference for areas of lush, thick, vegetation. One of the telltale signs that an individual is operating under the influence of this spirit is they are not adverse to criminal activity and have a history of preying upon others—especially other criminals as the cobra is cannibalistic in nature. Although the individual may explain this behavior away as a previous life before their point of maturity, or pass it off as a joke.

Python: The python spirit is one of restriction and constriction. It manifests as demonic dryness, drought and interference/destiny alteration to block God's blessings (his anointing, marriage, promotion, expansion, healing, wealth, etc.,). Further, this spirit exacerbates the everyday pressures of life—particularly financial, to create beliefs of failure, despair, impending calamity and abandonment by God. Any efforts the victim makes toward escape and upward mobility, triggers increased compression.

Viper. Vipers are masters of camouflage. The viper spirit is an enemy, detractor and conspirator that stealthily blends into the scenery. This is the enemy that hides in plain sight—usually an individual you have met in passing that you think nothing of, but who is deeply invested in your harm, betrayal and/or abandonment. Vipers are typically information gatherers, busy bodies and can be malicious gossips which correlates to the ability of the viper's mouth to open 180 degrees. This reptile is also infamous for its fangs—long, hanging and capable of rotating, but can fold up and rest on the roof of its mouth when not in use so are in a sense—hidden, adding to the ability of the spirit to hide their intentions to inflict severe pain and harm. Furthermore, their fangs inject toxins that may cause nausea, vomiting, diarrhea, rapid heart rate, blurred vision, increased sweating and salivation. These symptoms are exactly what the spirit operating in a human host seeks to conjure once they have released information designed to maim, shock and devastate their victim. The desire is to make the believer, "sick" from the news of betrayal. An individual with this spirit is often in cahoots with an individual with a stronger serpent spirit, namely the cobra or python spirit, or an individual housing both.

Squirrel – *The squirrel spirit is one that is opportunistic, motivated by self-interest and greed, and seeking to rob the children of God of their peace and/or resources.* The spirit is associated with individuals living two or more secret lives. Many squirrel species are known to have three separately located nests or homes—leaving a few resources in all and wandering between them. If indeed you have a bird feeder you know firsthand that it is hard to keep squirrels away once they discover a food source. They will eat beyond greed—to a point of gluttony and many become aggressive—even snatching food from children if and when they perceive the food source is dwindling. I call this spirit the spying thief as squirrels are known to stealthily watch other squirrels to discover where they have buried their food so they can return to steal it at another time.

The Narcissist – Ideal human host, shell or guesthouse for demonic hijacking (See armadillo, frog, raccoon, squirrel, hyena, serpent) The experience you are undergoing currently is most likely with a narcissist. Fundamentally, the narcissist can be classified into two types, vulnerable and grandiose and tends to have three personas—their public persona, private persona and secret persona. The narcissist you are dealing with may be attached to varying combinations and degrees of the demons defined.

Wanderer/Vagabond: The wandering and vagabond spirit can be described as a wilderness spirit. It is a roaming spirit as there is an absence of peace and great spiritual unrest. It is a spirit that has not planted roots independent of others. The person attached to this spirit will lack recognizable fruit or fruit with true sustenance. This individual is typically homeless, living from pillar to post or in a shared living situation. Their name will not be present on the lease, mortgage or deed of wherever they currently reside. This person actively seeks out believers to latch onto or leech off for the basic necessities of food and shelter. Initially they may appear willing to partner financially, but eventually they will divert and drive their resources into their own secret exploits. They will not be committed to equality in responsibilities for the household or for its financial care and stability. And when demands for equality, transparency and respect commence, this individual will search out and move on to another willing host. In layman's terms, this spirit is usually operative in the con or user.

Agents of Darkness – Agents of darkness are individuals that consciously and willfully engage in the occult to varying degrees for the achievement of desired objectives or in the advancement of the kingdom of Satan. These individuals may identify as witches or warlocks, satanists, practice Santeria, Palo Mayombe, New Ageism, Spiritualism or voodoo. Others may utilize manipulation and control and/or recite spells, chants, incantations, word curses, ill wishes, engage in root work, witchcraft prayers, payment transactions to purveyors of darkness, participate in seances, rituals, blood sacrifices and/or ceremonies that are devoid of the light, presence, and spirit of God. Many of these individuals believe that they are participating in God friendly/supported activities, however, they are deceived for any desired results that manifest are undoubtedly undergirded by the powers and principalities of darkness. As such, these individuals are in stark opposition to God—whether intentionally or unintentionally, knowingly or unknowingly.

Exodus 22:18 KJV
Thou shalt not suffer a witch not to live

Leviticus 19:26
Ye shall not…use enchantment, nor observe times (astrology).

Leviticus 20:27
Deuteronomy 18:10-11
Individuals that practice the dark arts—white magic, black magic, etc., know of spiritual things on a perfunctory or shallow level but do not possess spiritual knowledge and wisdom. As the fear of God is the beginning of knowledge, wisdom, good understanding and leads to life. Many of these individuals are unaware that these practices create a covenant with forces and entities of darkness, or build altars of reverence to Satan, fallen angels, demons and familiar spirits which cements their allegiance. Although many are fully aware, willfully entering satanic pacts and accepting their place as a soldier of Satan.

Unless you are spiritually acute, have consulted a spiritual leader or been informed by the Holy Spirit, it is difficult to ascertain whether you are being attacked by witchcraft or in one of life's storms. Each 747 woman's experience with witchcraft will be different and each person will experience attack at varying degrees. The Holy Spirit revealed that I was under demonic attack several times in a myriad of ways. Once I recall waking from a decent night's sleep with a demonic ditty playing in my head. I repeated the chant aloud a few times before receiving revelation about what I was chanting. It was indeed an incantation intended to program me to work hard, but regress, move backward and receive no fruit from my labor. I remember the incantation even now, "grind and reverse…grind and reverse."

Dishonorable Mentions:

Balaam – The spirit of Balaam is one of insolence, disobedience and rebellion. The rejection of God's sovereignty is specifically attributed to the individual's quest/lust after financial gain. The spirit is one of a stout-heart and bullhead as the individual continuously seeks God's approval to move forward with the pursuit of their lustful desire after having already received an answer from God not to do so. The story of Balak and Balaam discussed in a future section discusses Balaam's initial obedience to the Lord before turning and assisting Balak, an enemy of the Israelites, with his desire to destroy them for the promise of gold and silver.

Reprobate – Refers to the state a person is relegated to after repeated offenses of disobedience and rebellion as taught to us by Apostle Paul in Romans 1. Sister Sharon, prophetess and creator of Motivation2Win, an online platform, states that one is turned over to a reprobate mind when they are committed to living out sinful passions and ungodly desires. A reprobate mind then becomes their inheritance and habitation. If you confused the enemy in your midst as a believer, you could have very well been dealing with a believer with a reprobate mind. I would add that a person with a reprobate mind consistently makes decisions that are either opposite, or do not align with the outcomes they profess to desire. You will know them by their fruit as they are the consummate self-saboteur-sabotaging their best laid plans to such a degree that all around them are baffled. Sister Sharon states that there are eight fruits or signs that can assist with the identification of a reprobate which are listed here:

1. Possess *knowledge of scripture and church*. Reprobates are aware of the art of attending church but do not have an intimate relationship with the Lord
2. Reprobates relish in *profanity*. Profanity should disturb your spirit as it grieves the Holy Spirit. If the person uses profane language without apology or remorse, this is a red flag.
3. *Scoff at the righteous*. Reprobates rebuff correction and are uninterested in right living. They bask in their rebellion.
4. *Sexually flirtatious*. Reprobates are extremely flirtatious. The flirtation Sister Sharon references is not modest or respectful. It is lustful in nature as the reprobate is plagued with spirits of lust.
5. *Busybodies* with propensity for *slander* and *gossip*. Reprobates love to expose people's personal pain and shame. They receive pleasure from exposing the brokenness of others.
6. *Desire to be served*. Reprobates desire to be worshipped. They may make statements that reveal their stance that you owe them for being who you are and most likely were before crossing their path.
7. *Fame seekers*. Reprobates desire fame and seek attention. They wish for their efforts to be known, seen and catapulted to the forefront.
8. *Mentally ill*. Reprobates struggle with mental illness. This struggle may be public or private. This is not to suggest that individuals combating and/or living with mental illness are reprobates. This is to state however that many reprobates do suffer from mental illness just as King Saul after multiple infractions of disobedience and rebellion.

Posture When Confronting The Demonic
1. The Bible states we will be persecuted

You may not consider what you are experiencing a form of persecution. Yet the mocking, jeering, ostracism and abuse is exactly that. You have been targeted because of your heart posture and faith in God. Although those around you would not state this is the case, the demonic influence on them and their lives would beg to differ. In their perspective, your faith in God and desire to please Him is simple-minded, foolish and reeks of weakness. They consider your meekness an invitation to manipulate, abuse and belittle you, assuming that you are unaware of the diabolical nature of snakes and wolves in sheep's clothing. The bible makes it clear that to be a believer in this world means you will face persecution for your beliefs and for choosing to walk with the Lord.

Matthew 5:10 -12
Blessed are they which are persecuted for righteousness' sake: for theirs is the kingdom of heaven. Blessed are ye, when men shall revile you, and persecute you, and shall say all manner of evil against you falsely, for my sake. Rejoice, and be exceeding glad: for great is your reward in heaven: for so persecuted they the prophets which were before you.

1 Peter 3:14
But even if you should suffer for what is right, you are blessed. "Do not fear their threats; do not be frightened."

2 Corinthians 12:10
Therefore I take pleasure in infirmities, in reproaches, in necessities, in persecutions, in distresses for Christ's sake: for when I am weak, then am I strong.

2. We are instructed to be courageous

Joshua 1:9
Have not I commanded thee? Be strong and of a good courage; be not afraid, neither be thou dismayed: for the Lord thy God is with thee whithersoever thou goest."

Isaiah 41:10
Fear thou not; for I am with thee: be not dismayed; for I am thy God: I will strengthen thee; yea, I will help thee/ yea, I will uphold thee with the right and of my righteousness

Proverbs 3:25
Be not afraid of sudden fear, neither of the desolation of the wicked, when it cometh

Psalm 56:11
In God have I put my trust: I will not be afraid what man can do unto me

Psalm 112:7
He shall not be afraid of evil tidings: his heart is fixed, trusting in the Lord

Psalm 3:6
I will not be afraid of ten thousands of people, that have set themselves against me round about

3. Jesus gives us power and the victory!

As believers we are to stand on the power, authority and victory of Jesus Christ our Lord and Savior. As co-heirs, joint heirs of Christ, no matter what it looks like, our enemies are defeated foes. You must believe that and stand on the truth and power of the word.

1 John 3:8
"For this purpose was the Son of God manifested: that he might destroy the works of the devil."

Psalm 91:13
"Thou shalt tread upon the lion and the adder: the young lion and the dragon shalt thou trample under feet"

Luke 10:19
Behold, I give unto you power to tread on serpents and scorpions, and over all the power of the enemy: and nothing shall by any means hurt you.

Psalm 110:1
The Lord said unto my Lord, Sit thou at my right hand, until I make thine enemies thy footstool

1 Corinthians 15:25
For He must reign till He has put all enemies under His feet. And since we are co-heirs, joint heirs of Christ, no matter what it looks like, our enemies are defeated foes.

John 16:33
In the world ye shall have tribulation: but be of good cheer. I have overcome the world!

4. Do not be judgmental, condemn or seek revenge.

Be obedient to Jesus' call for us to forgive and pray for our enemies. These individuals are human hosts and shells for demonic purposes, infiltration, seduction and attack.

Matthew 18:21-22
Then came Peter to him, and said, Lord, how oft shall my brother sin against me, and I forgive him? Till seven times? Jesus saith unto him, I say not unto thee, Until seven times: but, Until seventy times seven

Matthew 6:14-15
Be transparent about God's desire for none of us to go to hell. And however, hurt we may be, vengeance is mine saith the Lord and ultimately God does not desire to harm his children, for if we repent and humble

5. Everyone's experience is unique as it based on the lessons God has destined and purposed for them to learn, their anointing and calling

Be mindful that the specific spirits I have included above are specific to my experience. The Holy Spirit will reveal the spirits that are at work in your situation. It may include a few, most, or all of the spirits I have mentioned, or different ones altogether. No two believers will have identical journeys with Christ. However, we are to support each other, offer our testimonies, comfort one another, provide guidance, wisdom, strategy and love. Yet your walk and your race is yours alone. You may be blessed to have destiny helpers, burden bearers and/or fellow believers accompany you at times, but there are times you will be called to solitude, separation and prodded to walk alone. Your calling and the preparation for that calling is unique to who you are and who God calls you to be. The specific and varied assignments of the disciples after Pentecost, Paul's witnessing that he was sent to preach to the Gentiles (the uncircumcised) and Peter to the Jews (the circumcised), demonstrate this truth as well as Jesus' reaction and response to Peter in John 21 when he inquires of John's assignment. All of which demonstrate that there is a definite distinction between our walks and callings. They are unique and differentiated based on God's desired impact, the audience to whom we are called to minister, timing, our generational design, coding, personality, the angels assigned to us, our gifts, level of anointing, geographic location, and factors of which we may never know.

Galatians 2:7-8
"But contrariwise, when they saw that the gospel of the uncircumcision was committed unto me, as the gospel of the circumcision was unto Peter; (For he that wrought effectually in Peter to the apostleship of the circumcision, the same was mighty in me toward the Gentiles:)"

John 21:21

"Peter seeing him saith to Jesus, Lord, and what shall this man do? Jesus saith unto him, If I will that he tarry till I come, what is that to thee? Follow thou me."

Part IV

Emergency Exit

Emergency Exit

EXPOSURE OF THE ENEMY

At this point of the experience, God will expose the enemy and give you a level of information that only spiritual gifting or enlightenment by way of the Holy Spirit can offer. What is interesting to state here is that prior to this moment of exposure, which tends to be ushered in by the onslaught of the counterfeit, although you are an oblivious sleeping beauty, on a holy pause or dancing with destiny destroyers, you still believe this is your season for promotion and that a very specific thing you have been praying for will come to pass.

BATTLE IN THE NATURAL/PHYSICAL REALM

I should warn you now that this is an experience you will have to walk out on your own—both in the natural and spiritual realms. The battle that those around you and your enemy see with their natural eyes is one-dimensional. It is only the perfunctory level—merely one level of what is transpiring. And initially, you too believe that it is the only battle you are engaged in.

To those around you, what you are trying to explain to them is just another day in the life—it just points to a bit of drama in which you are currently enmeshed in. For most of them it is a serving of gossip that they will gladly share with another friend. In the beginning it seems that might be the case until the Lord begins to reveal deeper levels of what has taken place, and in many cases has been going on for some time.

As your revelation increases you will be led into a more in-depth understanding of what is taking place in real time and what is at stake. You will know that you are in the midst of this exposure experience because as Dr. Tony Evans states in his *"Detour to Destiny"* sermon, you will have just been blindsided by one of your greatest disappointments (the onslaught by the counterfeit). Something you believe God was doing for you, a prayer he was answering, a person you were interceding for in hopes of their deliverance, or an opportunity you believed had your name all over it, will now appear not only unlikely, but impossible.

Further exposure will lead you to the realization that you have just been skipped. Dr. Evans demonstrates the second part of this process or juncture with the example of Joseph who after interpreting a dream for both the Pharoah's chief butler and his chief baker, was left in jail as they were released from prison and returned to the palace to resume work. So now after the biggest disappointment of your life, as neither returned for Joseph as they stated they would, you too have now been forgotten or skipped for the promotion. You have been skipped over and looked past as the one chosen for marriage, for consideration of the business contract or bid, the seat on the board, as member of the council, sorority, clique, etc. The anguish and heartbreak of this moment will cause you -if you are anything like me- to initially respond in seething anger. You will confront your enemy, not for a fight necessarily, but to let them know that the jig is up! The enemy will be confused and confounded because the information (insider's information) you have will be astonishing to your enemy. Your enemy or group of enemies is not Holy Spirit-led, therefore they will be unable to fathom that the Lord led you to this information moment by moment, unveiling to unveiling, until you receive what is and has been going on in its entirety or have enough of the picture to know that you have been betrayed, and the colossal magnitude of the betrayal.

Trust me, if you have not gone through this experience, I assure you that you feel abandoned, embarrassed, bewildered and betrayed—BUT GOD has something else in store! It is what Dr. Evans enumerates as the "SURPRISE." It is what God, His hand, or more specifically, providence, the invisible hand of God on your life, has been preparing you for the entire time. Bishop Dale C. Bronner asserts, "God is not a God of time, but a *God of timing*." He has been preparing you for this moment all along. For you, the 747 woman, the surprise, Dr. Tony Evans references comes down to this—the point where your previously feeble, embryonic understanding of your identity meets your destiny.

BATTLE IN THE SPIRITUAL REALM

This is the real battle. This is the battle that can only be seen through spiritual eyes—specifically, yours. You may not realize it but this is indeed a fight between good and evil. It is a fight between your obedience to God and commitment to walking with him or your choice to forfeit your calling and stand in alignment with those that reject God. Those who are willfully disobedient, do not value relationship or connection with Him and who have chosen to sit with the unrighteous, unclean and rebellious. I must admit that initially I did not view this juncture in my life this way. Initially my thought was okay, "I'm not going to go that far with you Lord. I'm going to go on ahead and exercise my free will here. I'm deciding to stay with this person and I'll be okay. If I don't get the magnitude of the blessing you have promised me over the years, that's fine. I'm okay." And yes, here we go again with the full on Jonah-like response in all of its glory.

Yet I wholeheartedly believed that I had the right to do it and that God would understand. After all I had always been taught that God gives us freewill—the ability and grace to make our own choices. Never mind that I had asked God in prayer if the person loved me, and heard a small still voice utter the word "*strange*," as in a *strange love*. I did not look it up in the Concordance at this time because when I initially entered the relationship it was not described as such and I wanted desperately to believe that what I heard then about the relationship had not changed, although I knew the person, their commitment to God and feelings for me had—regardless of what they were saying. Yet, my determination to walk this path persisted. Even after hearing Dr. Nina D. Bronner, the first lady of The Word of Faith Family Cathedral, state, during one of the *Women of the Word* (W.O.W) ministry meetings she hosts monthly with her daughter, Prophetess Neiel Zimbron, "God is saying, "SHUT THE

DOOR!" my heart was slow to respond. Dr. Nina proclaimed it repeatedly—at least seven times, each time louder than the last. Yet I rationalized that the message was not for me. My friend, who did not know much about my relationship, nor what I was experiencing as we had not spoken in some time, turned to me as if to say, "She is talking to you..." I heard her. I heard them. But my heart did not budge. I was open to forgiving this person and reconciliation.

It was not until God jolted me out of my sleepwalking state to set me straight and illustrate what was at stake, and released immediately after a barrage of daily messages to inform me of the magnitude of my decision. One morning I was even awakened to a gentle voice at the far corner of my room. I had previous experiences where I would hear a gentle whisper upon waking sharing information previously unknown to me to guide me or bring me into some new level of understanding, and I have always chalked it up to being an angel. This particular morning I heard a disembodied voice that sounded particularly compassionate. "Zebidiah." "Who?" I remember thinking. I had heard the name Zechariah, but Zebidiah? Who is that? And this is when it got really interesting for when I researched the matter it led me to the Prophet Ezra— particularly when he humbled himself, repenting and weeping before the Lord in an attempt to turn away God's wrath for many of the Israelites had enraged God due to their marrying *strange* women.

I guess it was now time to look up the word. I opened the Biblical Dictionary, Index and Concordance in The Holy Bible Authorized King James Version published by Bible House in Charlotte, North Carolina and read the words, "foreign, unfamiliar." The love I inquired about was something the Holy Spirit would not identify as love. In addition, the word strange is also used in the bible when God describes false gods and all manners of idolatry.

Emergency Exit

Genesis 35:2
Then Jacob said unto his household, and to all that were with him, Put away the *strange* gods that are among you, and be clean, and change your garments

Ezra 10:1-2
Now when Ezra had prayed, and when he had confessed, weeping and casting himself down before the house of God, there assembled unto him out of Israel a very great congregation of men and women and children: for the people wept very sore. And Shechaniah the son of Jehiel, one of the sons of Elam, answered and said unto Ezra, We have trespassed against our God, and have taken *strange* wives of the people of the land: yet now there is hope in Israel concerning this thing.

Shortly after, a council of the princes and elders decided that whomever would not divorce and depart from these strange women would lose his possessions and spiritual inheritance. And that whosoever would not come forward to confess their sin and disavow it within three days would forfeit their spiritual and natural inheritance in addition to whatever possessions they currently had. After the three days Ezra addressed the priests regarding the matter.

Ezra 10:10-12
And Ezra the priest stood up, and said unto them, Ye have transgressed, and have taken *strange* wives, to increase the trespass of Israel. Now therefore make confession unto the LORD God of your fathers, and do his pleasure: and separate yourselves from the people of the land, and from the *strange* wives. Then all the congregation answered and said with a loud voice, As thou hast said, so must we do.

And one of the first priests listed that had agreed to Ezra to divorce his strange/foreign wife and come forward was, you guessed it, Zebidiah son of Immer (Ezra 10:20). Zebidiah, a Levite priest that history denotes as having defiled himself by marrying an idolatrous woman. Yet he agreed to divorce and depart from her to retain his spiritual inheritance, position in the kingdom and remain in the will of God. There were a number of priests led to depart from wives God deemed unclean, rebellious, worshippers of idols and false gods during this time. The Lord wanted His children to come out from under them because they would cause the priest to veer from the path chosen for them and jeopardize their divine callings.

My thought? "Hmmm, how accurate, interesting and timely." Yet, I'm going to be honest here, I was still in denial about the extent of my freewill. I believed God would be upset but that he loved me so dearly that he would understand. After all, I'm just forfeiting a huge blessing for a smaller one. I am content enough with the goodness and blessings he has already given me. No harm in that. Yet, over and over again I received messages that if I decided to move forward with the relationship, it would not merely be a forfeiture of blessings, but a conscious decision to cast aside and reject the God of Israel. In not choosing God's way, whether I expressed it or not, I was choosing disobedience, rebellion and Satan. Wait a minute!

In the spiritual realm my decision was akin to choosing darkness over light. I do not know why it did not click previously, but this was the game changer. How could I willfully choose not to follow the one who created me, who throughout the years has been so faithful, loving, forgiving, understanding, present, kind, gracious and merciful? Shortly after this revelation, Prophetess Tiphani Montgomery, Head and Founder of the Covered By God Ministry and Movement, stated she was leading a fast for the year. Would you believe the fast was specifically geared to tear down the idols God said many of her congregants were placing before Him? Further, it would be deemed a marriage fast as its purpose was to remove idols and counterfeits so that the children of God could be led to their true kingdom spouses.

747 woman, after God goes to great lengths to reveal what is at stake spiritually -and He will- He will then call you to separate yourself. He will move you to desire solitude in Him before the fight. Maybe you did not

realize one would be approaching. Well neither did I. Yet before this showdown, you feel an unshakeable pull to leave your current surroundings to solely be in His presence, even if just for a day or two. Some of you may not have that luxury. But trust me when this moment comes, you will find the time and the money. I was fortunate enough during this time to be able to retreat to the mountains of North Carolina with a prayer partner. You may choose to visit a relative's home you cannot reach without a long ride or trip—just to get a moment of solace and alone time with God. It will be somewhere safe and isolated, where you can tap into your spirit, get a moment of respite, rejuvenate your strength and your will to fight because if you decide to continue to walk this out with the Lord, you will need it.

Part V

Full Upright Position

Full Upright Position

HOW TO DEFEAT THE ENEMY

ARSENAL FOR SPIRITUAL WARFARE

The Armor of God
Ephesians 6:13-17 KJV
Wherefore take unto you the whole armour of God, that ye may be able to withstand in the evil day, and having done all, to stand. Stand therefore, having your loins girt about with truth, and having on the breastplate of righteousness; And your feet shod with the preparation of the gospel of peace; Above all, taking the shield of faith, wherewith ye shall be able to quench all the fiery darts of the wicked. And take the helmet of salvation, and the sword of the Spirit, which is the word of God: Praying always with all prayer and supplication in the Spirit, and watching thereunto with all perseverance and supplication for all saints;

Worship

Exodus 17:9-11 (NLT)
And Moses said unto Joshua, Choose us out men, and go out, fight with Amalek: tomorrow I will stand on the top of the hill with the rod of God in mine hand. So Joshua did as Moses has said to him, and fought with Amalek: and Moses, Aaron, and Hur went up to the top of the hill. And it came to pass, when Moses held up his hand, that Israel prevailed: and when he let down his hand, Amalek prevailed.

Exodus 17:9-11 (NLT)
Moses commanded Joshua, "Choose some men to go out and fight the army of Amalek for us. Tomorrow, I will stand at the top of the hill,

holding the staff of God in my hand. So Joshua fought the Amalekites as Moses had ordered, and Moses, Aaron and Hur went to the top of the hill. As long as Moses held up the staff in his hand the Israelites had the advantage. But whenever he dropped his hand, the Amalekites gained the advantage

Praise and Thanksgiving

Acts 15:25-26

And at midnight Paul and Silas prayed, and sang praises unto God: and the prisoners heard them. And suddenly there was a great earthquake, so that the foundations of the prison were shaken: and immediately all the doors were opened, and every one's bands were loosed. And the keeper of the prison awaking out of his sleep, and seeing the prison doors open, he drew out his sword, and would have killed himself, supposing that the prisoners had been fled. But Paul cried with a loud voice, saying, Do thyself no harm: for we are all here. Then he called for a light, and sprang in, and came trembling, and fell down before Paul and Silas, And brought them out, and said, Sirs, what must I do to be saved? And they said, Believe on the Lord Jesus Christ, and thou shalt be saved, and thy house. And they spake unto him the word of the Lord, and to all that were in his house. And he took them the same hour of the night, and washed their stripes; and was baptized, he and all his, straightway. And when he had brought them into his house, he set meat before them, and rejoiced, believing in God with all his house.

Not only did their praise cause the prison doors to open, but their praise caused the heart of the prison keeper to open, ask what he needed to do to be saved and after being told, took them to his house for safety.

Prayer

James 5:13

Is anyone among you in trouble? Let them pray.

Psalms 17:6
I call on you, my God, for you will answer me; turn your ear to me and hear my prayer.

1 John 5:14
This is the confidence we hae in approaching God: that if we ask anything according to his will, he hears us

Jeremiah 29:12
Then you will call on me and come and pray to me, and I will listen to you

1 John 5:15
And if we know that he hears us—whatever we ask—we know that we have what we asked of him

Psalm 4:1
Answer me when I call to you, my righteous God. Give me relief from my distress; have mercy on me and hear my prayer

Philippians 4:6
Do not be anxious about anything, but in every situation, by prayer and petition, with thanksgiving, present your requests to God.

Fasting

When referring to casting out demons, Jesus stated:

Matthew 17:21
Amplified

[But this kind of demon does not go out except by prayer and fasting]

KJV
Howbeit this kind goeth not out out by prayer and fasting.

KJV
Esther 4:16-5:8

Release of Your Testimony

Revelation 12:11
"And they overcame (the devil) by the blood of the Lamb, and by the word of their testimony; and they loved not their lives unto death"

Psalm 66:16
"Come and hear, all you who fear God, and I will tell what he has done for my soul"

Psalm 22:22
"I will tell of your name to my brothers; in the midst of the congregation, I will praise you"

Acts 26:18
"To open their eyes, so that they may turn from darkness to light and from the power of Satan to God, that they may receive forgiveness of sins and a place among those who are sanctified by faith in me"

Matthew 5:14-16
In the same way, let your light shine before others, so that they may see your good works and give glory to your Father who is in heaven.

Praying in Tongues/Your Heavenly Language

Prevents Satan and other demonic spirits from monitoring your prayers.

1 Corinthians 14:2
"And these signs will accompany those who believe: in my name they will cast out demons; they will speak in new tongues."

Romans 8:26
"Likewise the Spirit helps us in our weakness. For we do not know what to pray for as we ought, but the Spirit himself intercedes for us with groaning too deep for words."

1 Corinthians 14:2

For he that speaketh in an unknown tongue speaketh not unto men, but unto God: for no man understandeth him; howbeit in the spirit he speaketh mysteries

1 Corinthians 14:2 (NLT)

For if you have the ability to speak in tongues, you will be talking only to God, since people won't be able to understand you. You will be speaking by the power of the Spirit, but it will all be mysterious

Additional and Necessary Protection for Battle

1. Professing the word and your beliefs as a Christian is powerful. Profess your belief in Elohim Chayim, the one and true living God—the Trinity, the Father, the Son and the Holy Spirit.
2. Profess your belief in the blood of Jesus Christ and his resurrective power for protection.
3. Ensure you have spiritual covering at this time. I am a member of a brick and mortar church and follow several online Christian ministries—all who have leaders whom I greatly respect, admire and know to be upstanding, righteous, and sensitive to the Holy Spirit.

THE AWAKENING

You now have a better idea of who you are in Christ and soon, what once was a vague and nebulous idea of your destiny will be unveiled in its entirety. At this time, your understanding that what you are experiencing is not the typical level of spiritual warfare you have experienced in the past should be apparent. In a span of days, your faith has increased exponentially. Your prayers have increased in vigor and intensity and are being answered with unprecedented speed. You will also see clear signs that prayers that you have been praying for years are now showing signs of near manifestation. At this time, your spiritual gifts may have been revealed, intensified and or even multiplied. At this time, I thought I might be kidding myself as the experience was new and foreign to me.

Yet confirmation came swiftly in the form of a YouTube segment released by Shannon Wells, Christian Life and Business Coach and founder of Shannon Wells Academy and the Promise Land Mentorship Program, entitled *"Get Ready To Receive Now!"*

PROPHETIC REVELATION (Position/Office)

During this time the Holy Spirit will give you revelation concerning your office/position in the kingdom of God. He may even reveal that your position was determined and established long ago, but for a particular season. For example, in 2012 I woke up for work, got dressed, exited my home to find my car was *gone*. It had been repossessed. I was in the midst of a custody battle for my daughter and the lawyer fees, childcare fees, and airplane fees from Georgia to New York among other things were pummeling me financially. I was shocked, devastated and at a loss for what I could do as without a car, there was no way for me to get to work. I ran to file for bankruptcy. I needed my car. Yet, the creditor stated I could only have the car if I paid $5000. That would pay the past due and the cost of transferring the car from a lease to a car loan. Obviously I did not have it. I called everyone and anyone I could think of that might have it or be willing to assist me. No luck. I mean I humbled myself and called people I had no business calling, but I was desperate. It did not matter. No one had it on hand and to be honest if they had it, they probably would not have lent it anyway as I had no idea how I would pay it back.

I recalled an acquaintance of mine stating that she recently did a fast with her church and God answered her prayer. I had heard of people fasting before but I honestly knew nothing about it. I began to google everything I could on fasting—biblical fasts in particular—Esther's fast, Daniel's fast, Jesus' fast, and determined my situation needed a miracle. I was desperate and needed definite assistance and it seemed desperation, having nowhere else to turn was an essential component of a water-only fast. I admit, I was scared. I remember thinking Lord, if you take me because I refuse to eat for seven days—at least I will be taken during an attempt to fast.

It was not easy, but I was way too desperate to pay attention to hunger pangs. I prayed, read the bible, and pushed through. During the fast I continued to try different avenues for the funds and all attempts proved futile. I turned over every rock, calling friends of friends and family members. Most scoffed and I am sure they talked about me for years to come. But I did not care. I needed a car. I needed my job and I would surely lose it without one as it was my only means for transportation at that time. Believe it or not, but Uber was not a thing yet—at least not in Georgia.

The last day of my fast, I remember crying during prayer and hearing "call your school." It was nonsensical to me for I had called the school two weeks ago to check to see if there was some kind of refund or credit available on my account. I remember what the young lady stated to me verbatim, "Ma'am you have exhausted all of the funds available—not for the semester, but in general." Not some—all. The loans I have taken out from the higher learning institutions I attended completely depleted any and all funds available to me. If I wanted to attain another Master's degree, I would have to pay out of pocket. If I wanted to earn my doctorate, no problem, as long as I covered the expense myself. Why would I ever call back? I was clear and certain that the young lady who explained it to me would not be welcoming at all if she answered my call a second time. She was irritated by my requests to repeat what she said the last time because I was certainly in denial. But what other recourse did I have? I had received no other solutions, hints, clues, or potential resolutions. My mom could not help me at the time. My sister could not help me at the time. So I called my school.

"Hi, this is Nonye Akuba. I am calling to inquire about the status of my account. Would you be able to tell me if there is a credit available on the account?" Of course it was the same young lady I spoke with the last time. Heavily annoyed, she sighed before blurting, "Ma'am..." I knew what she was about to say was "Didn't I tell you..." Instead, she started, "Ma'am," then said, "Wait, hold...wait, actually you do have a credit. You have a credit for $5001. I could not believe my ears! "I have a credit?" "Yes," she answered. "You have a credit of $5001, do you want me to process it for a refund?"

That is one of my most amazing and favorite testimonies. Everyone was shocked that I received the money, and by the time my mom and sister turned around to over me a few thousand for a down payment on a new car, my problem had already been solved. Glory be to God! I TESTIFIED to anyone that would listen. Anytime I want to encourage someone to fast, it is the testimony I share as it is my first experience utilizing fasting as part of my arsenal of spiritual weaponry. The joke I tell at the end of the testimony always sends the listener into hysterics because for the life of me I could not understand why God gave me $5001. Why not $5050 or $5500? Or just a cool $6000? I am certain He knew that it would have translated as, *"Ooow, shopping spree."* I'm certain His response to that was an adamant, "Ummm, no." For years, I believed it was simply a demonstration that he was *El Shaddai*, the *God of More Than Enough* as a dollar was technically more than I needed. I even chalked it up to being a demonstration of His humor. Either way I was fine with the amount as it exceeded the specific amount I asked for. It allowed me to keep my vehicle and to cease worrying about losing my job due to a lack of transportation. I was grateful and remain grateful for that blessing till this very day.

Yet, the other morning in prayer as I grappled with accepting that I may be called to walk in the prophetic, I heard a small, still voice whisper, "5001." I have learned to look up words and numbers whispered to me during prayer. I googled Strong's Concordance, the Hebrew version, which refers to the Old Testament and typed 5001. The literal definition? "To utter a prophecy, speak as a prophet." And the literal definition of the Greek version which refers to the New Testament? "That which has been arranged in order, a division, rank." I read further. The HELPS Word-studies Cognate definition reads, "reflecting God's perfect wisdom in ordering all creation. The NAS exhaustive Concordance states, "that which has been arranged in order, spec. a division, rank. The Thayer's Greek Lexicon, "that which has been arranged, thing placed in order."

I was in awe that a financial blessing by way of an answered prayer and biblical fast found acceptable to the Lord was also a revelation from the Lord—only I had no idea. Who would have guessed that this favorite testimony I have shared numerous times held the confirmation of who I am, and was born to be all along. Me, a prophet with spiritual ranking in God's sight. Even if I am the last of the last and the least, it is incredibly humbling and awe-inspiring to me for I neither believed I was worthy or qualified. It is indeed humbling now, yet I am also fully aware as I am sure God is that it is not a calling I ever wanted.

Yet during this time the Lord also revealed that I am a prophetic scribe. I have always known I was a gifted writer. However, God revealed I am a region of light, scribe for the kingdom, an author and leader of a movement (Hebrew/Greek Strong 5001, 747).

Spiritual Gifts

If the revelation of who you are in the kingdom by the Holy Spirit does not convince you that you are on the verge of an uncommon encounter with your divine purpose, the influx of spiritual gifts will. At this time, my ability to recall my dreams heightened and they were more vivid than ever. Not only did I recall my dreams with stunning clarity, but the meaning of my dreams were immediately understood. I believe I already had the gift of dream interpretation, but now I was receiving visions—quick, clear and brimming with revelations about my life and the lives and situations of many around me. Moreover, I was emboldened with a new level of confidence and surety when prophesying and sharing a word placed on my heart from the Holy Spirit for a believer that was contacting me for hope, assurance and confirmation. Many of you may have one particular gift that will be strengthened during this time or for which you may intuit that you have now received a double portion. Others of you may have one gift, but are now realizing that God has increased your anointing and given you multiple gifts. However this gifting stage manifests, it will and must be for God's glory. It would be a good idea to become familiar with the gifts of the Holy Spirit at this time so that you can accurately identify the move and directive of the Holy Spirit in your life and ministry.

I Corinthians 12:4-11 NIV
There are different kinds of gifts, but the same Spirit distributes them. There are different kinds of service, but the same Lord. There are different kinds of working, but in all of them and in everyone it is the same God at work. Now to each one the manifestation of the Spirit is given for the common good. To one there is given through the Spirit a message of wisdom, to another a message of knowledge by means of the same Spirit, to another faith by the same Spirit, to another gifts of healing by that one Spirit, to another miraculous powers, to another prophecy, to another distinguishing between spirits, to another speaking in different kinds of tongues, and to still another the interpretation of tongues. All these are the work of one and the same Spirit, and he distributes them to each one, just as he determines.

Romans 12:3-8
For by the grace given me I say to every one of you: Do not think of yourself more highly than you ought, but rather think of yourself with sober judgment, in accordance with the faith God has distributed to each of you. For just as each of us has one body with many members, and these members do not all have the same function, so in Christ we, though many, form one body, and each member belongs to all the others. We have different gifts, according to the grace given to each of us. If your gift is prophesying, then prophesy in accordance with your faith; if it is serving, then serve; if it is teaching, then teach; if it is to encourage, then give encouragement; if it is giving, then give generously; if it is to lead, do it diligently; if it is to show mercy, do it cheerfully.

Isaiah 11:2-3

The Spirit of the LORD will rest on him— the Spirit of wisdom and of understanding, the Spirit of counsel and of might, the Spirit of the knowledge and fear of the LORD— and he will delight in the fear of the LORD. He will not judge by what he sees with his eyes, or decide by what he hears with his ears;

Kingdom Mission

At this time your mission, at least for this season, should be coming into focus. My mission at this time in my life is clear. I have been called to write and publish my testimony. I have been called to write my testimony in such a way that it will serve as a roadmap for others who share many of the same experiences. I have been called to teach many of you how to identify, battle and be victorious when confronting certain junctures, experiences and enemies in life. And along with the call to write this particular testimony, I was called to begin my 7:47 ministry. I do not know if this will be my mission for the remainder of the time I have on this natural plane. I do know it is what the Holy Spirit has called me to do at this time and for this season. Please note, you may not be called to a traditional ministry as far as preaching at the pulpit, but you may be called to lead a ministry on social media, to teach, coach or to be a demonstration of a Christ-led woman of God in your particular industry—be it as an educator, entertainer, politician, business mogul, hair stylist, etc.

Revelation of Governing Demons & Principalities

During this time the Holy Spirit will reveal the demonic spirits, demons and principalities that have been working to suppress, derail and destroy your destiny. In the sermon entitled, *Anointed for Altercation*, TD Jakes implores us to understand that there is a demonic influence, principality or legion assigned to our lives by the kingdom of darkness. Although I started this section prior to hearing his sermon, I found comfort in knowing that I did not mistake what the Holy Spirit shared with me.

Although you may believe that this is an unnecessary step, useless fodder and information, it is not. In order to overcome an issue, problem, or enemy, you must name it first. Only when you name your adversary are you able to understand, study, evaluate and defeat it. If you recall when Jesus was confronted by the possessed man in Gadarenes, Jesus had asked the unclean spirit to come. The demon did not, but instead fell down in worship and stated, "What have I to do with thee, Jesus, thou Son of God most high? I beseech thee, torment me not" (Luke 8:28). After which, Jesus asked the demon his name. Jesus already knew the name of the demons possessing the man and their number for the man answered "Legion: because many devils were entered into him" (Luke 8:30). This question was asked for our benefit. For if you go into battle or war and assume you are only fighting one enemy when you are indeed fighting hundreds or thousands, your efforts will be unsuccessful. Now that was quite an exaggeration, but it is to demonstrate a point. Likewise, when a doctor recommends a full diagnostic test in an effort to address a healthcare issue, the physician will not be effective assuming there is only one issue if there are many. Thus, the Holy Spirit began to reveal the enemies, strongholds and principalities I was battling.

Disclaimer: *Let me quickly state that I do not encourage or condone any person engaging in spiritual warfare if you are not a fervent believer in Jesus Christ as your Lord and Savior, if you are not baptized, if you are not a born again Christian, and if you do not have a church home grounded in sound, biblical doctrine. Without the covering provided by His blood and the authority and dominion provided by the belief in His name, it is a dangerous undertaking with repercussions in both the spiritual and natural realms. I wholeheartedly believe, just as Reverend Kay ElBessing and his first lady, Minister Esther, of the Fresh Fire Prayer Ministry, in Maryland, have stated on numerous occasions and teach their followers, you cannot successfully fight and defeat demonic entities, or the demon possessed on the physical plane, or in the natural realm for it is their territory. They have the advantage in this realm. In order to defeat them in this realm without spiritual covering, you will have to become as evil as they are, invite demons to your aid and become a more treacherous demon. To defeat demons, the demon possessed, humans hosting demons legally and entirely, you must* *fight and defeat them in the spiritual realm. And that victory will manifest on the natural/physical plane. Furthermore, I encourage you to speak with a healthcare practitioner before entering any spiritual fast be it for one day, three days, seven, twenty-one, thirty, forty, etc.*

And a battle it was indeed. Yet, the naming of the entities I was battling allowed me to pray and make decrees against what was challenging and coming up against me specifically. Please understand that while it is important to name our enemies, God does not wish for us to be so preoccupied with demonology, demons and engaging them in warfare that we get distracted from serving Him, feeding His sheep and knowing our joy and victory rests in our salvation which is the gift of eternal life with our Savior in heaven. When confronted with satanic opposition we are to name the demon(s) attacking us, annihilate their influence in and on our lives and the lives of our loved ones, and move on to do what God has called us to do—unless your specific calling is to engage and destroy demonic spirits, entities and strongholds.

Luke 10:17
And the seventy returned again with joy, saying, Lord, even the devils are subject unto us through thy name. And he said unto them, I beheld Satan as lightning fall from heaven. Behold, I give unto you power to tread on serpents and scorpions, and over all the power of the enemy: and nothing shall by any means hurt you. Notwithstanding in this rejoice not, that the spirits are subject unto you; but rather rejoice, because your names are written in heaven.

Before this battle truly got underway, the Holy Spirit revealed that I have toiled with and been tormented by *Molek* (Molech), a Canaanite deity, associated with the practice of child sacrifice. In Leviticus 18:21 the Lord tells Moses to warn the Israelites against sacrificing their children in the fire.

The 7:47 Connection

Ezekiel 20:31

"When you offer your gifts—the sacrifice of your children in the fire—you continue to defile yourselves with all your idols to this day."

Jeremiah 7:31

"And they have built the high places of Tophet, which is the Valley of the son of Hinnom, to burn their sons and their daughters in the fired, which I did not command."

Believers and non-believers alike, whether they choose to believe it or not, enter into a covenant with Molech the moment they sacrifice a child. I am a woman who willfully had two abortions, one at eighteen and another at twenty-eight. I have spent most of my life either nursing or mourning aborted projects, relationships and dreams. And during the times when I really desired children, at thirty-two, just after having a daughter, and then again at thirty-five, when I desired to give her a sibling, I miscarried. I did not escape this demonic hold, or more specifically, Molek's demand for more blood from my life, more bloodshed, and more destruction. The innocent blood of my children cried out just as the innocent blood of Abel cried out after meeting death by Cain's hand—until I was taught about the spiritual implications of abortion. Yes, I do believe abortion violates the fifth commandment which states *Thou shall not kill*. In addition, I believe as taught by Prophetess Tiffani Montgomery and Kevin Ewing that in doing so we also enter into an unholy, unrighteous, demonic, wicked and evil covenant that must be denounced and renounced before reclaiming entry and permanent adherence to the new covenant sealed in the blood of Jesus Christ as stipulated in the Gospel. Do I curse or condemn any parties that have agreed to do so? I do not and am no position to judge anyone—ever. I am sharing and speaking to my own experience and belief, yet if this situation does apply to you, I would encourage you to research Prophetess Tiphani Montgomery's teachings on the matter and to purchase a book she recommends entitled, *Deliverance from Demonic Covenants & Curses* by Reverend James A. Solomon.

Shortly after renouncing the spirit of Molek operating in my life, the Holy Spirit revealed Balak as the perpetrator of the high levels of obstruction in my life. Balak, a Moab King, introduced to us in Numbers chapter 22 attempted to block the Israelite migration to Canaan by enlisting the prophet, Balaam, to put a curse on the Israelites. I would like to make clear that although the King James version of the bible identifies Balaam as a prophet, more than likely he was not a prophet of the God of Israel, but a high ranking/standing man of his time with the known and respected ability to access the spiritual or supernatural realm. Balak, envious and afraid of the favor placed on the Israelites by their God and His power to give them victory over their enemies, sought to use the power Balaam possessed to stop the Israelites' possession of their promised land. Yet, God instructed Balaam to refuse Balak's request. Not only did Balaam refuse Balak's request, but he blessed Israel three times instead. Eventually Balak persuaded Balaam, who was unable to resist the promise of wealth, to conspire with him by directing salacious and adulterous women to seduce the men of Israel away from their Lord and His commandments. Ultimately, their acquiescence gave the wretched co-conspirators the legal right required to wreak havoc on the people of God. Correspondingly, many of the enemy spirits in your midst may be operating under the authority of this principality. If so, you have experienced extensive warfare strikes geared to obstruct your path to destiny, seduce, turn away and abduct loved ones away from the love and commandments of Christ through ill-reputed soul ties and relationships. Many of which may appear to promise an increase in stature and wealth and/or use witchcraft as a means to oppress, devastate, demean and rob you. If you are confronted by incessant and hostile attacks by others to exert their will over your life in order to illicit your rejection of the commandments of God, it may very well be authorized and orchestrated by this false deity. This false deity works in tandem with the spirit of Balaam.

Lastly, the Holy Spirit revealed that a demonic entity the Prophet Isaiah referenced in Isaiah 13:21 was also at work and responsible for the relentless season of drought and barrenness in my life. I often leave my television on one of the Christian channels during the night as I sleep. At times I wake during the night to a sermon by a known televangelist on either TBN or Daystar. This particular time I was awakened as Reverend Fred Pryce, Jr. was teaching his congregation about a demon named Pan. Upon his description of the principality, I quickly realized that the demon he was referencing as the goat-like beast Isaiah identified as dwelling in a grim, dismal, sterile place so much so that he equated its habitation with the desert.

Isaiah 13:21
"But wild beasts of the desert shall lie there; and their houses shall be full of doleful creatures; and owls shall dwell there, and satyrs shall dance there."

Isaiah references this same beast again in Isaiah 34:14:
The wild beasts of the desert shall also meet with the wild beasts of the island, and the satyr shall cry to his fellow; the screech owl also shall rest there, and find for herself a place of rest.

In both instances, the prophet Isaiah seeks to paint a picture of what befalls the wicked, and how continual, willful disobedience of God's instruction and dismissal of His loving kindness and tender mercies can lead to a reality devoid of his presence, love and grace.

Stephen Ricks, professor of Hebrew and semitic languages and Associate Dean of General Education and Honors, Brigham Young University explains that in Greek mythology, "a satyr was a creature of the hills and woods, half man and half animal, who follows Dionysus and Pan." Correspondingly, Edwin L. Brown, a scholar of Classical Philology, describes Pan as the god of the wild, shepherds and flocks. Roman artistic depictions of the creature give him the physical attributes of a goat, which are reflected in his horns, hindquarters and legs and would be reminiscent of a faun or satyr. He is associated with being the god of fields, narrow valleys and harsh, jagged terrain.

Upon reflection, it made sense that a goat-like demon given authority over desolate and dearth places would have the physical prowess to navigate the sometimes mountainous and desert-like environments in which Isaiah described and where many types of goats thrive. It is also logical to believe how a demon said to be a god of shepherds and flocks would be an antithesis to what Jesus called his followers to do. As Jesus's great commission to us as spoken to Peter speaks of his desire for us to feed his lambs, and his purpose as stated by him is to give us abundant life, a demon assigned to scatter Jesus's flock as he launches attacks meant to deceive us into believing life is unpalatable, thereby gathering us into throes of apathy and non-belief, is not only conceivable but applicable to what I was experiencing.

John 21:15-17
So when they had dined, Jesus saith to Simon Peter, Simon, son of Jonas, lovest thou me more than these? He saith unto him, Yea, Lord; thou knowest that I love thee. He saith unto him, Feed my lambs. He saith to him again the second time, Simon, son of Jonas, lovest thou me? He saith unto him, Yea, Lord; thou knowest that I love thee. He saith unto him, Feed my sheep. He saith unto him the third time, Simon, son of Jonas, lovest thou me? Peter was grieved because he said unto him the third time, Lovest thou me? And he said unto him, Lord, thou knowest all things; thou knowest that I love thee. Jesus saith unto him, Feed my sheep.

John 10:10
I have come that they may have life and that they might have it more abundantly.

Jeremiah 23:1
Woe to the shepherds who are destroying and scattering the sheep of My pasture!" declares the Lord.

Ezekiel 34:6
Because you push with side and with shoulder, and thrust at all the weak with your horns until you have scattered them abroad.

Revelation 12:9
So the great dragon was cast out, that serpent of old, called the Devil and Satan, who deceives the whole word; he was cast to the earth, and his angels were cast out with him."

I can attest that the opposition I have experienced has been illogically relentless, unyielding and oppressive. I have lived in an utterly infertile land with signs of growth few and far between. I have had to eat from hand to mouth, and yet, at the same time have experienced the inexplicable mercy, compassion and tenderness of God and astounding miracles—miracles that have sustained and protected me. And although none have catapulted me into my promise land, I am wholeheartedly persuaded that the only position for me to take is that of Job.

Job 13:15
Though he slay me, yet will I trust in him

Job 19:25
For I know that my Redeemer lives, and that in the end He shall stand at last on the earth

Part VI

Prepare For Takeoff

HOW TO ADVANCE TO YOUR PROMISE

TD Jakes has referenced these destiny affirming, life-altering, showdown battles in our lives as moments—and according to him we must grasp it! Jakes states that these moments are the point where you commit to God's will for your life, as in totally—without reservation. It is the moment when everyone around you may not have known just how serious your walk with Christ is as you may not have made your beliefs public. The vast majority of people may not know the degree that you read the bible, attend church, intercede, attend bible study, pray, fast, lay hands on believers in need of healing, etc. You may indeed be one of your region's biggest demon slayers, yet it is unbeknownst to the majority of people that know you. But in this moment, you step up to center stage to unabashedly say to the enemy as I have stated before, "I AM A CHILD OF THE MOST HIGH GOD AND I WILL NOT BE MOVED!"

This bold step is not done in haste or without waiting for the Holy Spirit to let you know it is time to do so. You may want to follow the steps that proved successful in my 7:47 journey. Yet you must be silent until God gives you the gumption or signal to move. The bible says by two or three witnesses a matter is confirmed. God will always confirm his will. I have recounted the strategy I was led to follow below:

Publish an authentic, honest, powerful and specific public testimony:

An authentic testimony via social media post or video works perfectly. There may be a long period of time between this testimony and the next step, but sharing your testimony is a powerful tool against the enemy.

Revelation 12:11
And they overcame him by the blood of the Lamb and by the word of their testimony, and they did not love their lives to the death

Psalm 22:22
I will tell my people what you have done; I will praise you in their assembly

Psalm 105:1
Give thanks to the Lord and proclaim his greatness. Let the whole world know what he has done

Isaiah 12:4
Give praise to the Lord; proclaim His name! Make His works known among the peoples; declare that His name is exalted

Psalm 119:46-47
I will speak about your written instructions in the presence of kings and not feel ashamed

Release a prophetic word:

Many of you are still recovering or quivering Jonahs just as I was at this point, but just as Hannah said when she had grown tired of Peninnah bullying her and provoking her—just as David tired of Goliath's mockery of our God, you too must get to a point where your soul wishes to proclaim just as Hannah, "My mouth has been enlarged over my enemies" (1 Samuel 2:1) This may be released as a live or video on social media or you may be sent directly to confront the enemy on their turf. I am uncertain how this will take form in your life, but you will know exactly how to confront the enemy based on your situation. Wherever and however you are sent, be bold!

I am not saying that what you have been called to do is easy or remiss of fear. But what I am saying is that Christ calls us to be bold and courageous. And the quicker we past the tests sent our way, the quicker we will be promoted. You may fear embarrassment, humiliation, the lack of acceptance of your message and the lack of approval you are sure to face. But this choice, moment and prophecy is for your own deliverance, victory and most of all for God's glory. For whether you know it or not, you were chosen to slay this/these Goliaths in your life. And by doing so, victory is certain as long as you continue to live inside God's will and remain obedient. In addition, your testimony rapidly converts many bystanders causing them and some of the soldiers in the enemy's camp to repent. It also frees others to boldly stand in their spiritual gifts, anointings and kingdom purpose. Many of the individuals that are watching have either never believed in God, rejected God, previously turned away from God, or have been neglecting their relationship with God. This step is powerful and requires all the faith you have accumulated in your life over the years until now and an understanding of what you are going through. It has been directly imparted to you by the Holy Spirit. This prophecy will be a specific word for your enemy and those attached to him or her. Even if you have been holding the word God gave you for some time, God's timing is exact. It will be a Rhema (on time) word for your enemies when he tells you to release it. However, it will prove freeing for others as well.

John 4:39-42
And many of the Samaritans of that city believed on him for the saying of the woman, which testified, He told me all that ever I did. So when the Samaritans were come unto him, they besought him that he would tarry with them: and he abode there two days. And many more believed because of his own word; And said unto the woman, Now we believe, not because of thy saying: for we have heard him ourselves, and know that this is indeed the Christ, the Saviour of the world

The Prophetic Word Will Include:

1. **Exposure of the Enemy**
   For there is nothing covered, that shall not be revealed; neither hid, that shall not be known. Therefore whatsoever ye have spoken in darkness shall be heard in the light; and that which ye have spoken in the ear in closets shall be proclaimed upon the housetops (Luke 12:2-3)

2. **God's Review of the Events and Impending Judgement**
   The Lord standeth up to plead, and standeth to judge the people (Isaiah 3:13)

   'O ye house of Israel, I will judge you every one after his ways (Ezekiel 33:20)

3. **God's Promise to Fight Your Enemies**
   For the Lord your God is he that goeth with you, to fight for you against your enemies, to save you (Deuteronomy 20:4)

   Hint: It is important to ensure that you have forgiven your enemies and if indeed your enemies need judgment have the full understanding that when it comes to vengeance, "Dearly beloved, avenge not yourselves, but rather give place unto wrath: for it is written, Vengeance is mine; I will repay, saith the Lord (Romans 12:19)

4. **Extreme Obedience - Forgive Enemies and Press Forward**
   Ye have heard that it hath been said, Thou shalt love thy neighbour, and hate thine enemy. But I say unto you, Love your enemies, bless them that curse you, do good to them that hate you, and pray for them which despitefully use you, and persecute you (Matthew 5:43-44)

   But this one thing I do, forgetting those things which are behind, and reaching forth unto those things which are before, I press toward the mark for the prize of the high calling of God in Christ Jesus. (Philippians 3:13-14)

5. **Plea to the Enemy to Repent and Return to the Love of God**
   If my people, which are called by my name, shall humble themselves, and pray, and seek my face, and turn from their wicked ways; then will I hear from heaven, and will forgive their sin, and will heal their land (2 Chronicles 7:14)

Boldly walk in your gifting

At this time, the spiritual gifts that God has stored up for you to accomplish your specific mission(s) and step into your calling/position in the kingdom will begin to pour in. Which will lead you to your next and final blow to the enemy. Hint: It must be noted that anytime you have to engage the enemy you should be armed in the whole armor of God.e In addition, this should be a period of separation, fasting, prayer and worship. Your contact with anyone that is not a believer, born again or a worshiper of Christ in spirit and truth should be heavily avoided, if not extremely limited—unless God has given you specific instructions to minister to them, check on them, etc. This should be a period of fasting and consecration (none or limited exposure to worldly music, television and anything or anyone that can risk grieving the Holy Spirit or __ his presence)

During this time, I spoke prophetic messages from the Holy Spirit to many and the accuracy was confirmed by the believer on the spot. I performed a public laying of hands on a stranger as the Holy Spirit told me to pull over and lay hands on a growth on her back as she walked down the street. At this time you will find it advantageous to move when the Holy Spirit says move. God is testing you. He wants to ensure that he can trust you and that you truly have the faith you have demonstrated during your wilderness season.

Some of these experiences will be private while others will be public. I recall accompanying my daughter to the mall to purchase an outfit from a clothing store she adores called Garage during this time of separation. My daughter entered the fitting room to try on a few outfits she was considering purchasing. I took a seat directly outside the room she'd chosen. The Holy Spirit immediately revealed that the young lady working the fitting room was a painter or artist and that it was the path he had ordained for her. There was nothing that would suggest this young lady was a painter. But I was obedient. At that time I happened to be listening to a prophetic word from a sister I follow on YouTube. "Excuse me," she said. "Are you listening to a sermon?" I replied no, and walked closer to her to reveal the reel I was watching on instagram.

Almost immediately, without any thought I asked, "Do you draw? Are you an artist? Or painter?" She looked shocked. I humbly stated, "I apologize, please do not be alarmed. I walk in the prophetic and the Holy Spirit has revealed that you draw." She looked disarmed, but responded, "Yes, I am a musician and I paint." I then stated, "The Holy Spirit wants you to know that he has gone before you on this path. You have the free will to choose whatever career you like, but this is the path that he has specifically anointed and ordained for you." Shock is the only way I can describe her response. She stated "I haven't drawn in five months, but last night I was staring at one of my paintings and asked God, what did he want me to do with my life and what path was I supposed to take" for the young lady was multi-talented in the arts.

The young lady then shared that she was considering attending undergrad in the fall but was uncertain about a major. I informed her that the Holy Spirit was stating her path and major should include her gift to paint and to draw—but again, it would be her decision. The Holy Spirit then led me to inform her not to allow anything keep her from registering and attending school in the fall as I continuously heard "false burdens." I shared with her that she needs to be okay with allowing people in her life to learn how to seek God for themselves. She can pray for them, but she cannot babysit their salvation and has to move forward in her destiny. Again, she looked shocked and stated, "My mom has asked me not to go home this weekend. She has asked me to stay with her, but I am supposed to go home to get baptized." The Holy Spirit led me to tell her to move forward with her plans for baptism and that her mom would be fine. Suddenly it seemed as if a light began to emanate from this young lady. She seemed refreshed and relieved.

In hindsight, it was a quite funny watching my daughter emerge from the dressing room for she had never witnessed me walk in my gift to that degree before. When we left the store she asked, "How did you know that, Mom?" The day marks the day my daughter became a believer in my anointing and realized that Mom is not crazy after all.

Please be sensitive to the Holy Spirit at this time as he will let you know which experiences you can mention to others and which ones you should not. None of these small missions should be posted on social media for self-aggrandizement. For to God be the glory! Further, at this time you will be surrounded by nonbelievers, many who may think you have had a nervous breakdown, are disillusioned, fraudulent, judgmental and self-righteous. Yet, understand that the experiences with the strangers you have encountered may be the difference between them turning toward or away from God. It may be that the timely word to a total stranger, the full healing offered to a total stranger in the name of Jesus Christ may cause the person to testify and bring their friends and family to Christ. This step was critical.

Although I have gone to great lengths to describe how I defeated my enemy in detail, I realize you may need to employ a different strategy to defeat the enemies in your midst. Whatever strategy you employ, I pray it will be Holy Spirit led and totally annihilate what Bishop TD Jakes asserts are the only three stumbling blocks, pitfalls or temptations the devil has in his arsenal which is based on the revelation of 1 John 2:16 which reads, "For all that is in the world—the lust of the flesh, the lust of the eyes, and the pride of life—is not of the Father but is of the world."

These tactics and how to defeat them are illustrated for every believer's benefit when Satan confronted Jesus in the wilderness. Jesus was presented with three temptations—all of which he forthrightly and righteously dismissed. The first temptation Satan used to confront Jesus was the lust of the flesh as Matthew 4:32-3 states "And when he had fasted forty days and forty nights, he was afterward an hungred (hungry). And when the tempter came to him, he said, if thou be the Son of God, command that these stones be made bread." The second temptation Satan utilized was the lust of the eyes. In Matthew 4:8-9 the text reads, "Again the devil taketh him up into an exceeding high mountain, and sheweth him all the kingdoms of the world, and the glory of them; And saith unto him, All these things will I give thee, if thou wilt fall down and worship me." The last temptation Satan employed was that of the pride of life which appeals to a person's need to be overly praised by man and showered in accolades, in a bid to feed their arrogance and sense of superiority. This is demonstrated when Satan tempts Jesus to jump off the mountain for the bible states the angels would rush to his aid as the Son of God. Unswayed by the need to prove his position and station, Jesus retorted, "It is written again, Thou shalt not tempt the Lord thy God."

Part VII

Take Off and Climb

Take Off and Climb

POTENTIAL FLIGHT HAZARDS

Fear

During this journey fear may materialize in several different ways. You may fear the potential of your enemies to harm you. You may fear setting out on a new path, new journey, or just setting out on your own without previous companions. One of the hugest fears you may face may be the fear of what others will say or think about the new and improved focused, empowered you that has decided to follow the calling God has placed on your life. You will have to get beyond this as you will be unable to please God unless you do. You will have to get beyond the fear of what people may say about you launching out to start a new ministry, business, non-profit or whatever it is that the Holy Spirit has instructed you to begin. You must start it without worry about who will or will not like it. Typically they are not the audience to whom you are called to minister, which means your ministry is none of their business and their opinion of it does not matter. Even more likely is that they are not believers in Christ, and even if they are, it is in word only and they know nothing about picking up the cross. Yet, as a believer you must follow Christ, not only in word but in deed, regardless of how your partners, loved ones, friends, acquaintances, old friends, lovers, or foes feel. You cannot allow your past or the beliefs of those in your past define you or fetter you to what they know of you and what boxes they have constructed for you. You must press forward and launch out into the deep and be a fisher of men as we are instructed.

Luke 9:62 KJV
And Jesus said unto him, No man, having put his hand to the plough, and looking back, is fit for the kingdom of God.

Luke 5:4

When He had stopped speaking, He said to Simon, "Launch out into the deep and let down your nets for a catch."

Luke 12:51-53

"Do *you* suppose that I came to give peace on earth? I tell you, not at all, but rather division. For from now on five in one house will be divided: three against two, and two against three. Father will be divided against son and son against father, mother against daughter and daughter against mother, mother-in-law against her daughter-in-law and daughter-in-law against her mother-in-law."

Doubt

None of us are immune to ever experiencing doubt. You may doubt the validity of your calling, or you may doubt the level of success you may attain in terms of effectiveness, engagement, impact, etc. Based on my experience, when doubt crept in I prayed for the Lord to help my unbelief. I fasted, I read the word, made sure I did not allow any words fall from my mouth that spoke against what I needed to do, and I asked for confirmation again, and again, and again. I am a huge proponent of speaking the word to my mountains, against my enemies, to my doubts and to my future. I have been utilizing the word as a weapon for protection, to regain peace, for promotion, advancement and victory since reading Joyce Meyer's *Battlefield of the Mind* and Norman Vincent Peale's *the Power of Positive Thinking* in my twenties. I would suggest reading these books and books like it that stand on the word along with the bible, which should be your primary source for strength, comfort, healing, clarity, power and truth. It is said that it takes five positive thoughts to counteract or neutralize one negative thought. The New York Times calls it the 5:1 ratio. I interpret this phenomenon to mean that whenever a thought, idea or suggestion (TIS as taught by the late Frederick Price as the weapons of the devil) comes up against my plans and intentions for my calling, it is time for me to launch an onslaught of the word (bible verses) to counter everything the deceiver is trying to plant in my mind.

Whether the thought, idea, or suggestion forms internally or comes from an external source, I know I must destroy it from the root. Yet, most importantly, to combat doubt you must remember that if you have been called to it, whatever it may be, Elohim will help you accomplish that which he has called you to do. Jesus is your victorious advocate, partner, helper and ally. We must suspend our doubt and when we find it difficult to do, we can still come to Jesus in our frailty just as the father who confessed his doubt regarding his son that was possessed.

Mark 9:21-24
And he asked his father, How long is it ago since this came unto him? And he said, Of a child. And ofttimes it hath cast him into the fire, and into the waters, to destroy him: but if thou canst do anything, have compassion on us, and help us. Jesus said unto him, If thou canst believe, all things are possible to him that believeth. And straightway the father of the child cried out, and said with tears, Lord, I believe; help thou mine unbelief.

The possessed boy's father understood that in order for him to experience the miracle he requested for his child, what would be required of him was faith. Throughout the bible Jesus implores his disciples to believe and is touched by the unmovable faith of many who believed He was able to do the impossible. Jesus vehemently warns believers against doubt and unbelief for doubt can dismantle the best laid intentions, plans, hopes and visions of the believer. In addition, it appears to greatly grieve our Lord. Yet, faith is the currency of the believer in the kingdom of God, and by it not only are we free but we activate miracles, signs and wonders.

Matthew 15:28
"Then Jesus answered and said unto her, O woman, great is thy faith: be it unto thee even as thou wilt. And her daughter was made whole from that very hour."

Matthew 8:5-13
And when Jesus was entered into Capernaum, there came unto him a centurion, beseeching him, And saying, Lord, my servant lieth at home sick of the palsy, grievously tormented. And Jesus saith unto him, I will come and heal him. The centurion answered and said, Lord, I am not worthy that thou shouldest come under my roof: but speak the word only, and my servant shall be healed. For I am a man under authority, having soldiers under me: and I say to this man, Go, and he goeth; and to another, Come, and he cometh; and to my servant, Do this, and he doeth it. When Jesus heard it, he marvelled, and said to them that followed, Verily I say unto you, I have not found so great faith, no, not in Israel.

James 1:6
But let him ask in faith, nothing wavering. For he that wavereth is like a wave of the sea driven with the wind and tossed

Matthew 8:26
And he saith unto them, Why are ye fearful, O ye of little faith?

Matthew 14:31
And immediately Jesus stretched forth his hand, and caught him, and said unto him, O thou of little faith, wherefore didst thou doubt?

I John 5:4 AMP
For everyone born of God is victorious *and* overcomes the world; and this is the victory that has conquered *and* overcome the world—our [continuing, persistent] faith [in Jesus the Son of God].

Luke 17:6
And the Lord said, if ye had faith as a grain of mustard seed, ye might say unto the sycamine tree, Be thou plucked up by the root, and be thou planted in the sea; and it should obey you

Mark 9:23
Jesus said to him, "If you can believe, all things are possible to him who believes."

John 14:12
Verily, verily, I say unto you, He that believeth on me, the works that I do shall he do also; and greater works than these shall he do; because I go unto my Father.

Seeking Human Approval

Although you may not fear what people around you may say or feel about you during this time, it still may be extremely important for you to have their approval, be part of the clique, the in crowd, be invited to all the parties, girl and couple vacations, and social media photo ops. Yet, to fully follow Christ and proclaim your commitment to doing so will undoubtedly rub most the wrong way. You will be considered everything from a killjoy to a self-righteous, judgmental, lost or disillusioned crackpot. Many will avoid you, most will drop off and hope you do not notice and whomever is left will call you repeatedly to get the deets on why and how you arrived at this conclusion so they can blast it to any and everyone who will stop to listen. Others who you may not have heard from in ages may now request to follow you on social media while others will unfriend you.

Interestingly enough, those already following you may quietly play the background curious to see where all this is heading, or for pure amusement. News flash! You are not at liberty to care about any of it. You may not respond, berate, or allow any of these offenses to put a chink in your armor. What God has called you to do is much too important to the kingdom for you to get bogged down in petty and toxic minutiae. And if having the ability to ignore the rumor mill, criticisms and impending drama is too much to ask, then you really only have two choices. The first is to turn back and hope they -whomever they may be- will forgive your temporary lapse in judgement and nervous breakdown. The other choice is to allow their judgments, the rescinding of their invitations, friendships and the like to roll off your back while strengthening your resolve to attain what God has called you to attain and hold out for what he has promised you. This will not be done without a deliberate decision to do so, a deliberate change in your thinking and a deliberate effort to harness your intentions toward becoming the person you must become in order to manifest all God has asked you to manifest in this realm. In order to be successful in this undertaking you must let go of old parts of you, toxic and cyclical behaviors, thinking and responses that previously allowed others to feel comfortable around you or illicit certain reactions from you. You must let go of your tendency to play blind, small, or unconscious as it no longer serves your new mindset or where you are heading.

Romans 12:2
Be ye transformed by the renewing of your mind

Ephesians 4:23 NKJV
But ye have not so learned Christ, if so it be that ye have heard Him and have been taught by Him as the truth is in Jesus: that ye put off, concerning your former manner of living, the old man which is corrupt according to the deceitful lusts, and be renewed in the spirit of your mind, and that ye put on that new man, which after God is created in righteousness and true holiness.

Galatians 1:10
For do I now persuade men, or God? or do I seek to please men? for if I yet pleased men, I should not be the servant of Christ.

1 Thessalonians 2:4
But as we were allowed of God to be put in trust with the gospel, even so we speak; not as pleasing men, but God, which trieth our hearts.

Ephesians 6:6
Not with eyeservice, as menpleasers; but as the servants of Christ, doing the will of God from the heart;

If you seek to blend in with the crowd, this is not the path for you. If you are easily offended, bristle when derided, or if you are easily swayed by public opinion and disapproval, you might as well turn back now. For your desire to please God must overpower, outrank and outweigh your desire to fit in. Man's opinion cannot trump your desire to reach your fullest potential and destiny. Over the years I have had to train myself to ensure I desired to reach my goals more than the people around me wanted me to fail. Now my desire to reach the goals God has placed before me is more important than any enjoyment that people who are typically shallow, disingenuous and disloyal can offer. And most times the doors they shut on me because of my decision are not doors I need to enter anyway.

Luke 16:15
And He said to them, "You are those who justify yourselves before men, but God knows your hearts. For what is highly esteemed among men is an abomination in the sight of God.

Acts 5:29
Then Peter and the other apostles answered and said, We ought to obey God rather than men.

2 Corinthians 5:9
Therefore we make it our aim, whether present or absent, to be well pleasing to Him.

Hebrews 13:6
So that we may boldly say, The Lord is my helper, and I will not fear what man shall do unto me

Disobedience/Delayed Obedience

In the section entitled Destiny Destroyers I share that disobedience is a destiny destroyer when practiced by those around you or demonstrated in your own relationship with God. To obey another is to show them reverence, honor and respect. It is to demonstrate an understanding that they are the authority and to trust that they know what is best for you. The Concordance in the King James Bible defines disobedience as a condition of *being unable to persuade, obstinate rejection and sometimes denotes a refusal to hear*. Which suggests that the Lord views disobedience as rejection and he takes it personally. When King Saul chooses to be disobedient, dismissing the Lord's instructions, Samuel admonishes him by stating that obedience is more pleasing to God than sacrifice.

1 Samuel 15:22
And Samuel said, Hath the LORD as great delight in burnt offerings and sacrifices, as in obeying the voice of the LORD? Behold, to obey is better than sacrifice, and to hearken [listen and then carry out] than the fat of rams.

If additional clarification is required on disobedience please revisit that section. What I would like to point your attention to now to ensure you do not miss your connection to your destiny is that disobedience not only includes a refusal to heed the instruction of God, but also delayed adherence to instruction. By this I am asserting that the time you take to be obedient, even though you may eventually follow God's instruction, can be considered disobedience.

Psalm 119:60
"Without delay I hurry to obey your commands"

Luke 24:25
Then Jesus said to them, "O foolish ones, how slow are your hearts to believe all that the prophets have spoken:"

In order to be obedient you must trust and have faith in the Lord. Obedience suggests our wholehearted acceptance of Him, His way and His will. When we are obedient we assert our belief that what he has asks of us is our top priority.

Matthew 22:37
Jesus said unto him, Thou shalt love the Lord thy God with all thy heart, and with all thy soul, and with all thy mind.

Matthew 6:33
But seek ye first the kingdom of God, and his righteousness; and all these things shall be added unto you

Matthew 16:25
For whosoever will save his life shall lose it: and whosoever will lose his life for my sake shall find it

We must believe that when He asks us to follow his instruction to complete a particular mission, He has asked us to do so for a reason and it requires our timely submission to the task. To be hesitant is to lack faith and trust that God is able to protect you and see that situation through to its expected end. It is to challenge the assertion that He always knows what is best. To tarry, delay, procrastinate or postpone when you are called to a thing by the Lord is to be disobedient. For as I have mentioned earlier, although God is not a God of time, but eternal existing outside of the constraints of time as the creator of time, He is a God of timing.

Habakkuk 2:3
For the vision is yet for an appointed time, but at the end it shall speak, and not lie: though it tarry, wait for it; because it will surely come, it will not tarry.

We never know what plan or purpose of God hinges on our obedience. And during this season, our promise or the fulfillment thereof is contingent on our ability to follow instruction. As much as this journey is one of discovery, finding out who we are and what God wants us to do for this next phase of our lives, it is a time of testing and stretching. During this time God is testing if we can be trusted to carry out his will and if we are committed to the process, however painful it may be, to develop our capacity for victory. God is testing if we indeed trust Him and love Him above all else. Our willingness and capacity for obedience is one of the earmarks that God utilizes to determine and/or measure the depth and sincerity of our love for Him and to qualify or disqualify us for His purposes.

1 John 2:3-6
And we can be sure that we know him if we obey his commandments. If someone claims, "I know God," but doesn't obey God's commandments, that person is a liar and is not living in the truth. But those who obey God's word truly show how completely they love him. That is how we know we are living in him. Those who say they live in God should live their lives as Jesus did.

Dishonorable Mentions:
Ungratefulness, Impatience, Grumbling & Complaining

I believe one of the most illustrative examples of ungratefulness, impatience, grumbling and complaining is witnessed when studying the Israelites and their journey to their promise land of Canaan. Many believers would say that their delay into their promise land was due to their grumbling and complaining while others would state it was due to their disobedience. I definitely believe the first generation of Israelites were locked out of the promised land due to their disobedience, but I would assert that it was not only disobedience but a posture of ungratefulness and impatience which led to their incessant grumbling and complaining, and the combined effect of these offenses ultimately led to disobedience and shut them out of their promise. When studying the book of Exodus there are ten separate accounts of the Israelites grumbling and murmuring to Moses due to either their ungratefulness, impatience, lack of faith (doubt) or a combination of all mentioned.

Ungratefulness – Numbers 11:4-34 The Israelites tire of eating the Manna God has provided from heaven and instead long for fish, cucumbers, melons, leeks, and the onions of Egypt.

Impatience – Exodus 32:1-6 The Israelites tire of waiting for Moses to descend from Mount Sinai from his meeting with the Lord and ask Aaron to fashion a new god for them to serve.

Grumbling & Complaining – Numbers 11:1-3 Just days after their departure from Mount Sinai, the bible notes more complaints. Although we are not told the specific reason for the displeasure they express to Moses, it is enough to cause God to burn many of the Israelites with fire.

Disobedience – Exodus 16:11-20 Moses tells the Israelites they are not to save any of their daily portion of Manna for the following day as per God's instruction. Despite the warning, many do and the manna breeds warms and starts to stink.

Lack of Faith – Numbers 14:1-4 When the twelve spies return from surveying the promise land of Canaan, their account of giants in the land scares the Israelites and they express a desire for a new leader that will return them to Egypt.

Numbers 14:20-23
And the LORD said, I have pardoned according to thy word: But as truly as I live, all the earth shall be filled with the glory of the LORD. Because all those men which have seen my glory, and my miracles, which I did in Egypt and in the wilderness, and have tempted me now these ten times, and have not hearkened to my voice; Surely they shall not see the land which I sware unto their fathers, neither shall any of them that provoked me see it:

If you need further convincing, I invite you to use your own life as an example. Think about the times when you believed someone was letting you down, or not keeping up their end of a bargain, or when you allowed yourself to focus on all the negative attributes of a particular situation, or how long it was taking for a person to do whatever necessary to get you to a desired end. Given this line of thinking, it is a natural progression to get to a point where you no longer wish to believe or engage the person— and by no means would you consider obeying them. The more the Israelites allowed themselves to entertain ingratitude, impatience, discontent, grumbling and complaining, the more it affected their faith and unwillingness to believe in God which made disobedience a logical next step.

Unfortunately, they neglected to remember that they were not dealing with a mere mortal but the one and only true living God who demonstrated time and time again that they were His children and He would not forsake them. Yet, we do not want to be locked out of our promise land because we are ungrateful, impatient, and complaining during this process of testing. It would be quite tragic to get this far in the process only to forfeit our divine kingdom purpose and God's promises to us because we lack the spiritual foresight and tenacity to accept and trust what God is doing right now in our lives regardless of the adversity and what it may look like to the natural eye. As such, I implore you to refuse to make the same mistakes as that first generation of Israelites. Stay your mind on God's loving kindness and tender mercies because ingratitude, impatience, grumbling and complaining are spoilers of the vine that will beckon disobedience and prevent us from making the connection to your promise.

We are to go through our wilderness and testing seasons and sojourn to our promise lands with an attitudes of gratefulness and patience. For God rewards those who patiently wait on Him. Isaiah 30 states, ". Make no mistake, at times we will mess up, foul out and fumble the ball. Sometimes we will certainly miss the mark." Romans 3:23 states, "For we all have sinned, and come short of the glory of God." Thankfully, God's grace is available to us. However, we must not take advantage of the grace given to us.

Psalm 103:8
"The Lord is merciful and gracious, slow to anger and plenteous in mercy"

Psalm 103:10
"He hath not dealt with us after our sins; nor rewarded us according to our iniquities"

Psalm 103:12

"As far as the east is from the west, so far hath he removed our transgressions from us"

Acts 15:11(NLT)
We believe that we are all saved the same way, by the undeserved grace of the Lord Jesus."

Ephesians 4:7
But to each one of us grace has been given as Christ apportioned it

Jude 4 (Amp)
For certain people have crept in unnoticed [just as if they were sneaking in by a side door]. They are ungodly persons whose condemnation was predicted long ago, for they distort the grace of our God into decadence *and* immoral freedom [viewing it as an opportunity to do whatever they want], and deny *and* disown our only Master and Lord, Jesus Christ.

When we make decisions and demonstrate behaviors that exhibit disobedience because they are out of alignment with the will of God and violate His commandments, we must not assume it is trivial in His eyes because He gives us grace. Our gratitude for this gift and understanding of it should lead us to repent with contrite hearts, humble spirits and then try again.

Acts 3:19 (NLT)
Now repent of your sins and turn to God, so that your sins may be wiped away.

2 Chronicles 30:9
...For the LORD your God is gracious and merciful, and will not turn away his face from you, if ye return unto him.

James 4:8
Draw nigh to God, and he will draw nigh to you. Cleanse your hands, ye sinners; and purify your hearts, ye double minded.

Zechariah 1:3

Therefore say thou unto them, Thus saith the LORD of hosts; Turn ye unto me, saith the LORD of hosts, and I will turn unto you, saith the LORD of hosts.

Psalm 51:17
The sacrifices of God are a broken spirit: a broken and a contrite heart, O God, thou wilt not despise.

Although God's grace is sufficient, we must be exceedingly clear that it is only made available to us through the advocate we have in Jesus Christ. It is only through his blood and his sacrifice that we are able to repent, be forgiven and try again when we disobey, for he is indeed our advocate and intercessor.

1 John 2:1
My little children, these things write I unto you, that ye sin not. And if any man sin, we have an advocate with the Father, Jesus Christ the righteous. And he is the propitiation for our sins: and not for ours only, but also for the sins of the whole world.

Romans 3:24
Yet God, in his grace, freely makes us right in his sight. He did this through Christ Jesus when he freed us from the penalty for our sins.

Ephesians 1:6-7
So we praise God for the glorious grace he has poured out on us who belong to his dear Son. He is so rich in kindness and grace that he purchased our freedom with the blood of his Son and forgave our sins.

Hebrews 7:25
Therefore he is able, once and forever, to save those who come to God through him. He lives forever to intercede with God on their behalf.

Romans 8:34
Who is he that condemneth? It is Christ that died, yea rather, that is risen again, who is even at the right hand of God, who also maketh intercession for us.

Not only is Jesus are intercessor and advocate, but we have been given the Holy Spirit who dwells within in us, and who was specifically sent to us as our Helper. The Holy Spirit has equipped us with the truth, guides us and empowers us to obey God and carry out the missions he sets before us.

John 14:16
And I will pray the Father, and He will give you another Helper, that He may abide with you forever—the Spirit of truth, whom the world cannot receive, because it neither sees Him nor knows Him; but you know Him, for He dwells with you and will be in you.

Romans 8:26-27 (NLT)
And the Holy Spirit helps us in our weakness. For example, we don't know what God wants us to pray for. But the Holy Spirit prays for us with groanings that cannot be expressed in words. And the Father who knows all hearts knows what the Spirit is saying, for the Spirit pleads for us believers in harmony with God's own will.

Honorable Mentions

There are two lines of thinking I want you to be careful to avoid. Both lines of thinking are particularly deadly as they have the potential to deter you from your destiny if entertained as they will erode your confidence. If you allow the first thought to settle it will only be a moment before you are hit with a barrage of negative thoughts and goaded into inaction. So let's be clear. When that first toxic thought pops in your head to challenge the validity or accuracy of what you have heard from the Holy Spirit or what has been impressed on your heart, kill it immediately. While it is true that you have undergone an experience many people you know have not, that does not negate its validity. Other people's rejection of and refusal to believe what you have stated about your experience and your path is their right to exercise. You must be certain that you know beyond a shadow of a doubt that if the Lord allowed such a tumultuous, and painful experience to happen, rest assured that your purpose is hidden somewhere in the pain.

The second thought you must resist is that if you were meant to set out on this kind of path it would have happened long ago, or that it is too late for you to start a new ministry, business, embrace a new spiritual identity, etc. I assure you it is not. You are not considering anything I did not grapple with myself. I wish the trajectory of one's life moved forward in neat, straight lines, but it does not. If we look back, at times our journey was a straight line, at other times it jutted to the left, and then to the right before inclining, then descending and then spiraling to catapult us forward. None of our journeys have been a linear path and thank goodness because how boring, predictable and mundane would that be? Life's direction keeps us guessing and more importantly for the believer it keeps us dependent on and trusting in God. If that does not assist your resolve, remember that Moses and his brother Aaron were called to confront Pharoah at the tender ages of eighty and eighty-three according to Exodus 7:7. Keep moving, keep believing as what you are carrying is important to the kingdom. Do not let anything cause you to deny your Lord and Savior and his call on your life. They are people waiting on who you are becoming and the information you are carrying. Do not let them down and by no means should you ever do anything that would compromise your salvation. If it came down to it, I would rather be uncertain and move forward than to play it safe, do nothing, and later find out I blew it.

I Peter 2:9-10
But you are a chosen people, a royal priesthood, a holy nation, God's special possession, that you may declare the praises of him who called you out of darkness into his wonderful light.

2 Timothy 1:10
He ha saved us and called us to a holy life—not because of anything we have done but because of his own purpose and grace.

1 Corinthians 7:17

Nevertheless, each person should live as a believer in whatever situation the Lord has assigned to them, just as God has called them.

Luke 9:23

"…Whoever wants to be my disciple must deny themselves and take up their cross and follow me. For whoever wants to save their life will lose it, but whoever loses their life for me will find it."

Matthew 10:32-33

Therefore whoever confesses Me before me, him I will also confess before my Father who is in heaven. But whoever denies Me before me, him will also deny before My Father who is in heaven.

Everything discussed in this section truly can be summed up in refusing to allow your flesh to lead your spirit. As tempting as it may be to abort the mission and turn back, or to try to be the person you used to be, it is not possible.

Ignoring Spiritual Fatigue

Spiritual fatigue is real. And if you are not careful, you can sabotage the progress you have made up into this point if you are not honest about how you are feeling at every moment during your journey. At times you will feel exhilarated, spurned by small and big victories alike. As you receive signs and messages more often with stunning clarity and certainty, you will be both astonished and amused. At other times you will feel alone, sorrowful, and even depressed as you are still in a season of separation. Even the blowback from your enemies in the spiritual and natural realm may momentarily cause thoughts of defeat.

It is important at these times to remember that you are human and require periods of rest, time to recharge and communion with the Lord without the sole focus of spiritual warfare. Ironically, what I am suggesting you do did not come easy for me. I did not want attacks to heighten because of any decision by me to let up. Yet, ignoring spiritual fatigue leaves a gaping opportunity open for the enemy to bombard you with thoughts, ideas and suggestions that are counter to what you have been called to do and how you have been called to do it. You may even be tempted to abandon ship and began to entertain thoughts you normally would not because you are too exhausted to fight them. Yet I discovered that resting in the Lord does not mean you are sleeping on the job or lazy, it is a form of trusting the Lord to protect you, cover and still guide you during periods of replenishment. It is a time of ultimate vulnerability as you must be honest about being worn out, your frailty, and your need for him while you suspend your disbelief and take stock in everything you know Him to be—relying on him fully. Even the prophet Elijah came to a point of spiritual exhaustion where he felt defeated, began to fear his enemies and even asked God to take his life. Twice the Lord asked Elijah about his location as if to say, "Elijah why have you abandoned your post? What or who is plaguing you?" The Lord responded with compassion and allowed Elijah to replenish and rest, sending an angel to provide for his needs, and then graced him with assistance in the form of Elisha, who would be his successor, before calling him to serve again.

1 Kings 19:3-8
Now Ahab told Jezebel all that Elijah had done, and how he had killed all the prophets [of Baal] with the sword. Then Jezebel sent a messenger to Elijah, saying, "So may the gods do to me, and even more, if by this time tomorrow I do not make your life like the life of one of them." And Elijah was afraid and arose and ran for his life, and he came to Beersheba which belongs to Judah, and he left his servant there. But he himself traveled a day's journey into the wilderness, and he came and sat down under a juniper tree and asked [God] that he might die. He said, "It is enough; now, O LORD, take my life, for I am no better than my fathers." He lay down and slept under the juniper tree, and behold, an angel touched him and said to him, "Get up and eat." He looked, and by his head there was a bread cake baked on hot coal, and a pitcher of water. So he ate and drank and lay down again. Then the angel of the LORD came again a second time and touched him and said, "Get up,

and eat, for the journey is too long for you [without adequate sustenance]." So he got up and ate and drank, and with the strength of that food he traveled forty days and nights to Horeb (Sinai), the mountain of God.

1 Kings 19:9 AMP
There he came to a cave and spent the night in it; and behold, the word of the LORD *came* to him, and He said to him, "What are you doing here, Elijah?"

1 Kings 19:13 AMP
When Elijah heard *the sound*, he wrapped his face in his mantle (cloak) and went out and stood in the entrance of the cave. And behold, a voice came to him and said, "What are you doing here, Elijah?"

1 Kings 19:15-16 AMP
The LORD said to him, "Go, return on your way to the Wilderness of Damascus; and when you arrive, you shall anoint Hazael as king over Aram (Syria); and you shall anoint Jehu the son of Nimshi as king over Israel; and anoint Elisha the son of Shaphat of Abel-meholah as prophet in your place.

Your relationship with the Lord can handle you admitting your fatigue, and you will be astonished by the ways God will communicate with you to let you know he understands. I remember sharing how tired I was in prayer. The next week, Pastor Reverend Kay ElBlessing, the pastor of Fresh Fire Prayer Ministry, a ministry based in Maryland that I follow online, announced that he believed God was leading his children into a time of rest. I was relieved and believed I received confirmation that I could tweak my morning devotional time and reduce the rigorousness of my fast. Likewise, this may be a fasting season for you, yet you may wish to stop but feel uncomfortable about doing so. Sometimes breaking my fast for a day or allowing myself to eat a few hours earlier than usual was beneficial. Many days I awoke at the time I believe the Lord has called me to pray, but I may have had to cut back on my affirmations or commit them to memory just to allow myself a bit more sleep. If spiritual exhaustion applies to you, seek the Lord's guidance and then allow The Holy Spirit to lead you to the divine strategy that will give you the rest you need without compromising the mission God has set before you.

Allowing your flesh to lead your spirit

As believers we are to be led by the spirit. It is tempting to be led by the flesh as the flesh tends to want what it wants, when it wants it. During a fast, I desire to hear from the Lord, to break a stronghold or yoke, and/or to intercede, but my flesh will suggest that I end the fast a few hours or even a day early, order a philly cheese steak, Wild West shrimp from Longhorn—just the most unhealthiest food choices ever will be front and center in my mind unless I ask God for grace and assistance. It is the nature of our flesh. It seeks to appease our appetites, and man before God—each and every time succumbing to ego, lust, pride, and outward approval. Our flesh does not want to be different, deemed weird, strange and not a part of the "in crowd." Our fleshy nature wants to go along to get along. At times it is fine with being different as long as it is a different everyone surrounding us wants to be, envies or can accept. Yet, when the difference causes rejection and ridicule our flesh quickly wants to change, morph and revert back into what would be more acceptable. Even if the change would be contrary to who God has called us to be—not only during this season, but until we leave this natural plane—our flesh would urge us to do it. It is incredible how the flesh will proposition you, bargain with you and rationalize doing something completely counter to what you know you must do. The call of the flesh is strong and can be so strong that you can literally feel the pull of your former life. Yet, to be a disciple for Christ is to walk in the spirit and to die to the flesh, not only when it feels good, or when it is opportune to do so, but even when it is challenging.

Galatians 5:16
This I say then, Walk in the Spirit, and ye shall not fulfil the lust of the flesh. For the flesh lusteth against the Spirit, and the Spirit against the flesh: and these are contrary the one to the other: so that ye cannot do the things that ye would

Galatians 5:24-25
And those who are Christ's have crucified the flesh with its passions and desires. If we live in the Spirit, let us also walk in the Spirit.

Matthew 26:41
Watch and pray that you may not enter into temptation. The spirit indeed is willing, but the flesh is weak.

Departing from friends and ending friendships that do not honor God is difficult. No one, at least I do not enjoy judging anyone for their behavior or speech. Yet, if you share my belief that we are who we surround ourselves with, the decision to jettison many relationships will be unavoidable. In my case, as will be the case for many of you, you will immediately come under persecution and be labeled as self-righteous, a goody two shoes, weirdo, or fraud. This is one of the costs you must bear as to remain in certain relationships and environments puts your unpolluted and uncontaminated communication with God at risk. To walk with anyone that does not demonstrate, not perfection, but a reverence for or fear of God, or who embraces and relishes in the flesh, is to actively court misfortune and risk your salvation.

Romans 8:13
For if you live according to the flesh you will die; but if by the Spirit you put to death the deeds of the body, you will live

Galatians 6:8
For he that soweth to his flesh shall of the flesh reap corruption; but he that soweth to the Spirit shall of the Spirit reap life everlasting.

Romans 7:5
For when we were in the flesh, the motions of sins, which were by the law, did work in our members to bring forth fruit unto death.

During the times when we are tempted to engage in speech or behaviors that are contrary to who we are in Christ, we must humble ourselves as the Apostle Paul in recognizing the duality that exists between the desire to walk with Christ and the desire to do what is sinful and unpleasing to Him.

Romans 7:15 NKJV
For what I am doing, I do not understand. For what I will to do, that I do not practice, but what I hate, that I do.

Yet we must remember that God always provides a way of escape and desires that we flee temptation.

1 Corinthians 10:13
No temptation has overtaken you except such as is common to man; but God *is* faithful, who will not allow you to be tempted beyond what you are able, but with the temptation will also make the way of escape, that you may be able to bear *it*.

1 Corinthians 10:13 is illustrated by Joseph's actions when propositioned by Potiphar's wife to engage in an adulterous tryst.

Genesis 39:7-12
And it came to pass after these things, that his master's wife cast her eyes upon Joseph; and she said, Lie with me. But he refused, and said unto his master's wife, Behold, my master wotteth not what is with me in the house, and he hath committed all that he hath to my hand; There is none greater in this house than I; neither hath he kept back any thing from me but thee, because thou art his wife: how then can I do this great wickedness, and sin against God? And it came to pass, as she spake to Joseph day by day, that he hearkened not unto her, to lie by her, or to be with her. And it came to pass about this time, that Joseph went into the house to do his business; and there was none of the men of the house

there within. And she caught him by his garment, saying, Lie with me: and he left his garment in her hand, and fled, and got him out.

As every 747 woman's walk is different, so too will our battles against our flesh. For me, it is difficult to disengage from particular kinds of music, television shows, places and my way of approaching a single lifestyle—which, although it would be monogamous, it would not mean refraining from pre-marital sex. Although that is completely off the table for me now, I still struggle with disengaging from certain kinds of music and television shows. In all honesty it is an everyday struggle. I cannot count the times I have wanted to listen to a rap song that I know is out of order and would grieve the Holy Spirit. I must be honest about the times where I have diligently searched for a clean version of a song, or enumerated the reasons in my head in an attempt to justify why it is okay for me to watch a particular show. Sometimes I win the battle and shut down the ill-conceived idea, sometimes I do not. Yet, I am very clear that if and when I do succumb to the flesh, when I do not lean on the power of the Holy Spirit and forget to ask God for assistance, there is a cost. And without whole-hearted repentance, I can jeopardize the message the Holy Spirit wants me to write about or share with a believer. I may give a watered-down, impotent word because I have polluted the potency of what needed to be communicated because the Holy Spirit departed from me as I engaged in a behavior that was unbecoming of my calling. And so, for me it is not worth it. I do not wish to be off even a little bit when the Holy Spirit beckons me. Yet when I do fall, as we all do and will, I am totally and completely grieved.

Although I have found that when I to stay connected to God, and invite the Holy Spirit to dwell within me each morning whilst I command my day, overcoming the desires of the flesh is possible. I believe one of the best ways to walk in the Spirit is by giving the Holy Spirit complete, unrestricted, and unhindered access to my mind, body, spirit and soul.

Romans 13:14

But put ye on the Lord Jesus Christ, and make not provision for the flesh, to fulfill the lusts thereof!

Negative Words/Prophecies

At the risk of sounding redundant, I must reiterate the power of our words at all times and during all seasons, but especially when in preparation for spiritual ascension and in times of spiritual warfare. Many times our very own words upend our success and sojourn onto higher ground. In moments of anger, frustration, disappointment, fatigue and opposition it is human to experience doubt and discouragement. Though in these times it is vital to the manifestation of our promotion, appointment, calling or matriculation into our promised land to be extremely vigilant over the words we allow to fall from our lips, making certain that we do not speak defeat, failure or calamity.

Just as we must call to memory scriptures to obliterate doubt, we must courageously speak over and boldly vocalize the truth over negative words that we allow to escape from our mouths with the word. We must immediately cancel them with the word to ensure they are impotent, ineffective and unable to bring about a negative prophecy or build a stronghold in the situations, adverse circumstances or crises we are facing.

Proverbs 18:21

Death and life are in the power of the tongue, And those who love it will eat its fruit.

Matthew 12:37

For by your words you will be justified, and by your words you will be condemned

Jeremiah 23:29

Is not my word like as a fire? Saith the Lord; and like a hammer that breaketh the rock in pieces?

Psalm 107:20
He sent his word, and healed them, and delivered them from their destructions.

Hebrews 4:12
For the word of God is quick, and powerful, and sharper than any two edged sword, piercing even to the dividing asunder of soul and spirit, and of the joints and marrow, and is a discerner of the thoughts and intents of the heart.

Isaiah 55:10-11
For as the rain cometh down, and the snow from heaven, and returneth not thither, but watereth the earth, and maketh it bring forth and bud, that it may give seed to the sower, and bread to the eater: So shall my word be that goeth forth out of my mouth: it shall not return unto me void, but it shall accomplish that which I please, and it shall prosper in the thing whereto I sent it

If indeed we are able to avoid the many pitfalls that may litter our paths during this experience, our destinies as 747 women will began to unfold in a clear and tangible way. We are becoming completely aware, totally present and active participants in this process of healing, discovery and triumph as God unveils our purpose in his kingdom. Ultimately this process includes our death, resurrection and rebirth. We have died to our former selves which were not only beholden to the opinions and approval of man, but we have died to the parts of us that were held captive by fake friends, relationships and circumstances unbecoming of our true identity. Yet, the Lord has made us new and has resurrected us in front of the very same people who tried to oppress us, humiliate us, sully our name and in the worst case scenario, leave us for dead. Those very same people now have front row seats to our rebirth. We are now on the precipice of who we must be to accept our calling and fulfill the divine plan God has for our lives.

1 Corinthians 5:17

Therefore, if anyone is in Christ, the new creation has come: The old has gone, the new is here!

1 Peter 1:3

Praise be to the God and Father of our Lord Jesus Christ! In his great mercy he has given us new birth into a living hope through the resurrection of Jesus Christ from the dead

Galatians 5:1

Stand fast therefore in the liberty wherewith Christ hath made us free and be not entangled again with the yoke of bondage

Psalm 23:5

Thou preparest a table before me in the presence of mine enemies: thou annointest my head with oil, my cup runneth over

1 Thessalonians 5:24 NIV

The One Who called you is faithful and will do what He promised

Part VIII

Cruise Control

The 7:47 Connection

LIFT VS. WEIGHT

Many of us are accustomed to experiencing that tense feeling in our bodies or knot in our stomachs when the stewardess makes the final announcement to be seated. We ensure we are fastened snugly in our seatbelts, change our mobile phones to airplane mode and try to act unworried as the plane starts down the runway. We never give it much thought, yet the moment when the airplane breaks away from the asphalt and ascends is exactly what we experience when we decide to move forward with our journey. In our minds we know that we want to live on a higher plane, on a higher level of blessing and favor but we have not quite been able to attain the level of which we desire. Oftentimes it feels like negative forces are besetting us from every side to keep us grounded. Yet, just as a plane must confront and overcome the force of gravity working to keep it grounded, we must also confront and overcome the naysayers, distractors, depressors, and destroyers hurling our pasts at our heads and the circumstances that seem determined to deter or defeat our desire to take flight. We do not seek violent or hostile confrontation to overcome the onslaught of opposition. Instead, we are steadfast in efforts to ensure our determination, commitment and power to lift is greater than any other thing's power to keep us down.

When considering an airplane about to take flight, weight, which NASA describes as the force caused by gravity, works against its flight as it always seeks to pull matter in a downward direction toward the center of the earth. In order for a plane or even a bird to take flight, its wings must use the force of lift, to break through or pass the force of weight. This lift in birds is derived from its muscles, and in planes it is derived from the engine. In the 747 woman, our lift is derived from our spiritual muscles which include our ability to hold our peace, remain focused, and stay committed to the process when confronted with those who do not wish our ascent. The power of our lift is determined by our commitment to praise, worship and consistent prayer to God. To fast, keep our tongues about what God has promised us, and to stay our minds on what is before us. Lift for the 747 woman includes our escape from negative and limiting mindsets, people, memories, situations and habits that no longer serve us or are unnecessary for where we are headed.

I am in no way suggesting that lift is easy as many times we must defiantly move forward in the face of rejection from loved ones who are uncomfortable with and offset by the destruction of constricting boxes they constructed for us. At other times we must refuse to be moved by the lack of support and faith from those we believed would always have our backs. Yet when we press forward and fully commit to lift, we begin to see signs, wonders and glimpses of our promised land that encourage us to hold fast to our faith that we are closer to victory than we have ever been before and that our circumstances will change, not for a few months, a year or a season, but that we will reach what TD Jakes calls our *inflection point*, the point in which our circumstances will forever be changed, ushering us into a surety of purpose and stability. It is the point where you break out of the prison of patterns, where you never go through what you went through ever again in your life, where you come up and never go back down again.

TURBULENCE

When we focus on pushing forward past the weight of our struggles and circumstances to lift off, we eventually arrive at clear skies. We may finally figure that it is time to let up on the intensity of our prayer and fasting, praise and worship, only to be shocked when it seems all you know what has broken out. "What is this?" we may ask ourselves as we experience another round of fierce opposition as we assumed we reached the point of inflection.

The 7:47 Connection

I honestly believe that opposition is most prevalent when we are on the verge of breakthrough. Turbulence refers to the often sudden, chaotic and at times, violent changes in the air or atmosphere around an airplane during flight. It is unexpected and cannot be accurately predicted but the likelihood of turbulence can be determined by observing the factors or indicators that have the potential to create it. Yet, as I read on about the six types of turbulence that can beset an aircraft, I learned that turbulence does not need to end in calamity or the plane falling thousands of feet to its end. And surprisingly, one's response to turbulence should not be to fight it, just as our response to the opposition meant to curtail our growth, progress and triumph should not be to confront, but to transcend it. Bishop Dale C. Bronner states that when relentless opposition and strife arises, our ability to *transcend it*, reflects the *trance ending*—which is a witty, revelation of the word. And the only way for the trance that has held us captive for months, if not years to be defeated is by moving above and beyond it and disallowing it the opportunity to make us give up.

Accordingly, our response to turbulence, in order to defeat turbulence during our ascension, we must respond as seasoned pilots would. One response includes slowing down, another includes navigating around the conditions or, more specifically, revising the route. Yet another option may be to change altitude. Pilots have the option of changing their altitude higher or lower. As a 747 woman, when beset by turbulence our response should be to either slow down, navigate around adverse conditions, revise the route if indeed a new route is confirmed in prayer, or to climb higher. The 747 woman must maintain the new ground we have covered. We are not to drop in altitude or turn back. In the face of turbulence which in our case is most probably due to demonic interference, interruption, obstruction and impediments, we must continue to pray for God's grace, mercy, loving kindness and compassion, ask for the faith, capacity and courage to forge past whatever is trying to hold us back and down—no matter how difficult or painful, and be at the ready with every spiritual weapon we have developed thus far. Emotional, knee jerk reactions will not and cannot be tolerated or allowed.

PUSHING PAST THE PAIN

I wish there was some kind of formula I could offer for the pain to disappear in an instant. There isn't one. I wish I could tell you that once you pray, fast and plead the blood, the pain will immediately dissipate. It will not. The only way to get past the pain is to go through the pain. You must go through the feelings of betrayal. You must wade through the humiliation and embarrassment. You must muster the strength to guard against being drowned in the disbelief and devastation. You have experienced a loss and there is no sense in denying it. As Pierre Teilhard de Chardin states, "…[You] are a spiritual being having a human experience," and part

of this experience is dealing with pain and loss. As such, you must healthily move through the five stages of grief—denial, bargaining, anger, depression and acceptance. The key is not getting stuck at any one stage.

But at times you will feel stuck. You will feel like you cannot take another second, minute, hour or day of the gut-wrenching pain. Keep going. Keep praying. Keep fasting. Keep believing. Continue to confess your trust in God, and your trust in the process. Hold fast to the promises God gave you. He has not changed his mind. He is only updating the strategy, swapping out some of the players and rerouting you to a different connection. He is not a man that he shall lie. He has not lied before and he will not start now.

Numbers 23:19
"God is not a man, that he should lie."

You may be tempted to turn back. You cannot. Even if you did, you are no longer the person you were. You no longer see the situation or the people involved in the same way. You are no longer naïve to the deception, trickery or the wiles of the devil and how he uses others for his purposes. You may have known the devil will use strangers, acquaintances, family and friends in theory, but now you know it from experience. And not in a perfunctory sense as far as using someone to irritate you, or momentarily steal your joy, but know that is possible for someone to be assigned to you in order to seriously cause you and your destiny irreversible harm. Yet, Jesus bears testament of Satan's strategy to use loved ones to attack and derail us when he admonishes the demonic spirit in Peter.

Matthew 16:23
But Jesus turned and said to Peter, "Get behind thee Satan! You are a stumbling block to me' you do not have in mind the concerns of God, but merely human concerns."

During this process I have had to pinch myself several times just to ensure what I was experiencing was real. Witches? Warlocks? Intentional, belligerent opposition and rejection of Elohim—God the Father Almighty, His Son Jesus Christ and the Holy Spirit? Who is unaware of the sovereignty of God? Whose fear of our Great and Dreadful God has not been peaked by the many accounts on YouTube of believers that were allowed to visit hell and to return in order that we may believe?

It is difficult for me to wrap my mind around a person's decision to willfully offend God. It is difficult to believe someone I loved was consorting with witches, hex throwers and spell casters whose intent was to harm me, hurt me and get me out of the picture. Yet it happened, and by doing so they inadvertently turned my loved one into a hex throwing, demon worshipping spellcaster too. For once you open a gateway or portal to the demonic, you do not get to determine how that demonic influence or entity will show up in your life or in the lives of those around you that you claim to love. You have given that demon a foothold and/or stronghold in your life which means that they have the authority to operate as they will. Can you say drama-filled experience? Can you say painful? Yes. Excruciatingly so.

But why does it have to be so painful, you ask? Especially when you firmly believe your Lord and Savior is Jehovah-Rophe—the God that heals. You must understand and believe the truth of that statement is undisputable, for Jesus Christ is indeed our healer. He is also our liberator. I know he is my healer because I have been healed, not just in this situation but many times before. I know now that He is a liberator because I have been freed. I literally woke up and the confusion, demonically imposed stupor, fog and disillusionment were gone. I felt as if I was rescued from a satanic cage, literally moving from a catatonic state back to the ambitious, wise and insightful self I had always been—in one day. I wanted nothing to do with anyone related in any way to the mentally, emotionally and spiritually, life-altering, tumultuous experience.

John 8:36
If the Son therefore shall make you free, ye shall be free indeed.

Isaiah 53:5
But he was wounded for our transgressions, he was bruised for our iniquities: the chastisement of our peace was upon him; and with his stripes we are healed.

Yet, being free and being healed does not mean that the pain of losing a loved one—no matter how far off the path they have gone, isn't very real. And we must always remember that there is a lesson in the pain. Unfortunately, pain is built into the sin as not only a consequence, but as a reminder for us to never choose rebellion, disobedience, idol worship, or jettison discernment again. It is a reminder to check everyone by the spirit—not once, not twice, but repeatedly—always.

Again, I attest that although I am still dealing with the pain, I have been liberated and healed. When you break a limb—be it your arm or your leg, does the pain immediately dissipate during the healing process? After you undergo surgery and enter recovery, do you not experience pain even after the surgeon states you are healed of the ailment? So it is with your current situation—healing, but not without pain. The process cannot be avoided, bargained away or cheated. You will have to endure the pain, engage it, accept it, and then move beyond it. The great thing about it is that you do not have to do it alone. I hate to sound cliché, but Jesus really is right there with you. The book of Isaiah portrays Jesus as comforter and healer of our emotions.

Isaiah 61:2-3
"to comfort all that mourn; to appoint unto them that mourn in Zion, to give them beauty for ashes, the oil of joy for mourning, the garment of praise for the spirit of heaviness."

Jesus wants us to rely on him for healing, comfort and to make sense of what happened because he understands. He has been on the receiving end of disappointment and betrayal. I am a firm believer that when Jesus was in the Garden of Gethsemane and told his disciples he was going to pray, he not only prayed to our Father regarding the weight of the task before him as the Savior of mankind, but regarding the pain and heartbreak associated with Judas' betrayal and Peter's denial. Thus, this painful experience is not foreign to our Lord.

Matthew 26:22
"Then he said to them, "My soul is overwhelmed with sorrow to the point of death."

Luke 22:44
"And being in agony, He prayed more earnestly. Then His sweat became like great drops of blood falling down to the ground."

As painful as the experience is, one thing is sure, you no longer desire to have anyone in your inner circle that is not sold out for Christ, and cannot even risk having an inner circle not sold out for Christ. It is dangerous to the success of your calling. Notwithstanding, the relationship you once knew is no more. Opened eyes cannot be unopened. What you have seen cannot be unseen. Once you know, you know. Further, many of you have received an edict and injunction directly from God regarding His will that you may not turn back or entertain certain relationships. It is painful to deal with a "no" for which you have no control to change or alter. It causes an emotional upheaval, at least it did for me, being unable to control the outcome of the situation. The prophet Samuel also experienced the pain associated with God, making a firm decision about leaving behind someone he loved as seen in his struggle with God's decision to remove King Saul from power.

1 Samuel 16:1
"The Lord said to Samuel, "How long will thou mourn for Saul, seeing I have rejected him from reigning over Israel? Fill thine horn with oil, and go, I will send thee to Jess the Bethlehemite: for I have provided me a king among his sons."

According to Mathew chapter 26 while in the Garden of Gethsemane, Jesus prayed to our Father, three times regarding the mission before him to offer himself as a living sacrifice for all of humanity. In this manner, the bible not only demonstrates Jesus's humanness, and his ability to identify with our entire experience, but it teaches us how difficult and painful it can be at times to conquer one's flesh and submit to God's will. I believe TD Jakes refers to this as the crushing and that is exactly how it feels as we lay down our lives to pick up our individual crosses and follow the Lord, not according to how we see fit, but according to his divine plan.

Matthew 26:39
"O my Father, if it be possible, let this cup pass from me: nevertheless not as I will, but as thou will."

Matthew 26:42
O my Father, if this cup may not pass away from me, except I drink it, thy will be done.

Matthew 26:44
"And he left them, and went away again, and prayed the third time, saying the same words."

During this time you will still be separated from most people and you will still need to employ every weapon in your arsenal for spiritual warfare as it will assist the healing process—especially praise, worship and professing the word over your future. Resist the temptation to give up. You must resist the negative replay of words, arguments, events, and abuse—if trauma applies to your situation. Yet, each and every day you must choose God, choose yourself and choose the thoughts and words you will allow yourself to think and say. Each day you must deliberately choose life and choose victory.

John 10:10
I am come that they might have life, and that they might have it more abundantly

Philippians 4:8
Finally, brethren, whatsoever things are true, whatsoever things are honest, whatsoever things are just, whatsoever things are pure, whatsoever things are lovely, whatsoever things are of good report; if there be any virtue, and if there be any praise, think on these things.

Matthew 11:28-29
Come unto me, all ye that labour all ye who are heavy laden, and I will give you rest.

During this journey, I must admit that I have arrived to a new level of understanding regarding the pain of my experience. I have heard it said that pain positions one for promotion. I now know that to be true. Before his passing, Chadwick Boseman stated to a sea of recent, bright-eyed hopeful Howard University graduates, "Sometimes you need to feel the pain and sting of defeat to activate the real passion and purpose that God predestined inside of you." I felt that. Reverend Dr. Trunell D. Felder of New Faith Baptist Church surmises that prior to your calling, God will in a sense pluck you right from the path you had all intentions on marching down because it would risk the success of the calling on your life and purpose. The Reverend Dr. Felder states that it will appear to everyone around you to be a demotion. Yet Dr. Felder purports that what we have just experienced is an inverted promotion, a promotion disguised as a demotion. What we are experiencing is not abasement, but advancement. Thus, if we abandon the process due to the pain, we will forgo and forfeit seeing the glory of God in our lives.

Press Forward

I must say that during this journey I have done my best to choose thoughts that would assist me in my desire to move forward. I was not always successful, as a matter of fact, I struggled with looking ahead and letting go of dashed dreams, promises and plans I believed I was leaving behind. Even after the Holy Spirit revealed what was at stake, if I did not press forward and urged me to reveal a prophetic word for those who had recently shared the experience, moving beyond the pain and perceived loss was difficult. I hope you can understand when I say I imagined that I felt similar to Joseph—left in a pit to die, or at the very least abandoned with the full intention for me to never get up again. But God!

Job 33:30
To bring back hi soul from the pit, to be enlightened with the light of the living

Psalms 35:7
For without cause have they hid for me their net in a pit, which without cause they have digged for my soul.

Psalms 40:2
He brought me up also out of a horrible pit, out of the miry clay, and set my feet upon a rock, and established my goings.

I reached a pivotal point in my healing when I began to wholeheartedly believe that trusting God meant there was a definite brighter and bigger future ahead of me compared to the potential of what I believed was behind me. My healing accelerated when I began to understand that each day I pressed forward successfully meant that I could choose to do the same thing the next day. As previously stated, I wished the healing of my heart was instantaneous, but it was not. Over time I began to draw from the resurrective power of our Lord and Savior.

Ephesians 1:19-20
I pray that you will begin to understand how incredibly great His power is to help those who believe Him. It is that same mighty power that raised Christ from the dead and seated Him in the place of honor at God's right hand in heaven.

Isaiah 40:29
He gives power to the faint and weary, and to him who has no might He increases strength {causing it to multiply and making it to abound]

Ephesians 6:10
Finally, be strong in the Lord and in his mighty power

Soon I became steadfast in my commitment to break free of all one-sided, non-reciprocal, petty, intrusive, toxic, two-faced, stagnating, negative, vision-constricting, at times disrespectful, and/or demonic relationships and soul ties. Each day I chose to work toward purpose over mulling over the pain became a win for me. Each day I chose to press forward and refused to accept a fate akin to Lot's wife after fair warning not to look back, was another notch in my belt.

Philippians 3:13-14
Brethren, I count not myself to have apprehended: but this one thing I do, forgetting those things which are behind, and reaching forth unto those things which are before, I press toward the mark for the prize of the high calling of God in Christ Jesus.

Genesis 19:17
And it came t pass, when they had brought them forth abroad, that [the angel] said, Escape for thy life; look not behind thee, neither stay thou in all the plain/ escape to the mountain, lest thou be consumed.

Genesis 19:26
But his wife looked back from behind him, and she became a pillar of salt.

When the Holy Spirit called me to write this book, I honestly believed I was in no shape to do so—mentally, emotionally or spiritually. I firmly believed that I needed all my strength to pray, fast, and fight my enemies in the spiritual realm. The rest of my energy needed to be geared toward my healing and goal attainment. Yet, the Holy Spirit did not let me rest. "Write the book," not now, but right now is what I heard. In addition, a couple of experiences made it plain that He would not take no for an answer. It was clear that my desire to wait on writing the book, or to not write it at all was non-negotiable. So I began to write—reluctantly, as I nursed my wounds, fought off creditors, raised my daughter, attended work, side-hustled as an Uber driver, started a new career in real estate, lost friends that deemed me crazy, delusional and heretical—and through the gaslighting, stalking, hovering, vandalism, smear campaign, character assassination, witchcraft, demonic attacks, ridicule and judgment, I wrote and planned for my ministry. In all honesty, I definitely wondered why the process had to be as difficult as it was. Yet, Bishop Dale C. Bronner teaches, "The Holy Spirit is not concerned about your discomfort, he's concerned about your development."

And then one day while praying, the Holy Spirit reminded me of the ten men with leprosy Jesus healed. If you recall, their healing did not happen at once, but on their way walking to tell the priests of their healing. That is exactly what the Holy Spirit wanted me to understand. You will be healed on your way—on your way to the book's completion, on your way to the beginning of your ministry, and on your way to building your new career. I can honestly say I have gone from wiping tears each day to completing a book, launching a new ministry, a new career, locating a spiritual coach and then a business mentor to taking all steps necessary to live a fully empowered life. And so, whatever it is that you have been called to begin, begin it. Even if you do not feel ready, healed, prepared or well rested, start the process. You will heal on the way. If Jesus did it for the ten men with leprosy and for me, he can and will do it for you.

Luke 17:11-19
And it came to pass, as he went to Jerusalem, that he passed through the midst of Samaria and Galilee. And as he entered into a certain village, there met him ten men that were lepers, which stood afar off: And they lifted up their voices, and said, Jesus, Master, have mercy on us. And when he saw them, he said unto them, Go shew yourselves unto the priests. And it came to pass, that, as they went, they were cleansed.

During this journey, I have found it extremely beneficial to minimize and then eradicate any and all murmuring and complaining. But this has not been an easy task. I have pleaded with myself to not be like the Israelites whilst in the wilderness. Some days I did better than others. Yet, each day I did my best not to complain about the pain and fatigue, or to pray for the situation to be easier, but to ask God to expand my capacity and transform me into the person He envisioned me to be by stretching my perspective, understanding, wisdom, character, and heart to be triumphant.

YOU WILL BE VICTORIOUS

I cannot begin to imagine what your idea of victory might be or what you believe needs to happen before you claim victory. You may not see it fit to claim victory until your enemies are plastered all over the internet hanging from the gallows, or on the six o' clock news as your watch their fall from grace. I understand the temptation, but I am pretty sure that is not where God wants you to lay your hope or attention. What happens to our enemies, when it happens and how it happens is not our concern, but rest assured, God protects and avenges harm to his children.

Luke 18:7
And shall not God avenge his own elect, which cry day and night unto him, though he bear long with them? I tell you that he will avenge them speedily…"

Romans 12:19
Dearly beloved, avenge not yourselves, but give place unto wrath: for it is written, Vengeance is mine; I will repay, saith the Lord.

Psalm 7:15
He made a pit, and digged it, and is fallen into the ditch he made

Proverbs 26:27
Whoso diggeth a pit shall fall therein: and he that rolleth a stone, it will return upon him

While I know this to be that is true, I tend to believe your victory is in escaping a situation, friendship, business relationship, work environment, or a romantic partner that is not God's will for your life and then sharing your testimony in the hopes of freeing someone else facing the same trauma. An even greater victory than that, however, is in your recent, steadfast commitment to your kingdom purpose as you successfully execute any and all missions the Holy Spirit has laid on your heart. We know now that victory—true, deep and far-reaching, does not come without pain. We also know there will be obstacles, barriers and mountains to overcome, but as long as we keep God first, whatever we've lost during the process, however weary we may get, if we keep our hope in Him, we will be victorious.

Matthew 6:33
Seek ye first the Kingdom of God And His righteousness, And all these things shall be added unto you.

1 Corinthians 15:57
But thanks be to God! He gives us the victory through our Lord Jesus Christ

Galatians 6:9
And let us not be weary in well doing: for in due season we shall reap, if we faint not.

The 7:47 Connection

1 John 5:4

For whatsoever is born of God overcometh the world: and this is the victory that overcometh the world, even our faith.

Part IX

Cleared to Land

YOU ARE ANOINTED

I am certain you will attest to the fact that this process is one of growth and transformation. It most certainly requires the death of our old self, ushers in our resurrection and then rebirth. If you find that hard to believe, then I suggest asking a few close friends if they have noticed a change in you. Even if they do not fully believe in what God is doing in your life, you will definitely get a response somewhere along the lines of you are changing or acting differently. Yet, if you still have not embraced the truth of your carnal death, resurrection and rebirth, I assure you that by the time this experience is over, you will walk in full awareness of Christ's love for you, your call to express the love He has shown you to others, and the expanse of your anointing.

I understand that while you may be aware that you walk in God's anointing, you may not know what it specifically entails or means for your life. In the Bible, the word anointing can signify the confirmation of God's elect into an office or ministry, particularly as king or priest, and usually encompasses a move of, or covering of the Holy Spirit.

1 Samuel 16:13
Then Samuel took the horn of oil and anointed him in the midst of his brethren: and the Spirit of the LORD came upon David from that day forward.

1 Kings 19:16 (NKJV)
Also you shall anoint Jehu the son of Nimshi as king over Israel. And Elisha the son of Shaphat of Abelmeholah you shall anoint as prophet in your place.

Yet, as you may know, this is only one facet of the anointing of God. While it is true that the anointing may involve the pouring of oil over one's head to denote as previously mentioned, a new appointment of kingship or priesthood, many of us understand the anointing as the power to imbue healing.

Mark 6:13
And they cast out many devils, and anointed with oil many that were sick, and healed them.

Another function of the anointing you may be familiar with is its capacity and purpose to guide and teach us.

1 John 2:27
But the anointing which ye have received of him abideth in you, and ye need not that any man teach you: but as the same anointing teacheth you of all things, and is truth, and is no lie, and even as it hath taught you, ye shall abide in him.

Moreover, many of you may be fully versed in the power and function of the anointing over your lives, while others may consider yourself anointed, but may not be able to express what it means. Although you may be clear on your possession of a level of favor, grace and protection that is not only inexplicable, but defies the norms and/or experiences that befall others that have faced the same predicament. If you are anything like me, then it seems you escape dire circumstances by the skin of your teeth, every, single, time.

Psalms 20:6
Now know I that the LORD saveth his anointed; he will hear him from his holy heaven with the saving strength of his right hand.

2 Samuel 22:51
He is a tower of deliverance to His king, And shows loving kindness to His anointed, To David and his descendants forever

Psalm 84:9
Behold our shield, O God, And look upon the face of Your anointed

Psalm 28:8
The Lord is their strength, And He is a saving defense to His anointed

Am I saying we dodge the trials and tribulations that go along with the human experience? Absolutely not. But what I am asserting is that many circumstances that have the potential to leave a lasting negative impact on our lives, or that can jeopardize our destiny are diverted, averted and quelled. Not necessarily immediately, although oftentimes that is the case, but fundamentally what I am asserting is what Paul stated in Romans 8:28.

Romans 8:28
"And we know that all things work together for good to them that love God, to them who are called according to his purpose"

I cannot state with one hundred percent surety to be able to fathom or express all that God's anointing encompasses in its full breadth or capacity, yet I can offer a soft framework what I believe it envelopes. In Roadside Service, one of the many sermons where T.D. Jakes teaches on the anointing of God, he asserts that to be anointed means to be effective. When in context, it points to effectiveness in the ministry, office, mission, or purpose for which God has called you. I believe this to be so.

In addition, I believe that the anointing of God announces you. It establishes that you have been set apart for a specific purpose and endorses you to ensure acceptance to those to which you are called to minister or serve. When the appointed time comes upon the chosen vessel, the anointing increases the light that emanates from the person's entire being. Their aura will be undeniable. The anointing emboldens them with strength, irrefutable enlargement, agile capability, capacity, focus, potency, influence and affluence much more than their contemporaries. Doors open, yokes break, captives are freed, broken hearts are mended, backsliders and nonbelievers return and begin to worship the Lord. There are increased accounts of inexplicable angelic assistance, demonic portals close as angelic portals open, disagreeable, suppressing and tempestuous climates and atmospheres shift, seats and positions are arranged to accommodate the anointed as they emerge as the head, and not the tail, above, and not beneath, and enter, encounter, and engage new stages, levels and spiritual dimensions for the Glory of God. Dr. James Akanbi, Head of God's Mercy Revival Ministries, states, "with anointing, natural faculties are heightened while divine intuition and nudges take over from natural instincts. Human beings that were formerly nonentities suddenly become celebrities…Anointing cannot be defined in any other way than to describe it as divine presence/ the invasion of supernatural substance for the purpose of accomplishing divine design."

1 Samuel 10
Then Samuel took a vial of oil, and poured it upon [Saul's] head, and kissed him, and said, Is it not because the LORD hath anointed thee to be captain over his inheritance?

1 Samuel 16:13
Then Samuel took the horn of oil, and anointed [David] in the midst of his brethren

Judges 6:12
And the angel of the LORD appeared unto [Gideon], and said unto him, The LORD is with thee, thou mighty man of valour

Isaiah 45:1
Thus saith the Lord to his anointed, to Cyrus, whose right hand I have holden, to subdue nations before him; and I will loose the loins of kings, to open before him the two leaved gates; and the gates shall not be shut

Hebrews 1:9
Thou hast loved righteousness; and hated iniquity; therefore God, even thy God, hath anointed thee with the oil of gladness above thy fellows

Psalm 45:7
Thou lovest righteousness, and hatest wickedness: therefore God, thy God, hath anointed thee with the oil of gladness above thy fellows

Isaiah 61:1-2
The Spirit of the Lord God is upon me; because the Lord hath anointed me to preach good tidings unto the meek; he hath sent me to bind up the brokenhearted, to proclaim liberty to the captives, and the opening of the prison to them that are bound; to proclaim the acceptable year of the Lord, and the day of vengeance of our God; to comfort all that mourn

God lovingly anoints his chosen elect, yet we must not forget that the anointing is not to be misused, mishandled or misrepresented. It is not to be glamorized or used to taunt others. It is not a flashy piece of jewelry adorned around one's neck to evoke jealousy or envy for it comes with a costly price, a heavy price that most are not willing to pay. In addition, it involves great responsibility and accountability.

Luke 12:48
"For unto whomsoever much is given, of him shall be much required: and to whom men have committed much, of him they will ask the more.

In the preceding pages it was my intent to illustrate this piece as truthfully and honestly as possible. The journey to the release of the fullness of one's anointing, for many of us involves unspeakable pain, rejection, loneliness, reproach, seasons of solitude, separation, embarrassment, humiliation, mockery, betrayal and abandonment. The road to the activation of the anointing involves the believer's death, resurrection and then rebirth, a season of accusation, acquittal, redemption and then lastly, accepting that you have been chosen for a specific purpose and such a time as this. It is my hope that my experience has caused you to examine the anointing on your life. If indeed you identify with my journey, even if your pain has not been as extensive or intense, I invite you to explore the next section where I share what the Holy Spirit has revealed to me as the attributes of the 747 Anointing.

Part X

Prepare For Landing: Your Final Destination

THE 747 ANOINTING

THE ABIDING ANOINTING

According to the Biblical Dictionary, Index and Concordance in The Holy Bible Authorized King James Version published by Bible House in Charlotte North Carolina, abide means to sojourn, encamp, sit down, to remain. As I mentioned earlier, a seer shared with me that the Lord wanted me to walk with Him years ago. I replied, "okay," or "I know," and preceded to ask about what I thought was more pressing. How foolish of me, but at that time I can only assume that I did not truly understand the levity of what was being proposed or better yet, what was being decreed. Yet as I look on my life, at no time has the Lord left me. At no time have I felt abandoned or felt as if a prayer went unanswered—never. A delay—possibly, but never a denial. No matter who rejected me, abandoned me, betrayed me, or who I rejected, abandoned or betrayed, I can say with unwavering certainty that the Lord has kept me—and if I can go so far, I would say he has kept me to a degree that defies logic and reason even when my experience is considered by my most blessed and favored loved ones.

Colossians 2:6
Therefore as you have received Christ Jesus the Lord, so walk in Him.

John 15:7
If you abide in Me, and My words abide in you, ask whatever you wish, and it will be done for you.

John 15:4-5

Prepare For Landing: Your Final Destination

Abide in Me, and I in you. As the branch cannot bear fruit of itself unless it abides in the vine, so neither can you unless you abide in Me. I am the vine; you are the branches; he who abides in Me and I in him, he bears much fruit, for apart from Me you can do nothing.

The abiding anointing may even include a visitation at the appointed time to confirm your calling or ensure your readiness. I must confess that during a prayer session I believed I was visited by the angel of the Lord. Weeks prior to this time, I heard several instructions regarding my prayer room. I was instructed to clean off the table, to purchase an altar and a standing cross to sit upon it. Previously I had a blanket that I would kneel upon that was laid before my bible and whatever prayer points and bible scriptures I'd handwritten. Yet, over the next few weeks I carried out what I believed I was led to do. And then one day, during the wee hours of the morning as I prayed, I felt someone had come into the room to check it in a sense—to literally look at the set up. To this day I am unsure of what parameters earned a pass or fail, but I believed I had been qualified. I must say that I vacillated regarding the inclusion of this particular testimony and finally decided to bring it to prayer. I received the unction to move forward and include it. Just now I opened up the Biblical Dictionary, Index and Concordance to look up visitation. Do you know what the first definition states? Well, I will share it. It defines visitation as an "Inspection, special time. In day of."

Revelations 3:20
Behold, I stand at the door, and knock: if any man hear my voice, and open the door, I will come in to him, and will sup with him, and he with me.

Genesis 21:1
The Lord visited Sarah as he had said, and the Lord id to Sarah as he had spoken

1 Samuel 2:21
The Lord visited Hannah

Psalm 65:9
You visit the earth and cause it to overflow

Exodus 4:31
The people believed, and when they heard that the Lord had visited the children of Israel, and that he had seen their affliction they bowed their heads and worshipped

Ezekiel 38:8
After many days you shall be visited

Jeremiah 15:15
The Lord, you know; remember me, and visit me

The Abiding Anointing ultimately is a covenant God has made to be with us, sojourn with us, encamp around us, sit down with us and remain.

Matthew 28:20
And behold, I am with you always, to the end of the age

Hebrews 13:5
I will never leave you nor forsake you

John 14:16
And I will pray the Father, and He shall give you another Comforter, that He may abide with you forever

FIRE ANOINTING

I cannot state that every member of the 747 ministry will experience exactly what I have experienced. You may have the full expanse of the 747 anointing, some of it, or maybe even more than I list or have experienced. I can only include what I have experienced and do so to assist you with determining if this particular anointing describes your own.

As such, I recall engaging in fierce prayer one night whereas I was single-mindedly focused on praising and worshiping the Lord. I praised, sang, danced, spoke in tongues, declared bible scriptures and fully submitted myself to the Holy Spirit. When I knelt to pray, I saw a vision of myself aflame, not harmed, but on fire as a ring of fire surrounded me. This experience happened in the midst of my last spiritual warfare experience and I immediately knew the fire represented the presence of the Holy Spirit and the fulfillment of God's promise to protect me from enemies and their devices. I was astonished as I had never heard of anyone speak of such an experience. I turned to the internet to see if maybe someone else shared the account of the same. Lo and behold, there are many accounts of other believers praying to the degree that the Holy Spirit alights on them. Again, this is not essential to the 747 anointing but is a sign that your anointing is authentic, powerful, confirmed, activated and endorsed.

Matthew 3:11
I indeed baptize you with water unto repentance. but he that cometh after me is mightier than I, whose shoes I am not worthy to bear: he shall baptize you with the Holy Ghost, and with fire:

Hebrews 12:28
Therefore, since we receive a kingdom which cannot be shaken, let us show gratitude, by which we may offer to God an acceptable service with reverence and awe; for our God is a consuming fire

Exodus 3:2
And the angel of the Lord appeared to him in a blazing ire from the midst of a bush; and he looked, and behold, the bush was burning with fire, yet the bush was not consumed

Revelation 1:14
His head and his hairs were white like wool, as white as snow/ and his eyes were as a flame of fire

2 Chronicles 7:1
Now when Solomon had finished praying, fire came down from heaven and consumed the burnt offering and the sacrifices, and the glory of the Lord filled the house

1 Chronicles 21:26
And David built there an altar unto the Lord and offered burnt offerings and peace offerings, and called upon the Lord; and he answered him from heaven by fire upon the altar of burnt offering

1 Kings 18:24
Then you call o the name of your god, and I will call on the name of the Lord, and the God who answers by fire, He is God.

2 Kings 1:10
Elijah answered the captain, "If I am a man of God, may fire come down from heaven and consume you and your fifty men!" Then fire fell from heaven and consumed the captain and his men.

Deuteronomy 5:24
And ye said, Behold, the Lord our God hath shewed us his glory and his greatness, and we have heard his voice out of the midst of the fire: we have seen this day that God doth talk with man, and he liveth.

PROVISION ANOINTING (MANNA)

When I look back on my life and my journey thus far, the anointing I have seen demonstrated day in and day out, season to season, consistently and powerfully leaves me in speechless awe and irreversible humility. This anointing has ensured that I have always had food on the table and a roof over my head. I may have had to go without some of the preferred bells and whistles for a time, like the latest trendy wardrobe and cable, for a short season, and recall living without hot water too, but have never been blind to the goodness of God even at those times in my life. Complete strangers have paid my mortgage and utilities, offered costly essential services at a deep discount, or for free outside of any social or welfare program. I have received monetary gifts and cashapps never petitioned for but needed. I have been penniless—literally, needing to attend a particular event that cost more than the means I had to go, and have received miraculous provision to do so. I have gone to work without gas to get home, and have found a twenty dollar bill in the elevator on the way to my car.

I have a close friend that reminds me of my own testimony on several occasions. We joined a live together in which the prophet leading the call asked us to pray for the nations. I prayed as hard as I could, not to receive anything but to intercede as I was asked to do. The prophet then asked for each of us to give five dollars. I only had nineteen dollars in my account, yet I offered the five dollars without question. The prophet than stated that those that give would receive a monetary blessing the next day. I was not concerned with that part. I only desired to be obedient to what the prophet asked of me.

On the way to work, during a phone conversation with my girlfriend, she asked me if I heard the part about the blessing, I said yes and went on to the next topic. That evening on my way home from work I stopped to get gas. I said to myself fourteen dollars will get me home. I checked my account to ensure nothing in my account had gone awry, as in no debit taken out that I was not expecting. Yet, when I looked into my account, I was unable to move. I quickly called the bank because something was wrong. My balance read that I had received a deposit of over one thousand dollars. Hallelujah! To this day I do not know from where that money came. For weeks I waited for an update from the bank. I called continuously to request information regarding the error. Yet, to this day, I still have that bank account and have never heard anything about that particular deposit being incorrect.

Romans 8:32
He that spared not his own Son, but delivered him up for us all, how shall he not with him also freely give us all things?

Matthew 6:31-33
Therefore take no thought, saying, What shall we eat? or, What shall we drink? or, Wherewithal shall we be clothed? (For after all these things do the Gentiles seek:) for your heavenly Father knoweth that ye have need

of all these things. But seek ye first the kingdom of God, and his righteousness; and all these things shall be added unto you.

Luke 12:24
Consider the ravens: for they neither sow nor reap; which neither have storehouse nor barn; and God feedeth them: how much more are ye better than the fowls?

Matthew 7:11
If ye then, being evil, know how to give good gifts unto your children, how much more shall your Father which is in heaven give good things to them that ask him?

Psalms 34:10
The young lions do lack, and suffer hunger: but they that seek the LORD shall not want any good thing.

Philippians 4:19
But my God shall supply all your need according to his riches in glory by Christ Jesus.

In this past season, the one that has followed my greatest spiritual warfare battle thus far, the assault on my finances has been crippling and nearly debilitating. Yet during this season God has revealed himself to be even more faithful than I previously believed and has utilized the season to reveal who should continue this journey with me and who I need to let go. And when those who I believed I could count on in my worst times, showed me that I could not, there was God and God alone using the few loved ones I had left and what was in my hand to provide for and bless me.

Oftentimes you will hear me refer to this anointing as the Manna Anointing, as even with a full-time position, for weeks on end I still had to Uber. For if I did not go out that day, my daughter and I would not have eaten that evening. The bills mounted up, fell behind, the creditors threatened, my credit rating disintegrated, the maintenance of my home, and whatever image I thought I may have had crumbled. So-called friends and family members ducked me, ignored emergency messages, took out their popcorn and waited on standby for my fall, but I praised Him anyway. And through it all He kept me, and He kept my daughter.

Psalms 37:25
I have been young, and now am old; yet have I not seen the righteous forsaken, nor his seed begging bread.

Exodus 16:12
I have heard the murmurings of the children of Israel: speak unto them, saying, At even ye shall eat flesh, and in the morning ye shall be filled with bread; and ye shall know that I am the LORD your God.

Exodus 16:15
And when the children of Israel saw it, they said one to another, It is manna: for they wist not what it was. And Moses said unto them, This is the bread which the LORD hath given you to eat.

John 6:31
Our ancestors ate the manna in the wilderness; as it is written: 'He gave them bread from heaven to eat.'"

OVERCOMER'S ANOINTING

In the King James Bible, to *overcome is defined as to gain victory*. The online AV, or Authorized Version originally published in 1611 defines *overcome as to conquer; vanquish; to subdue as, to overcome victories in battle*. The second definition reads *to surmount/ to get the better of; as, to overcome difficulties or obstacles*. Yet another definition states *overcome as to gain superiority; to be victorious*. And it defines an *overcomer as one who vanquishes or surmounts*.

Now I must admit that no one has ever referred to me as an overcomer, but I am sure many would state that I have overcome seemingly insurmountable odds. I often hear "You don't look like what you've been through," as Bishop Dale C. Bronner often affirms to his Word of Faith Cathedral congregation. A very close friend of mine has often stated the same to me during many of our testimony-filled conversations. When I consider the anointing on my life, I attribute this specific blessing as the Overcomer's Anointing on my life for if I shared my testimony and story, most people would believe I was being untruthful. Yet, time and time again my experience has been of the three young men, Shadrach, Meshach, and Abednego, who were thrown into the fiery furnace due to their refusal to worship King's Nebuchadnezzar's golden image. The bible states that not only did the boys emerge from the furnace unsinged, but the king noticed another figure in the furnace with them.

Daniel 3:19-27

And he commanded the most mighty men that were in his army to bind Shadrach, Meshach, and Abednego, and to cast them into the burning fiery furnace. Then these men were bound in their coats, their hosen, and their hats, and their other garments, and were cast into the midst of the burning fiery furnace. Therefore because the king's commandment was urgent, and the furnace exceeding hot, the flames of the fire slew those men that took up Shadrach, Meshach, and Abednego. And these three men, Shadrach, Meshach, and Abednego, fell down bound into the midst of the burning fiery furnace. Then Nebuchadnezzar the king was astonished, and rose up in haste, and spake, and said unto his counsellors, Did not we cast three men bound into the midst of the fire? They answered and said unto the king, True, O king. He answered and said, Lo, I see four men loose, walking in the midst of the fire, and they have no hurt; and the form of the fourth is like the Son of God. Then Nebuchadnezzar came near to the mouth of the burning fiery furnace, and spake, and said, Shadrach, Meshach, and Abednego, ye servants of the most high God, come forth, and come hither. Then Shadrach, Meshach, and Abednego, came forth of the midst of the fire. And the princes, governors, and captains, and the king's counsellors, being gathered together, saw these men, upon whose bodies the fire had no power, nor was an hair of their head singed, neither were their coats changed, nor the smell of fire had passed on them.

Prepare For Landing: Your Final Destination

Each time I have gone through the fiery furnace, if God did not extinguish the fire, He made me fireproof so I could walk through the fire. As such, built into the essence of this anointing is an ability to thwart long lasting immobility. A woman that has this anointing has the ability to move—to go over, under, around or through the obstacles when most would be sidelined. Be it a grave loss, calamity, or misfortune, the Overcomer's anointing propels the believer forward to eventual and undeniable victory.

1 John 5:3-5
For this is the love of God, that we keep his commandments: and his commandments are not grievous. For whatsoever is born of God overcometh the world: and this is the victory that overcometh the world, even our faith. Who is he that overcometh the world, but he that believeth that Jesus is the Son of God?

Revelation 2:7
He that hath an ear, let him hear what the Spirit saith unto the churches; To him that overcometh will I give to eat of the tree of life, which is in the midst of the paradise of God.

My close friend has also noted my uncanny ability to pivot or adapt during adverse circumstances. When one door closes, I almost immediately move on to my next move. It may not be the greatest move, but I will make a move according to my surveyance of the land and what opportunities I deem available before me or on the horizon. When I got laid off from AT&T in 2017 for the second time (yes that happened) I went directly to an arcade in Smyrna, Georgia called the Main Event and played Ms. Pacman until I coughed up power pellets. The very next day, I enrolled at a nearby school to become a licensed claim adjuster. I passed the test on the first try, but was unable to get into the field and then studied to become a drone pilot as I thought it would be a plus on my resume, passing that exam the first time as well. A great effort was put forth, yet it did not work and it appeared I was locked out of the labor market. No problem, I sold t-shirts. When that did not successfully meet my cost of living, I Ubered, when that failed as a long-term solution, I entered a program to train to be an entry-level construction worker. When that plan did not allow me to integrate my education and experience in the way I intended due to Covid-related hiring freezes, I accepted a job at a call center. The pivot. Adaptability. I pray and move quickly. I do not rail at God about my lot. I know better. I may cry and I may weep, but when I sense an open door I walk through it. And with God's grace, even if and when I am still grieved about some wrong, or ill-deserved hit, I am unable to sit still, grieve or pine for the closed door for long. I may still express my pain in prayer, but I grieve, nurse wounds and bandage myself while in motion. I firmly believe that being carried through nearly every lot, position, place of lack and abundance was to ensure my ability to be empathetic and of service to women of all stations and circumstances.

Philippians 4:11-12 (AMP)
Not that I speak from [any personal] need, for I have learned to be content [and self-sufficient through Christ, satisfied to the point where I am not disturbed or uneasy] regardless of my circumstances. I know how to get along and live humbly [in difficult times], and I also know how to enjoy abundance *and* live in prosperity. In any and every circumstance I have learned the secret [of facing life], whether well-fed or going hungry, whether having an abundance or being in need.

1 Corinthians 9:19-20
For though I am free from all *men,* I have made myself a servant to all, that I might win the more; and to the Jews I became as a Jew, that I might win Jews; to those *who are* under the law, as under the law, that I might win those *who are* under the law

Over time I began to refer to this particular anointing as the Joseph Anointing. The story of Joseph' chronicles his journey through great travail until he finally emerges victorious. I believe Joseph's journey, trumped only by that of Yeshua's, can serve as the foremost example of the Overcomer's Anointing. We follow the bible's account of Joseph's mistreatment, betrayal, oppression, false accusation and imprisonment. We listen or read intently as he demolishes obstacles, adapts, pivots, and then ascends to royalty while exhibiting the utmost humility, obedience to and faith in God. The magnitude of his rebirth is so astounding that his own brothers do not recognize that they are indeed addressing the brother they left in a pit to die before selling him into slavery.

Genesis 37:24-27
And they took him, and cast him into a pit: and the pit was empty, there was no water in it.

And they sat down to eat bread: and they lifted up their eyes and looked, and, behold, a company of Ishmaelites came from Gilead with their camels bearing spicery and balm and myrrh, going to carry it down to Egypt. And Judah said unto his brethren, What profit is it if we slay our brother, and conceal his blood? Come, and let us sell him to the Ishmaelites, and let not our hand be upon him; for he is our brother and our flesh. And his brethren were content.

Genesis 42:6-8
Now Joseph *was* governor over the land; and it was he who sold to all the people of the land. And Joseph's brothers came and bowed down before him with *their* faces to the earth. Joseph saw his brothers and recognized them, but he acted as a stranger to them and spoke roughly to them. Then he said to them, "Where do you come from?" And they said, "From the land of Canaan to buy food." So Joseph recognized his brothers, but they did not recognize him.

So too will be the degree of the rebirth of the 747 woman. Old friends and once familiar faces will no longer recognize you in your aura or demeanor. I would go as far to say that even your countenance will change as you will begin to walk in the fullness of your calling. It is a glow that no MAC counter or liquid detox can offer. It is the light bestowed upon you by Elohim, by our Lord and savior Yeshua the Christ and is indicative of your decision to walk with Him and follow your calling. It is both your reward for your obedience and faithfulness during the years of hardship, persecution, opposition and ridicule as well as a clarion call to others to follow the one and true living God. Your rebirth has ushered in your transformation, redemption, vindication and victory. Glory be to God! The Lord has indeed made you anew!

2 Corinthians 5:17
Therefore if any man be Christ, he is a new creature: old things are passed away; behold, all things are become new.

Matthew 9:17
And no one puts new wine into old wineskins for the old skins would burst from the pressure, spilling the wine and ruining the skins. New wine is stored in new wineskins so that both are preserved.

ROYALTY ANOINTING

Psalm 103:19 states The Lord has established his throne in heaven, and his kingdom rules over all. He is the Supreme Being over all gods and over all powers (Deuteronomy 10:17), the Most High Forever More (Psalm 92:8), the Alpha and the Omega, the First and the Last (Revelation 22:13), the Rock of the ages (Isaiah 26-4) who has given Yeshua, his Son, all power and authority.

Matthew 11:27
All things have been handed over to Me by My Father

Matthew 28:18
And Jesus came up and spoke to them, saying "All authority as been given to Me in heaven and on earth

Philippians 2:9
For this reason also, God highly exalted Him, and bestowed on Him the name which is above every name

Colossians 2:10
And He is the head over all rule and authority

1 Peter 3:22
Who is at the right hand of God, having gone into heaven, after angels and authorities and powers had been subjected to Him

John 3:35
The Father loves the Son and has given all things into His hand

According to the book of Revelation, Yeshua the Christ is King of Kings, and Lord of Lords. It is also written that Yeshua sprang from the order and line of Melchizadak, the King and Priest, who blessed God for Abraham's victory over his enemies and then blessed Abraham, prompting him to give Melchizedek a tithe of ten percent. It is the same line from which King David, who was considered both King and Priest was sired; King because he was heir to Israel by his father King Solomon, and a priest because at times he accessed God directly through no man or prophet.

Revelation 19:16
And He hath on his vesture and on His thigh a name written, King of Kings, and Lord of Lords.

Hebrews 7:14-17 (NLT)
What I mean is, our Lord came from the tribe of Judah, and Moses never mentioned priests coming from that tribe. This change has been made very clear since a different priest, who is like Melchizedek, has appeared. Jesus became a priest, not by meeting the physical requirement of belonging to the tribe of Levi, but by the power of a life that cannot be destroyed. And the psalmist pointed this out when he prophesied, "You are a priest forever in the order of Melchizedek."

Psalm 110:4
The Lord has sworn and will not change his mind, 'you are a priest forever after the order of Melchizedek'"—is the outgrowth of David's reflection on Genesis 14 in light of the Davidic covenant and the patterns of his own life.

Correspondingly, we too spring from the line of Melchizedek. We are royalty because of the kingship bestowed onto Christ, our brother, the Highest Priest, and are priest ourselves because we have direct access to God through Him. We are indeed co/joint heirs with Christ and are of a royal priesthood.

John 20:17
Jesus saith unto her, Touch me not; for I am not yet ascended to my Father: but go to my brethren, and say unto them, I ascend unto my Father, and your Father; and *to* my God, and your God.

Romans 8:29
For whom he did foreknow, he also did predestinate *to be* conformed to the image of his Son, that he might be the firstborn among many brethren.

Hebrews 2:11-12
So now Jesus and the ones He makes holy have the same Father. That is why Jesus is not ashamed to call them his brothers and sisters. For he said to God, "I will proclaim your name to my brothers and sisters. I will praise you among your assembled people." He also said, "I will put my trust in Him," that is , "I and the children God has given me."

1 Peter 2:9-10
But ye *are* a chosen generation, a royal priesthood, an holy nation, a peculiar people; that ye should shew forth the praises of him who hath called you out of darkness into his marvelous light: Which in time past *were* not a people, but *are* now the people of God: which had not obtained mercy, but now have obtained mercy.

Christian author, Alyssa J Howard, purports that we as believers are royalty via three biblical truths. The first truth comes by way of a royal birth when we receive the spirit of God by becoming born again in Christ. The second truth is via marriage as we the church and as believers, are the bride of Christ. The third truth that evidences our royal heritage is because God destined and declared us as royal.

Prepare For Landing: Your Final Destination

Romans 8:15-17
So you have not received a spirit that makes you fearful slaves. Instead, you received God's Spirit when he adopted you as his own children. Now we call him, "Abba, Father." For his Spirit joins with our spirit to affirm that we are God's children. And since we are his children, we are his heirs. In fact, together with Christ we are heirs of God's glory.

Revelation 19:7
Let us rejoice and be glad and give the glory to Him, for the marriage of the Lamb has come and His bride has made herself ready

Ephesians 5:25-27
Husbands, love your wives, just as Christ also loved the church and gave Himself up for her, so that he might sanctify her, having cleansed her by the washing of water with the word, that he might present to Himself the church in all her gory, having no spot or wrinkle or any such thing; but that she would be holy and blameless

Revelation 21:2
And I saw the holy city, new Jerusalem, coming down out to heaven from God, made ready as a bride adorned for her husband

Isaiah 62:3
Thou shalt also be a crown of glory in the hand of the LORD, and a royal diadem in the hand of thy God.

For many 747 women, our appointment comes directly from God. We are not formally trained, although we may opt to be at a later time. Our coronation into this Royal Priesthood is an unwavering inner knowing and conviction. Our anointing and marching orders were given to us directly by the Holy Spirit. Though we may have unofficially sat at the feet of many teachers, shepherds, reverends, pastors and church officials, through church membership, media—traditional and social, ultimately our ranking in the spiritual realm was bestowed upon us as an act of grace and predestined despite us in most cases.

This royal ranking ensures a posture of dignity, humility and servitude, not one of haughtiness or arrogance. We have been entrusted with authority and power and fully understand that to whom much is given much is expected. We are seated in heavenly places, walk in favor and witness God's frequent and consistent breaking of protocols for us. If and when our value in the earthly realm is temporarily diminished or deemed low in stature, beings and entities in the spiritual realm, be they submitted to the authority of God or in rebellion, know our stately spiritual identity and behave accordingly.

DOMINION ANOINTING

When considering the concept of dominion and how it relates to the Christian walk, many of us tend to think of the bible verses that speak of God's instruction for man to subjugate the fowl of the air, the beast of the land, fish of the sea and every living thing that moves on the earth.

Genesis 1:26-28
And God said, Let us make man in our image, after our likeness: and let them have dominion over the fish of the sea, and over the fowl of the air, and over the cattle, and over all the earth, and over every creeping thing that creepeth upon the earth. So God created man in his own image, in the image of God created he him; male and female created he them. And God blessed them, and God said unto them, Be fruitful, and multiply, and replenish the earth, and subdue it: and have dominion over the fish of the sea, and over the fowl of the air, and over every living thing that moveth upon the earth.

Yet, that is not the full spectrum of what the Dominion Anointing encompasses. In order to give the most concise definition of dominion I can offer, I would ask that you refer to Vine's Expository Dictionary of New Testament Words whereby dominion (Have...Over) is defined as "force, strength, might," [or more specifically], "manifested power," [and] is derived from a root *kra*," [meaning] "to perfect, to complete:" It then directs us to cross reference MIGHT, POWER and STRENGTH for a more comprehensive understanding. Yet, what was most notable in Vine's efforts to expound on the meaning were the synonyms utilized to convey the essence of word and concept. In order to accomplish this, several Greek words are employed. The first is *bia*, or force, the second, *dunamis*, or power, especially "inherent power," the third is *energeia*, which also means "power" but as it relates to power being exercised, as an operative power. The next synonym used is *exousia*, which means "liberty of action," [and] "authority" either delegated or arbitrary. The last is *ischus*, or strength" especially physical, or power as an endowment.

Daniel 7:27

And the kingdom and dominion, and the greatness of the kingdom under the whole heaven, shall be given to the people of the saints of the Most High, whose kingdom is an everlasting kingdom, and all dominions shall serve and obey him

I love Kenneth Copeland's approach to the concept of dominion as he maintains that it is a "God-given gift to His people that requires His supernatural Anointing. He states, this gift of dominion, "belongs to [the believer] but it isn't automatic. It takes faith, walking in love, and operating in the anointing." I believe that to be true. He further asserts that there are four components or keys that can assist the believer with understanding this anointing:

1. The anointing includes the ability to take dominion over every area of your life and do things you would otherwise not be able to do.
2. This anointing includes the ability to prosper financially which simply suggests that you take what belongs to you as a child of God
3. The anointing includes the ability to excel to the highest place which Copeland contends is long life in a strong, healthy body. I would also add that you are exalted to your God appointed position in the industry that God has preordained and set apart for you to dominate

4. The anointing includes the expectation that you will be blessed during famine

As 747 women the dominion anointing is part of our legacy as children of the Most High God and joint/co-heirs with Christ. This power is not derived from our sheer volition, but is a demonstration of the inherent power of the blood and resurrection of our Lord and Savior, Yeshua the Christ, which we are infused with, invigorated and empowered by as anointed believers.

Ephesians 1:21
Far above all principality, and power, and might, and dominion, and every name that is named, not only in this world, but also in that which is to come:

Psalm 145:13
Your kingdom is an everlasting kingdom, and your dominion endures throughout all generations.

1 Peter 4:11
Whoever speaks, as one who speaks oracles of God; whoever serves, as one who serves by the strength that God supplies—in order that in everything God may be glorified through Jesus Christ. To him belong glory and dominion forever and ever. Amen

Numbers 24:19
And one from Jacob shall exercise dominion and destroy the survivors of cities!

Revelation 12:11
And they overcome him by the blood of the Lamb

John 6:53
Then Jesus said to them, verily, verily, I say unto you, Except ye eat the flesh of the Son of man, and drink his blood, ye have no life in you.

Romans 8:11

If the Spirit of him who raised Jesus from the dead dwells in you, he who raised Christ Jesus from the dead will also give life to your mortal bodies through his Spirit who dwells in you

Ephesians 3:20-21
Now unto him that is able to do exceeding abundantly above all that we ask or think, according to the power that worketh in us, Unto him be glory in the church by Christ Jesus throughout all ages, world without end. Amen.

What is also worth noting is that as the anointing activates to its full potency, you will become more aware of your authority and dominion. Outside of the bible, and the previous definitions I have offered, one of the clearest illustrations of what it means to shift from lack of knowledge and understanding regarding our true identities to authority and dominion, can be heard in Dr. Cindy Trimm's Atomic Power of Prayer. During this prayer Dr. Trimm, internationally acclaimed life strategist, humanitarian, and bestselling author, not only leads us in prayer but illuminates the believer's, and in this case, the 747 woman's authority and dominion.

She posits that our dominion anointing includes our authority to break out, break free, and break through satanic shackles, anchors and cages. It galvanizes us to resist, release and plow through demonic mountains, boulders, barricades and blockades. We are anointed to excavate seeds of deception, lack, limitation and sabotage. We reverse, cancel and veto the lies, tyranny, bondage and oppression of Satan and the fallen angels that cause poverty, failure, hopelessness, malice, pride, pain and destruction. Our authority enlarges our mouths over our enemies to declare, decree and proclaim that the God of Israel is the one and only true God and that wicked provinces, territories and regions are overthrown and destroyed. We possess what is rightfully ours and our inheritances as children of the Most High God. We deliver ourselves, loved ones and captives from strongholds as well as the effects and bands of unholiness and unrighteousness. We demand that the glory of the Lord be ushered in and established in every inch, corner and quarter of every single natural and spiritual realm, dimension on, above and beyond the earth, and in the depths below thereby shifting atmospheres and climates. We command and demand that anyone and everyone refusing to proclaim and accept the kingship, lordship, authority, power, truth and light of our Lord and Savior Yeshua the Christ be forever subjugated to be His foot stool.

Deuteronomy 28:13
And the Lord shall make thee the head, and not the tail: and thou shalt be above only, and thou shalt not be beneath;

Job 22:28
Thou shalt also decree a thing, and it shall be established unto thee: and the light shall shine upon thy ways

I would be remiss if I did not mention that this anointing promotes the explosive arrival of astounding growth in wisdom, stature and courage. This growth diminishes the enemy's attempts to discourage, dissuade and depress us. The attacks and attempts to harm and impede us feel more like the annoyance of a gnat rather than a challenge from a lion. I undoubtedly still sense and perceive the attacks of witchcraft via broken focus and dream penetration, but the efforts and results of these attacks are dull and insipid at best. I now move into rooms, spaces and territories with my head held high, fully aware of the range and volume of who I am—blessings, lessons, triumphs, failures, value, misgivings and anointing. I do not second guess myself when I am not accepted, when some are repelled, or shun my presence and/or assistance. I accomplish the purpose, task and mission that the Lord has set before me. Whomever he has predestined for me to touch, bless, teach and uplift, it happens. Whomever he sends to touch, bless, teach and uplift me, it happens. Whomever rejects me is not my concern. I disengage from and disavow connection from anyone and anything incapable of seeing who I am as a child of the Most High God and I keep it pushing. They may think they are of God, but may be as counterfeit as a three dollar bill, or may have rejected God long before I showed up. Even still, they may very well be a full-fledged proclaimed child of God, but not designated for my ministry, or life and that is quite alright.

WEALTH ANOINTING

The International Standard Bible Encyclopedia teaches that the words wealth and wealthy are derived from welth, wel'-thi (hon, Chayil, nekhacim; euporia, "to possess riches," "to be in a position of ease" (Jeremiah 49:31). It further asserts that the possession of wealth was considered proof of the blessing of God (Ecclesiastes 5:19; 6:2). Likewise, the Authorized King James Version of The Holy Bible published by Bible House Charlotte, North Carolina defines wealth as having many possessions/possessions. It further contends that in the Old Testament, possession of wealth was regarded as evidence of God's favor (Psalm 1:3).

Jeremiah 49:31
Arise, get you up unto the wealthy nation, that dwelleth without care, saith the LORD, which have neither gates nor bars, which dwell alone

Ecclesiastes 5:19
Every man also to whom God hath given riches and wealth, and hath given him power to eat thereof, and to take his portion, and to rejoice in his labour; this is the gift of God

Ecclesiastes 6:2
A man to whom God hath given riches, wealth, and honour, so that he wanteth nothing for his soul of all that he desireth, yet God giveth him not power to eat thereof, but a stranger eateth it: this is vanity, and it is an evil disease

Psalm 1:3
And he shall be like a tree planted by the rivers of water, that bringeth forth his fruit in his season; his leaf also shall not wither; and whatsoever he doeth shall prosper.

The 7:47 Connection

I believe 747 women undoubtedly walk into the wealth anointing once they have demonstrated a commitment to obedience and to walk with the Lord. This is not an easy walk as I do believe it involves long seasons of testing, fasting, sacrifice, singleness and separation to ensure attunement with the Holy Spirit and adherence to the purpose for which you have been called. Even if you have children and are married, God can still separate you. Those relationships may undergo seasons of extensive difficulty and estrangement. Please note that I am not saying seasons of perfection as we all fall short of the kingdom of God. Yet God weighs and seeks out the secret places of our hearts and He knows and determines who worships Him, seeks Him and loves and fears Him authentically. And I wholeheartedly believe that they are the anointed believers he gifts with wealth. Is every woman gifted with the wealth anointing, a 747 woman? No, that is not what I am stating. But this is the way it may show up for a woman that identifies herself as a 747 believer.

John 4:23-24
But the hour cometh, and now is, when the true worshippers shall worship the Father in spirit and in truth: for the Father seeketh such to worship him. God is a Spirit: and they that worship him must worship him in spirit and in truth.

Romans 3:23
For all have sinned, and come short of the glory of God

Jeremiah 17:10
I, the LORD, search the heart, I test the mind, Even to give every man according to his ways, According to the fruit of his doings

Let me clarify my standing on the wealth anointing as I do not mean to say that wealth will fall in your lap. That is typically not the case. Hard work, dedication, seasons of planting, sowing and sleepless nights are required to reap the promises God has given you. Giving to the poor and those less fortunate, and I firmly believe, tithing is required for this particular anointing. Walking in humility, gratitude and acknowledging

Him in all your ways is mandatory. Yet, there are certain previously closed doors that now open to the touch. You now enter rooms that were formerly shut closed with ease. The Lord provides an abundance of ideas, opportunities and people assigned to your promotion, appointment, vindication and relocation from the pit to the palace. The people of which I speak will be believers themselves who have crossed over to their promised land or are on their way. They are equipped with the Holy Spirit, love, humility, authenticity, knowledge, wisdom and connections to get you exactly where God promised he would take you.

Proverbs 10:4
He becometh poor that dealeth with a slack hand: but the hand of the diligent maketh rich

Genesis 26:12
Then Isaac sowed in that land, and received in the same year an hundredfold: and the Lord blessed him

Isaiah 65:21
And they shall plant vineyards, and eat the fruit of them

Isaiah 30:23
Then He will give you rain for the seed which you will sow in the ground, and bread from the yield of the ground, and it will be rich and plenteous; on that day your livestock will graze in a roomy

Acts 10:1-4 (NLT)
In Caesarea there lived a Roman army officer named Cornelius, who was a captain of the Italian Regiment. He was a devout, God-fearing man, as was everyone in his household. He gave generously to the poor and prayed regularly to God. One afternoon about three o'clock, he had a vision in which he saw an angel of God coming toward him. "Cornelius!" the angel said. Cornelius stared at him in terror. "What is it, sir?" he asked the angel. And the angel replied, "Your prayers and gifts to the poor have been received by God as an offering!

Luke 6:38
Give, and it shall be given unto you; good measure, pressed down, and shaken together, and running over, shall men give into your bosom. For with the same measure that ye mete withal it shall be measured to you again.

Malachi 3:10 (NIV)
Bring the whole tithe into the storehouse, that there may be food in my house. Test me in this," says the LORD Almighty, "and see if I will not throw open the floodgates of heaven and pour out so much blessing that there will not be room enough to store it.

1 Peter 5:6
Humble yourselves therefore under the mighty hand of God, that he may exalt you in due time

Thessalonians 5:18
In everything give thanks: for this is the will of God in Christ Jesus concerning you.

1 Chronicles 16:34
O give thanks unto the Lord; for he is good; for his mercy endureth for ever.

Proverbs 16:3
Commit thy works unto the LORD, and thy thoughts shall be established.

Proverbs 3:6
In all thy ways acknowledge Him, and He shall direct thy paths

Isaiah 48:17
Thus saith the LORD, thy Redeemer, the Holy One of Israel; I am the LORD thy God which teacheth thee to profit, which leadeth thee by the way that thou shouldest go

What is most interesting, however, is the plethora of former acquaintances, friends, lovers, and in many cases, family members, who believe you do not deserve your season of elevation. From all outward appearances, it should not be you. They proclaim that you are too worldly, focused on wealth, or a heretical hypocrite while totally unaware of what you have gone through and been delivered from after years in the wilderness. They naively believe that they could walk in your shoes having totally wiped away from their memory the seasons they have witnessed of your hardship, betrayal, character assassination, ostracism and exile. Yet, I state again, God knows the heart. God promotes and demotes. And the table from which you now indulge is the table He has set for you in the presence of those who spitefully used, disparaged, discouraged and discarded you as you prayed for them.

I Samuel 16:7
for the LORD seeth not as man seeth; for man looketh on the outward appearance, but the LORD looketh on the heart.

Psalms 75:7
But God is the judge: he putteth down one, and setteth up another

Luke 6:28
Bless them that curse you, and pray for them which spitefully use you.

Psalms 23:5
Thou preparest a table before me in the presence of mine enemies: thou anointest my head with oil; my cup runneth over

As I write these words, I bear witness to the Lord's promise of a wealth anointing decreeing and establishing prosperity and financial stability over my life. This anointing breaks generations of lack, poverty, quality of life-crippling debt, financially related stress, embarrassment and despair and is a cornerstone of the 747 anointing.

Psalm 115:14-15
The LORD shall increase you more and more, you and your children. Ye are blessed of the LORD which made heaven and earth

Psalm 112:1-3
Praise ye the LORD. Blessed is the man that feareth the LORD, that delighteth greatly in his commandments. His seed shall be mighty upon earth: the generation of the upright shall be blessed. Wealth and riches shall be in his house: and his righteousness endureth for ever.

Job 22:25
Yea, the Almighty shall be thy defence, and thou shalt have plenty of silver.

Proverbs 10:22
The blessing of the Lord, it maketh rich, and he addeth no sorrow with it.

Am I there yet? Not quite. Yet there has been a significant shift in the financial climate and atmosphere around me. There has been notable changes in my mindset and my surroundings as well as my shift to people, places and environments that will support growth and promotion of that magnitude. I am unshakeable in my belief that this shift is from the Lord and is preparing me for what is to come. The road ahead requires work, it requires consistency, it requires preparation and you must be up to the challenge, yet the shift is evident.

Psalm 66:12
Thou hast caused men to ride over our heads; we went through fire and through water: but thou broughtest us out into a wealthy place.

Deuteronomy 26:9
And he hath brought us into this place, and hath given us this land, *even* a land that floweth with milk and honey

Deuteronomy 1:8
Behold, I have set the land before you: go in and possess the land which the LORD sware unto your fathers, Abraham, Isaac, and Jacob, to give unto them and to their seed after them

Numbers 33:53
And ye shall dispossess the inhabitants of the land, and dwell therein: for I have given you the land to possess it

There are several examples of women called by God, whom before their ascent in their ministry and in wealth, engaged in spiritual warfare with a narcissist. It almost seems par for the course. I am not stating that this is the sole qualifier for the 747 anointing, however, many of us will have this experience in common, in addition to seasons of intense infliction, attack, rejection and exclusion. There are many other women whose ministries testify of interaction with a narcissist as well. Although they have not attained the level of wealth of which I speak and their ministries are still in infancy, there is no doubt in mind that they are heading for the same level of victory and vindication. I would also like to share that I do not mention these stories to glorify riches. I am, however, glorifying the goodness and promises of God and to inform you of an attribute of the 747 anointing. For through us, and by our testimonies and ministries, God is drawing his sheep to Himself.

Matthew 5:16
Let your light so shine before men, that they may see your good works, and glorify your Father which is in heaven

Acts 13:47
For so hath the Lord commanded us, saying, I have set thee to be a light of the Gentiles, that thou shouldest be for salvation unto the ends of the earth

The assertion that a wealth anointing is included in the destination of the 747 woman is a serious one. You may be the first billionaire in your zip code, or you may be the first person to own an extremely lucrative business in your family, or you may be the first to discover or implement a groundbreaking technology, process or product. Only the Lord knows to the extent and degree that your earthly reward will manifest. Only the Lord knows when, where and how. What I do know is that you will be the first to attain a certain financial level in your family. But more importantly, although this degree of financial wealth will be passed down for generations to come, it is not solely for your financial gain. God also intends for you to be a selfless, spirit-led financier of the kingdom and kingdom interests. Your anointing includes the power to lay hands on, and/or use the power of your words to minister to believers the Holy Spirit identifies as suffering in lack and poverty. It is a very real and powerful anointing, and He expects you to walk in it.

THE ACCELARATION ANOINTING

One of the telltale signs that you are in the throes of the transformative establishment of your anointing is the many stories of God's ability to manipulate time to restore lost years and accelerate the manifestation of your promises. A few days ago I was listening to a timely word (reel) from Pastor Dwight Buckner, Jr., Senior Pastor at Generation of Hope Church in Atlanta, Georgia where he stated that the *divine acceleration of the Lord will overtake you*. And I was of course, finishing up the Wealth Anointing section and heading into the Acceleration Anointing section of this book. For me, it was additional confirmation of the Holy Spirit's desire for it to be included as part of the 747 anointing.

Acceleration can be defined as *an increase in the rate of speed* of something and although it is not listed in any of the Concordances I utilize as reference materials, the word speed is utilized. The Holy Bible Authorized King James Version published by Bible House in Charlotte, North Carolina defines speed as "haste, progress." And haste is defined as "to hurry, to escape thither (as to or toward that place). A portion of passage Isaiah 60:22 which states "I the Lord will," is referenced in the definition. The full verse in the King James Version reads, "I the LORD will hasten it in his time." The New International Version interprets the passage as "I am the Lord; in its time I will do this swiftly and in the Amplified Bible as "the LORD, will quicken it in its [appointed] time.

Thus not only does the speed of the Lord's blessing correspond to its velocity, but it refers to an appointed time for it to occur. In the case of the 747 the Acceleration Anointing goes hand in hand with the Wealth Anointing. Yet it goes even further applying to areas beyond your financial standing. It can include a speedy restoration of your health, marital status in terms of moving from singleness to marriage, or your marriage moving from a season of drought to rebirth and renewal. It can include the resurrection of relationships with family members, loved ones, job opportunities, or even previously abandoned business ideas being restored—and robustly. Whatever was stolen from you during your testing season will not only be restored, but God will give you the portion of joy, happiness, prosperity, health and new memories that you missed during your years, plus more. I am talking a double portion and heaping of the Lord's blessing that will overtake you and ensure that you do not feel left out of anything or separated from anyone that was divinely assigned to you or predestined for your life. I believe Helen Calder, of Enliven Ministries offers a great explanation for this concept. She defines divine acceleration as "a reminder that you can trust the timing of God. For He is faithful, He is sovereign, and He is powerful. He is also the God of the resurrection."

Author Atoyebi Samuel makes a keen differentiation when covering divine acceleration by stating that it does not "necessarily mean physical fast movement, [but] accomplishing a task faster than the human estimated time. Samuel points to the prayer by Abraham's servant before setting out to find a wife for his son Isaac in Rebekah. In Genesis 24:12 the servant states, "O Lord God of my master Abraham, I pray thee, send me good speed this day and show kindness unto my master Abraham" suggesting his desire to accomplish the task with speed and favor. The next verse indicates that suddenly he was near a well, attended by the daughters of the men of the city as the next verse, Genesis 24:13 states, "Behold, I stand here by the well of water; and the daughters of the men of the city come out to draw water." He then prays that the young woman that offers him water for himself and for his camels is to become Isaac's wife—and Rebekah did just that. Thus the story uses divine connection for a kingdom marriage to demonstrate divine acceleration. It did not happen at the speed of light, but quicker than the time it would have taken to identify Abraham's son's kingdom spouse if done in the absence of the gracing.

Yet I also believe that divine acceleration includes velocity and swiftness. This is demonstrated when Elijah is instructed by the Lord to travel to Jezreel, the same destination that Ahab was traveling to, but by chariot. Yet Elijah beat him there.

1 Kings 18:44-46 KJV
And it came to pass at the seventh time, that he said, Behold, there ariseth a little cloud out of the sea, like a man's hand. And he said, Go up, say unto Ahab, Prepare thy chariot, and get thee down that the rain stop thee not. And it came to pass in the mean while, that the heaven was black with clouds and wind, and there was a great rain. And Ahab rode, and went to Jezreel. And the hand of the LORD was on Elijah; and he girded up his loins, and ran before Ahab to the entrance of Jezreel.

1 Kings 18:46 AMP
And at the seventh *time* the servant said, "A cloud as small as a man's hand is coming up from the sea." And Elijah said, "Go up, say to Ahab, 'Prepare *your chariot* and go down, so that the rain shower does not stop you.'" In a little while the sky grew dark with clouds and wind, and there were heavy showers. And Ahab mounted *and* rode [his chariot] and went [inland] to [a]Jezreel. Then the hand of the LORD came upon Elijah [giving him supernatural strength]. He [b]girded up his loins and outran Ahab to the entrance of Jezreel [nearly twenty miles].

1 Peter 5:10
But the God of all grace, who hath called us unto his eternal glory by Christ Jesus, after that ye have suffered a while, make you perfect, stablish, strengthen, settle you.

Joel 2:25-26
And I will restore to you the years that the locust hath eaten, the cankerworm, and the caterpillar, and the palmerworm, my great army which I sent among you. And ye shall eat in plenty, and be satisfied, and praise the name of the LORD your God, that hath dealt wondrously with you: and my people shall never be ashamed.

Jeremiah 30:17
For I will restore health unto thee, and I will heal thee of thy wounds, saith the LORD; because they called thee an Outcast, saying, This is Zion, whom no man seeketh after.

Isaiah 61:7
For your shame ye shall have double; and for confusion they shall rejoice in their portion: therefore in their land they shall possess the double: everlasting joy shall be unto them.

Zechariah 9:12
Turn you to the strong hold, ye prisoners of hope: even today do I declare that I will render double unto thee;

When taking into account the Acceleration Anointing, many of today's leading kingdom leaders and motivation speakers, including but not limited to Bishop Dale C. Bronner, Les Brown and Pastor Mike Todd, compare the supernatural phenomenon to the growth of the bamboo. The Guinness Book of World records touts the bamboo as the fastest growing plant on the earth and it some parts of the world, namely Asia, many of its species can grow upwards of one hundred-sixty feet. Yet what should be of most interest to the believer is the unique growth process of the Chinese bamboo tree. It is recorded that the plant's root system takes five years to grow with daily watering and fertilization. After which the plant breaks through the ground and over the course of the next five weeks, the plant will grow ninety feet tall. What a feat! And this growth spurt is akin to the 747 believer's season of acceleration. The five years in which it takes to establish a strong, healthy root system is akin to the season of separation that God utilizes to toughen us, prepare us and ensure we know His voice. It points to the season directly prior to the wealth and acceleration anointings taking flight. It is the season where we are hidden, out of the loop, out of sight and for the most part becoming firmly planted in our relationship with God. Yet, when the season shifts, it is then time for us to burst on the scene with astonishing speed, tenacity and success to herald the mercy and goodness of the Lord.

Isaiah 51:14 KJV
The captive exile hasteneth that he may be loosed, and that he should not die in the pit, nor that his bread should fail.

Isaiah 51:14
The captive exile shall speedily be freed; and he shall not die [and go down] int o the it, neither shall his bread fail.

Isaiah 5:26
And he will lift up an ensign to the nations from far, and will hiss unto them from the end of the earth: and, behold, they shall come with speed swiftly

Isaiah 5:26 (NKJV)
He will lift up a banner to the nations from far, and he will whistle for them from the end of the earth. Behold, they will come speedily and swiftly.

THE ANOINTING OF GOD'S FIERCE RETRIBUTION

I must say that this is the anointing I grappled with including and finally understood that the Holy Spirit wanted its inclusion. This anointing definitely points to the judgment God doles out to those who harm his anointed. I use the word harm to mean the intentional and deliberate harm of his anointed.

Psalm 105:15
Do not touch My anointed ones, And do My prophets no harm

Luke 18:7-8
And shall not God avenge his own elect, which cry day and night unto Him, though he bear long with them? I tell you that he will avenge them speedily.

Habakkuk 3:13 (NIV)
You came out to deliver your people, to save your anointed one. You crushed the leader of the land of wickedness, you stripped him from head to foot

Isaiah 59:19
When the enemy shall come in like a flood, the Spirit of the LORD shall lift up a standard against him.

Psalm 28:8
The Lord is their strength, And He is a saving defense to His anointed

I am not suggesting that you will experience retribution of any sort for not liking a believer or someone that walks in God's anointing. Many people do not and will not like you regardless of whether you did something to them or not. You can give them the shirt off your back, explain, refrain, and do whatever else you can think of—and they still will not like you. More often than not, not only do they not like you, but they secretly resent you too. Now brace yourself because this may hurt. Whether you like it or not, these same people will still receive blessings from the Lord. The Lord makes available to them the same grace He extends to us, and it cannot be said enough that we all fall short of the glory of God (Romans 3:23).

Matthew 5:45
That ye may be the children of your Father which is in heaven: for he maketh his sun to rise on the evil and on the good, and sendeth rain on the just and on the unjust.

Romans 3:10
As it is written, There is none righteous, no, not one

However, this component of the anointing is not addressing those who dislike us. Rather, it speaks to the willful, deliberate intent to do the anointed spiritual, mental, emotional, reputational, financial and/or physical bodily harm. The operative words here are intentional, deliberate and harmful. People hurt each other every day, most times unintentionally, not pre-mediated and or is a case of a person simply taking themselves into account without being empathetic or compassionate toward others. I am not speaking of those instances. I am speaking of plans, campaigns, cauldrons and attempts to shut down and shut out God's children. I am speaking of heavily contemplated, pre-mediated and strategic measures to hurt the anointed whether they realize the person is anointed or not.

An example of this anointing is exemplified in 1 Samuel 25 where the story of King David and Nabal, the wealthy, yet surly man in Carmel is recounted. The story begins directly after the prophet Samuel's death when David sends ten of his men to ask Nabal, a shearer of sheep, if he would be so kind as to gift them some of his resources and supplies. David instructed his men to share with Nabal how they had protected his shepherds and showed them kindness. Yet Nabal was indignant, harsh and refused them. When David's men returned with the news, David sought to kill Nabal stating he returned evil for good. Yet Nabal's wife, Abigail, beautiful and intelligent, seeking to avoid the trouble her husband has brought on his head, secretly went to David and brought him heaps of wine, food and livestock. In turn David, enroute to march on Nabal with four hundred of his men, turned away his wrath. When Abigail returned from showing kindness to David and informed Nabal of what she had done, "his heart died within him, and he became as a stone. And it came to pass about ten days after, that the Lord Smote Nabal, that he died." Sharee, a strong, professed believer in Christ shared her experience with this anointing in an authentic and precise YouTube video entitled, "Touch Not the Anointed and Do The Prophets No Harm!" which enumerates how this anointing shows up in the lives of many of God's anointed today.

Isaiah 5:20
Woe to those who call evil good and good evil, who put darkness for light and light for darkness, who put bitter for sweet and sweet for bitter

Proverbs 4:16
For they cannot rest until they do evil; they are robbed of sleep till they make someone stumble

Proverbs 6:14
Who with perversity in his heart continually devised evil, who spreads strife

Isaiah 32:7
As for a rogue, his weapons are evil; He devises wicked schemes to destroy the afflicted with slander

Job 5:12
He frustrates the plotting of the shrewd, So that their hands cannot attain success

I have vigorously prayed for the healing of people who have turned around and stabbed me in the back. Stunningly, that same body part I prayed for, for which they have received healing, gets damaged again—the same exact place. In an instant their healing is revoked and every prayer result and fast I did on their behalf is seemingly reversed. I have had people betray me, slander and sully my name for me to watch them be brought to an open and public shame in the very next season. I have prayed for the healing of disease in a person, be informed they were healed, be dropped by the person months later, only to hear that the ailment returned—and worse. I have had people come after me to ruin me financially, emotionally and mentally, and in a year's time, meet their sick bed, an untimely demise, or their closest loved ones meet their premature deaths. And some have even dropped dead.

Psalm 110:5 (NLT)
The Lord stands at your right hand to protect you. He will strike down many kings when his anger erupts

Ezekiel 25:17
I will execute great vengeance on them with furious rebukes; and they shall know that I *am* the LORD, when I lay My vengeance upon them

Deuteronomy 32:35 (NKJV)
Vengeance is Mine, and recompense; Their foot shall slip in *due* time; For the day of their calamity *is* at hand, And the things to come hasten upon them.'

Deuteronomy 30:7
The Lord your God will inflict all these curses on your enemies and on those who hate you, who persecuted you.

Psalms 34:15-17
The face of the LORD *is* against them that do evil, to cut off the remembrance of them from the earth.

It is important that I be extremely clear that I do not relish in anyone's harm, nor do I pray against people whether they have hurt me or not. Not because I am some self-proclaimed goody two shoes. I do try hard to love and pray for my enemies, but I am not always successful. If I am aware a person does not care for me, perceive hostility or disingenuity, I will immediately become distant, indifferent and dismissive. I am working on that. But, hate them? No. Do I wish them harm or imminent death? No, not at all. I am literally too afraid to do so. Have I wanted to fight, react, pay back when wronged, slighted or offended? Absolutely. Have I done just that in the past? Absolutely. Yet God has brought me a long way. At this point in my life I fear God, the Father Almighty, the Great and Dreadful one and true living God of Israel and how He will feel about my reaction—especially if I start praying against one of His children—no matter the magnitude of their envy, foolishness or spiritual immaturity. We are not to go after or pray against others. To do so, as far as I am concerned, is a form of witchcraft. I will, however, pray for protection and ask God to fight for me and vindicate me.

Ephesians 4:26
In your anger do not sin": Do not let the sun go down while you are still angry,

1 Peter 3:9
Do not repay evil with evil or insult with insult. On the contrary, repay evil with blessing, because to this you were called so that you may inherit a blessing.

Romans 12:19 (NLT)
Dear friends, never take revenge. Leave that to the righteous anger of God. For the Scriptures say, "I will take revenge; I will pay them back," says the LORD.

Proverbs 19:23 (NKJV)
The fear of the LORD leads to life, And he who has it will abide in satisfaction; He will not be visited with evil.

Psalms 20:1 (NIV)
May the Lord answer you when you are in distress; may the name of the God of Jacob protect you.

Psalms 59:1
Deliver me from mine enemies, O my God: defend me from them that rise up against me

Psalm 94:22
But the Lord is my defence; and my God is the rock of my refuge

Nahum 1:7
The Lord is good, a strong hold in the day of trouble; and he knoweth them that trust in Him.

Now if I encounter something more sinister, as I have previously stated, I will request permission to engage in spiritual warfare and battle against the person(s). If indeed it is revealed that they are demon possessed, housing spirits of darkness and attacking me or my loved ones, then they are heading toward a real problem. The thing to commit to memory is that I ask for permission. Just as King David asked God for permission to attack the Philistines, I ask the Lord for permission to fight those attacking me. I can tell you now that it is only given if the person is identified as working against the kingdom of God—be it a witch, warlock, satanist, etc., When afflicted, persecuted or wrongly accused by other believers, we are to put them in God's hands and pray for them. A demonic being, entity, principality, or professed enemy of God, however, I will fight no matter how disadvantaged the enemy may think I am—just as King David fought Goliath—for God and with God, and the win will be evident and indisputable.

1 Chronicles 14:8-11
And when the Philistines heard that David was anointed king over all Israel, all the Philistines went up to seek David. And David heard of it, and went out against them. And the Philistines came and spread themselves in the valley of Rephaim. And David inquired of God, saying, Shall I go up against the Philistines? And wilt thou deliver them into mine hand? And the LORD said unto him, Go up; for I will deliver them into thine hand.

Nehemiah 4:14
Be not ye afraid of them: remember the Lord, *which is* great and terrible, and fight for your brethren, your sons, and your daughters, your wives, and your houses.

Jeremiah 51:20
You are my battle-ax and sword," says the LORD. "With you I will shatter nations and destroy many kingdoms.

Leviticus 26:7
And ye shall chase your enemies, and they shall fall before you by the sword. You will chase your enemies, and they shall fall by the sword before you.

Prepare For Landing: Your Final Destination

Deuteronomy 20:1
When you go to war against your enemies and see horses and chariots and an army greater than yours, do not be afraid of them, because the LORD your God, who brought you up out of Egypt, will be with you.

Deuteronomy 20:4
For the Lord your God is the one who goes with you to fight for you against your enemies to give you victory.

I do not say this to evoke fear in anyone for as a child of God, the same power is available to you as a believer. I would like to make clear that with this power comes immense responsibility. It cannot be wielded haphazardly, recklessly or irresponsibly. A 747 woman knows this innately. Furthermore you have repeatedly noticed swift consequences for those who have harmed or attempted to harm you. You may have experienced this several times in your life, but have been leery to mention it to others. You may have tried to talk yourself out of believing it to be true. Yet, if you are honest with yourself, you have noticed that those who have set out to harm you have been irreversibly hit or utterly destroyed to the point where you feel deeply and sincerely sorry for their suffering even though the person came after you! Simply put, God does not play about His children. He plays even less about those He has given a tremendous calling. He will ensure that they are available and ready for the appointed time, and woe to the person or thing that tries to block or stop it.

Isaiah 14:27 (NIV)
For the Lord Almighty has purposed, and who can thwart him? His hand is stretched out, and who can turn it back?

Job 42:1-2
Then Job replied to the LORD: "I know that you can do all things; no purpose of yours can be thwarted.

Nahum 1:9 (NIV)
Whatever they plot against the Lord he will bring to an end; trouble will not come a second time

HEALING ANOINTING

I am a healer. My mother, while not as spiritually zealous as I am, was a healer called to troubled adolescents, both male and female, women and the exiled. She was a brilliant, passionate educator, social worker, steward of social services , community activist and an incredibly effective manager having been awarded a Doctor of Laws, Honoris Causa, Honorary Degree from her almater Morgan State University before her passing. Yet she was a healer at her core. Like my mom and many healers I attract the wounded, broken, broken-hearted, abandoned, lost, confused, the lackluster or lukewarm Christian, the non-believer, etc. And many times I attract them during seasons when I need healing myself. Nonetheless, I pray and intercede. Most times I pray and fast for others more intensely than I do for myself.

James 5:16
Confess your faults one to another, and pray one for another, that ye may be healed

Ephesians 6:18
And pray in the Spirit on all occasions with all kinds of prayers and requests. With this in mind, be alert and always keep on praying for all the Lord's people.

1 Timothy 2:1
I exhort therefore, that, first of all, supplications, prayers, intercessions, and giving of thanks, be made for all men

2 Samuel 1:12
And they mourned, and wept, and fasted until even, for Saul, and for Jonathan his son, and for the people of the LORD, and for the house of Israel; because they were fallen by the sword

Esther 4:16

Go, gather together all the Jews that are present in Shushan, and fast ye for me, and neither eat nor drink three days, night or day: I also and my maidens will fast likewise; and so will I go in unto the king, which is not according to the law: and if I perish, I perish.

Many times I have taken on the burdens of others to such a degree that it has been to my own detriment—or at least that is how I initially perceived it. I now firmly believe that God does not forget about anyone who serves in such a way. Yet as 747 women, we can pour into others to the point of derailing our own assignments and destinies if we are not careful. We must be intentional and purposeful when engaging with others. We must remember that it is not our duty or responsibility to save them for that duty belongs solely to the Lord, and their destiny is known by the Lord. Yet, it is our responsibility to lead them to the Lord and to spark their desire to seek a relationship with the Lord. In addition, it is our responsibility to love them, encourage them, be authentic and honest, generous and kind, whilst interceding for them, demonstrating what is possible with God and attesting to His love for His children in all humility.

Galatians 6:2

Bear ye one another's burdens and so fulfill the law of Christ

Micah 6:8

He hath shewed thee, O man, what is good; and what doth the Lord require of thee, but to do justly, and to love mercy, and to walk humbly with thy God?

Psalm 138:8

The LORD will perfect that which concerneth me: thy mercy, O LORD, endureth for ever: forsake not the works of thine own hands

3 John 1:2

Beloved, I wish above all things that thou mayest prosper and be in health, even as thy soul prospereth.

Psalm 57:2
I cry out to God Most High to God who will fulfill his purpose for me.

Isaiah 43:11
I, even I, am the LORD; and beside me there is no savior.

Acts 4:12
Neither is there salvation in any other: for there is none other name under heaven given among men, whereby we must be saved

This is not to say everyone around me is wounded or could potentially put the fulfillment of my purpose at risk. That is not the case. Neither does it mean that those individuals that do come in my life for healing will always be in need of healing. I too, have been wounded and entered someone's life who assisted, or galvanized my healing and pointed me to the Lord and was then equipped to uplift someone else. Yet these kinds of relationships are typically not lifelong. I hate to be cliché but we have all heard the adage, "People enter your life for a reason, season or a lifetime." Usually the relationships that require the healing I speak of are assigned for a season. Yet I definitely have lifelong relationships with a very small group of women who know, love and serve the Lord. They are lifelong soul travelers of mine. They are individuals destined to travel with me from the cradle to the grave, or from whatever point we entered each other's lives until the Lord calls us home. They are carriers and beacons of light, walking testimonies of the grace and glory of the Lord. They are aware of and walking in their own callings. These women represent soul connections in my life that are irrevocable and irremovable. They have been blessed to be a blessing to me, or I have been blessed to be a blessing to them, or the exchange of blessings flow in a continual and reciprocal manner. Many times these women have entered my life as destiny helpers and burden bearers, and most often than not, they are also healers. The 747 woman can easily identify her soul connection relationships, and relationships assigned to her for a season to ultimately usher in that person's healing.

2 Timothy 2:2 (NIV)
And the things you have heard me say in the presence of many witnesses entrust to reliable people who will also be qualified to teach others

Acts 15:32-33
Judas and Silas, who themselves were prophets, said much to encourage and strengthen the believers. After spending some time there, they were sent off by the believers with the blessing of peace to return to those who had sent them.

Proverbs 18:24
A man that hath friends must shew himself friendly: and there is a friend that sticketh closer than a brother

Ephesians 5:7
For you were formerly darkness, but now you are Light in the Lord; walk as children of Light

As 747 women we are called to be healers because we can speak to the healing power of God. We may carry different anointings in terms of who we are assigned to and where we are assigned, but we are walking testaments of His healing power. Whether the Lord has healed us from toxic relationships—both romantic and platonic, financial ruin, disease, mental illness, unwarranted attack and smear campaigns, exile, betrayal, ridicule, rejection, reproach, violations—sexual, emotional, mental, physical, verbal, financial or spiritual, you know that you know that the Lord is Jehovah Raphe, The Healer. I have several testimonies that evidence the Lord's healing power in nearly every single aspect in which it exists. Many already know of my testimony of healing as far as my health and a doctor's prediction and preparation for me to accept a diagnosis of cancer. I disavowed every word he said in the name of Yeshua, the Christ—Yeshua the sacrificial lamb, and commenced a water-only fast for seven days. The doctor had to rescind his stance.

In 2010 I was told I had a growth in one of my breast. I was not fasting at that time, but poured my heart out to the Lord and asked for healing.

When I returned to the doctor's office I was informed that the growth was benign. Glory be to God! Furthermore, although I do not share it often, I am a survivor of many forms of abuse. I'll state that again. I am a survivor of MANY forms of abuse. And I would further assert that I have been healed and made whole. As per the Biblical Dictionary, Index and Concordance in The Holy Bible Authorized King James Version published by Bible House in Charlotte, North Carolina, "healed" or "healing" means to be made whole, cured, well from disease, a brokenheart and all manner of sickness. Whole is defined as possessing soundness. When I looked up soundness, it pointed to being healthy, received safe. Healthy is described as soundness of body and to have [hope] in one's countenance. Countenance is defined as the face, cheerful, like lightning. Lightning is defined as a flashing light. And safe as being secure, or free from harm. I am going to take some liberty here and state that when I state I have been healed and made whole I am asserting I am cured, healthy, secure from harm and my aura shines bright—radiantly reflecting the Lord who is my light and my salvation.

Matthew 9:22
"But Jesus turned him about, and when he saw her, he said, Daughter, be of good comfort; thy faith hath made thee whole. And the woman was made whole from that hour."

Matthew 14:36
"And besought him that they might only touch the hem of his garment; and as many as touched were made perfectly whole."

Luke 8:48
"And he said unto her, Daughter, be of good comfort: thy faith hath made thee whole; go in peace."

Psalm 27:
The Lord is my light and my salvation; Whom shall I fear? The Lord is the defense of my life; Whom shall I dread?

I am indeed healed and I am whole. I am also what many would call an orphan as both of my parents have passed on. I do not state any of it to be pitied. I state it to say that without a father, mother, husband, or much family, I rely on the Lord wholeheartedly. Do not misunderstand me, for I am blessed and highly favored no matter the current state of my life. I share my testimony because I can powerfully and unwaveringly speak of God's miraculous, healing grace because I have had to depend on Him more than most, and He has shown up for me repeatedly and consistently.

John 14:18
I will not leave you as orphans, I will come to you

Job 29:12
Because I delivered the poor that cried, and the fatherless, and *him that had* none to help him.

2 Kings 20:5
Turn again, and tell Hezekiah the captain of my people, Thus saith the LORD, the God of David thy father, I have heard thy prayer, I have seen thy tears: behold, I will heal thee:

Psalm 91:15
He shall call upon me, and I will answer him: I will be with him in trouble; I will deliver him, and honour him.

Luke 8:39
No, go back to your family, and tell them everything God has done for you." So he went all through the town proclaiming the great things Jesus had done for him.

Today I am completely aware of and standing in the healing anointing I carry. One of the ways my healing anointing has shown up in the past is through my words. I do my best to use my words to uplift, encourage and inspire faith and keep others' issues, concerns and mountains in confidence as they prayerfully war to obliterate them.

1 Thessalonians 5:11 (NLT)
So encourage each other and build each other up, just as you are already doing.

Ephesians 4:29
Don't use foul or abusive language. Let everything you say be good and helpful, so that your words will be an encouragement to those who hear them

Another way the Healing Anointing manifests in my life is through intercession. I am often led to pray for others due to approaching spiritual danger or physical trouble for which I have been given no material evidence, disease or loss. The Holy Spirit will even lead me to pray for strangers. I may come across a story about several people that are experiencing some sort of affliction, but there is always one or two the Holy Spirit places on my heart to intercede for specifically as if the burden was my own. By that I mean, I am led to pray as if it is my own ailment, mountain or attack and then ask Yeshua to remove it.

The other day I heard someone say that when it comes to others, God hears their prayers, but He *answers* yours. I suppose that is why I am led to pray for certain people who at times are facing insurmountable odds. I am not saying that God does not assist them, or answer them. I am not saying that they specifically need me as God has armies of believers He can call upon. I have considered that it could be my proximity to them or someone they know, or in the case of total strangers, it may be that my specific anointing covers that specific ailment. I am not certain. Although more than anything I believe that it is possible that they do not have the level of faith required to accomplish the petition for which they are seeking assistance so God uses the anointed and extreme believer to stand in the gap and pray on their behalf.

Prepare For Landing: Your Final Destination

Romans 15:30
Now I beseech you, brethren, for the Lord Jesus Christ's sake, and for the love of the Spirit, that ye strive together with me in your prayers to God for me

James 15;5
And the prayer of faith shall save the sick, and the Lord shall raise him up; and if he have committed sins, they shall be forgiven him

Ezekiel 22:30
I looked for someone who might rebuild the wall of righteousness that guards the land. I searched for someone to stand in the gap in the wall so I wouldn't have to destroy the land, but I found no one.

I would like to close by stating that the Healing Anointing I carry has intensified in potency as I have grown in faith and awareness of my identity. I am now comfortable with laying hands on myself and my daughter whenever I feel the need arises—be it a headache, cramp or even stumped toe. I will reach for my anointed oil and cast out whatever it is—pain, discomfort or ailment. I do not reject traditional medicine, nor do I avoid going to the doctor. That would be just plain foolish. Yet I do know that healing power is available to me.

Isaiah 53:5
But he was wounded for our transgressions, he was bruised for our iniquities: the chastisement of our peace was upon him; and with his stripes we are healed.

Psalm 103:2-3
Bless the LORD, O my soul, and forget not all his benefits: Who forgiveth all thine iniquities; who healeth all thy diseases;

Jeremiah 17:14
Heal me, O LORD, and I shall be healed; save me, and I shall be saved: for thou art my praise.

James 5:14-15
Is any sick among you? Let him call for the elders of the church; and let them pray over him, anointing him with oil in the name of the Lord: And the prayer of faith shall save the sick, and the Lord shall raise him up; and if he have committed sins, they shall be forgiven him.

I am certain that many will state those instances of healing are small and inconsequential. They may be right. Yet I believe as we grow in spirit and in faith, we grow in boldness and in power. Initially, I had to muster the small amount of faith to heal myself and my daughter. Each time the pain or ailment dissipated; my faith strengthened. So when the Holy Spirit led me to reach for my anointed oil and anoint the head of an individual fighting addiction, I did—without hesitation. And when the individual checked themselves into a rehabilitation center that very same evening, after vacillating for weeks, I knew it was by the healing power of the Holy Spirit. Just as I know when I laid hands on a stranger in the street I saw suffering from back pain, she too was healed. I did not take her information to check on her. I just know she was as the Holy Spirit led me to jump out of my car to lay hands on her. Yes, I did exactly that. And yes, she was both happy and excited that I did. I cannot wait until I see her again, either on this side or the next. Now if you were to ask me if I foresee myself laying hands on sickly believers and then thrusting them to the ground as many of the televangelists do, I would answer that I certainly do not. However, if I perceive the power of the Holy Spirit moving and feel the supernatural unction to lay hands on someone, I will obey the call to do so.

Acts 28:8
And it came to pass, that the father of Publius lay sick of a fever and of a bloody flux: to whom Paul entered in, and prayed, and laid his hands on him, and healed him.

1 Timothy 5:22
Lay hands suddenly on no man

Mark 16:17-18

And these signs shall follow them that believe; In my name shall they cast out devils; they shall speak with new tongues; They shall take up serpents; and if they drink any deadly thing, it shall not hurt them; they shall lay hands on the sick, and they shall recover.

THE EAGLE AND THE LIONNESS ANOINTINGS

As denoted in a previous section where animals were utilized by the Holy Spirit to identify and understand surrounding demonic influences, the following anointings are explained utilizing two specific animals to demonstrate the supernatural characteristics of the 747 Anointing—both of which are used extensively in the bible to demonstrate the supernatural. The anointings I will cite in the next sections are not unfamiliar to the seasoned Christian. Both the eagle and Lion/Lionness anointings are not new concepts. However, I have been tasked with elaborating on our current understanding of these anointings as they relate to the 747 Anointing.

For new believers reading this book who are not accustomed to the use of animals to define the supernatural, do not be alarmed or find it strange. As I stated previously, Jesus our Lord and Savior is referred to as the Lamb of God (John 1:29), the Lion of the tribe of Judah (Revelation 5:5) and is our Divine Scapegoat (Leviticus 16). Time and time again, Jesus refers to believers as his flock—his sheep. The parable of the sheep and the goats is yet another example of Jesus using animals or an earthly understanding to illustrate spiritual truths. Further, Jesus utilizes animal metaphors to prepare his disciples for their missions and as a way to highlight the walk of the believer and the potential perils that can befall them.

Matthew 10:16

"Behold, I send you forth as sheep in the midst of wolves: be ye therefore wise as serpents, and harmless as doves."

As such, I have listed the revelations received from the Holy Spirit regarding the Eagle and Lioness Anointings as they relate to the 747 Woman.

THE EAGLE ANOINTING

The eagle is referenced many times in the bible and there are many favored scriptures referencing the majestic bird. Many of you are acquainted with the concept of the eagle anointing, therefore, its attributes and the power it encompasses may not be new. However, for the reader who may not be, I am utilizing a work by Dr. James Akanbi to introduce you to, or familiarize you with the idea.

Dr. James Akanbi, in his book entitled, "The Anointed Eagle," states that the eagle anointing ensures "extraordinary exploits result." He further states that the specific anointing, "takes one out of [his/her] natural elemental operation to supernatural exploits…The anointing takes you out of what you can only naturally do into what's possible with divine ability."

Dr. Akanbi asserts, decrees and declares that this anointing encompasses the following attributes:

1. <u>Anointed Vision</u> – "As my God lives, your benefits and blessings shall no longer hide from you. You will see opportunities before others see them. God will make your provision to be bare before you, without any camouflage. Nothing shall cover your blessing, you will see it clearly. (Job 39:27-29)
2. <u>Above and Beyond Hazards</u> – "As my God lives, your life shall be above and beyond the hazards of life. You will be beyond the reach of demonic serpents and scorpions of life (Luke 10:19). He further decrees, "You will be a stranger to the experiences of low places of life. I command your life to jump out of valley of life; you will be in very high places and sit with nobles at high tables of life. Every move of the enemy to make your life to be subject to oppression of low places shall be aborted. You are an eagle-

believer, and your life shall correspond with scripture (Deuteronomy 28:13)

3. <u>Super Fresh Provision</u> – "You are expected to magnetize provision and attract supplies. So shall it be for you in life." (Philippians 4:13, Psalm 37:19)

4. <u>The Speedmaster</u> – "Right from now, you will no longer use [the] human calendar to achieve; the divine calendar shall be available to you. You will manifestly experience the supernatural speed of an eagle. Favour of one month shall cancel labour of many years. You will have the speed to achieve in one year what will take many more than 20 years to accomplish. God shall impart the eagle's dimension of speed into your life affairs. He further declares "Your life and affairs shall be beyond the reach of the enemy. Nothing shall by any means stop your progress; problems of life shall not compete favourably against you. You will always have an edge against troubles. Your way shall be a mystery from now on. Your speed of achievement shall be a mystery. No one shall be able to explain your way, it shall be supernaturally crafted." (Proverbs 30:19)

5. <u>Eagle's Fortified and Insulated Accommodation</u> – "As from today, they that hunt for you shall become victims of empty pursuit. They shall seek for you but shall not find you…From henceforth, you will become invisible in the radar of your enemy…The heaven shall jam the satanic internet of the enemy that is browsing for information about you. When they browse your name, your life data shall not show up. (Isaiah 43:2, Isaiah 54:17)

6. <u>Fidelity Teacher</u> – "Eagle tests before trust…the female eagle wants to be sure the male eagle will be a good father that will bear the eaglets on its wings (Deuteronomy 32:11) Eagle teaches fidelity, faithfulness and loyalty. Eagle tests before it will trust, God also tests his people before He trusts them and before He

eventually thrusts them into greatness. (Timothy 2:12, 2 Timothy 2:21, Job 23:10)
7. <u>Renewal and Restoration Expert</u> – Eagle is an expert when it comes to healing and renewal…Retreat must be a regular habit for an eagle-believer' we must know how to retire into [the] secret place of the Most High to pick His power for our goings…Beloved , you must live your life as someone with the understanding that you can't do things by your power or by your might except by the spirit of the Lord…Go to God daily for fresh outpouring of His spirit for you to be an overcomer in the contest of life. Be an eagle-believer; be smart to meet God regularly for His strength. (Isaiah 40:31, Zechariah 4:6, Proverbs 3:5-6)

Additional Eagle impartations Dr. James Akanbi asserts as part of the Eagle Anointing:

1. <u>Courage</u> – "We become bold…Eagle confronts predators by attack not by defence." (2 Timothy 1:17)
2. <u>Strength</u> – "Eagle has the capacity to carry a load that is double its own size." (John 10:10) [Isaiah 40:31]
3. <u>Powerful Mouth</u> – "Eagle's mouth is designed to 'rip and tear'…Almost nothing in the animal kingdom is beyond the powerful beak of an eagle. You are armed with a similar or more powerful mouth." (Isaiah 41:15-16)
4. <u>Slippery Blessings and Miracles</u> – "Eagles have something more than feet to grip their prey; they have what is known as Talons. The talons grip prey effectively; prey gripped with eagle's talons has no chance of escape. The talons are not just to grip, but also divinely fitted to carry eagle's prey. So the talons are in essence to grip and carry. The talons are known to be four times stronger than the strength of human hand and grip…Whatever you get from God is expected to be a permanent miracle and blessing. (John 15:16) He then decrees, "Your miracle shall no longer slip off your hands. You will experience abiding and permanent

miracles, your supernatural 'talons shall 'grip and carry' your blessings to your home and life."

5. <u>We Are Fitted with Divine Intelligence</u>: - "Eagles are one of the most intelligent among the birds in the world. They reason very close to humans...You are imbued with supernatural intuition as an eagle believer. You have all means of supernatural intelligence with the Spirit of God. The Spirit of God is the intelligence of God. When you get the Spirit inside of you, the intelligence of God is available to you." (2 Timothy 1:7)

6. <u>We Are Too Big For A Cage</u> – "You cannot cage an eagle! Or let me put it this way, Eagle is not meant to be caged. Eagle is divinely 'constructed' to be on the sky. Eagle is not a chicken to be roosted in a cage...There is a divine instinct in an eagle that is to fly, to soar and to mount up and up." (Isaiah 40:31) Dr. Akanbi argues, "You cannot be caged as well, embargo cannot work on your destiny, and limitation shall fail around you.'"

7. <u>The Devil Cannot Match Us</u> – "The enemy cannot match us on our territory...We are [in] heavenly places [with] Christ. Even right from our location here on earth we are expected to live in the heavenly places through heavenly power and practices [Ephesians 2:4-9] "We are supposed to always drag the devil to our own territory, he cannot survive there. When we speak in tongues, the devil is confused. When [we] kneel down to pray the devil is on his heels running. When we knock by faith, fear and trouble flee through the windows. When we stand in righteousness, the enemy losses ground to fight against us.

8. <u>Let Us Go Afishing</u> – "...Eagle is a great fishing machine. The eagle always has a river in its territory. Most eagles feed on fresh fish...Eagle [have] a strong vision capacity to see beneath water and the fish it aims to catch...It will wait for all the time it takes till it has a vantage position to make a catch. Fish is part of the daily diet of eagle. Eagle fishes with dexterity. Eagle [believers] must agree with Jesus. "And he saith unto them, Follow me, and

I will make you fishers of men." (Matthew 4:19) "Therefore go and make disciples of all nations, baptizing them in the name of the Father, and of the Son, and of the Holy Spirit." (Matthew 28:19)

THE EAGLE ANOINTING: A CLOSER LOOK
EAGLE-EYED VISION

Just as Dr. Akanbi asserts and many other Christian scribes, leaders and servants, the eagle has remarkably sharp vision. It is said that golden eagles have a clear eyelid that protects their eyes from dust and dirt. Traditionally, those that have studied the eagle anointing undoubtedly list the gift of sight as an anchoring component of this anointing and it is. However, I would take the understanding of the gift of sight from the eagle anointing even further by focusing our attention on the eagle's ability to turn its head 270 degrees. Although this certainly allows for a wider range of panoramic vision, this rotating feat is mainly due to the fact that their forward-facing eyes have limited mobility in the eye socket.

This fact is particularly significant for the 747 woman as it speaks to her uncanny ability to uniquely view and then assimilate information and patterns past, present and future for herself and others while holding fast to the vision - or better yet, while facing forward. As she assesses the aspects of a current situation that may be emotionally, mentally, financially or spiritually debilitating, she remains in motion and is committed to forward movement and advancement. She can look to the past introspectively for perspective and to glean the lesson, but she does not glare at the past, get bogged down by it, nor does she take residence in past situations or relationships. This characteristic allows her to walk and chew gum at the same time while holding steadfast to the vision and goal ahead. It is another component of the 747 anointing that keeps the 747 woman from getting stuck. A quick example would include my current financial standing; although I am currently working three jobs, and doing my best to abscond from the grips of debt and near poverty, I am receiving mentoring and tutelage from many that are earning hundreds of thousands yearly, and many are millionaires. I do not have much time to feel sorry for myself or my situation. If I stop to pity myself, I will miss the call, coaching session, conference and/or opportunity I have been asked to attend or in which to participate.

Accordingly, this vision anointing and head swiveling attribute allows her to see what others do not see, and eventually sharpens into a skill that allows for the proper identification and avoidance of ill-intentioned, disingenuous, predatory people and/or situations. The 747 woman has eyes behind her head in the truest sense. The 747 woman sees and hears what others do not see or hear. She sees the faces after snide remarks, perceives the intention behind actions meant to look innocent but have a more sinister goal. She perceives when conversations that should be between her and another surreptitiously include another listener or when those with whom she is in contact recruit others to see and watch what they will hope will soon be her fall or embarrassment. Others may not be able to perceive such violations and believe the 747 woman is ultra-sensitive or paranoid. Yet she is one hundred percent accurate in her perception. If it is perceived, then the Holy Spirit has revealed it and she must take action by distancing and/or removing herself. She must ensure her circle is not negatively infiltrated or contaminated solely because her purpose cannot be sabotaged or derailed. Our greatest teacher and Savior, Yeshua the Christ, demonstrated his keen perception, spoke of the failure of his followers during his time on earth to utilize it, and allowed the scripture to illustrate its effective use in many believers.

Luke 8:46
And Jesus said, somebody hath touched me: for I perceive that virtue is gone out of me

Mark 8:17-18
And when Jesus knew it, he saith unto them, Why reason ye, because ye have no bread? Perceive ye not yet, neither understand? Have ye your heart yet hardened?

John 4:19
The woman saith unto Him, Sir, I perceive that thou art a prophet

2 Kings 4:9
And she said unto her husband, Behold now, I perceive that this is an holy man of God, which passeth by us continually.

Philippians 1:9-11
And this is my prayer: that your love may abound more and more in knowledge and depth of insight, so that you may be able to discern what is best and may be pure and blameless for the day of 'Christ, filled with the fruit of righteousness that comes through Jesus Christ—to the glory and praise of God.

1 John 4:1
Beloved, do not believe every spirit, but test the spirits to see whether they are from God, for many false prophets have gone out into the world

Matthew 10:16
...be ye therefore wise as serpents, and harmless as doves

THE FIGHT IS NOT FAIR

Many believers, including Dr. Akanbi, cite the eagle's ability to swoop down on its enemies and take them to territory where they cannot function or gain their equilibrium and suggests we as carriers of the eagle anointing are empowered to do the same. This is true. I would like to reiterate that when trouble and opposition arise, as 747 women we are called to do just as our name suggests. As Planes will fly to a higher altitude to avoid, or soar above turbulence, accordingly, the 747 woman flies high above drama and disengages from direct confrontation with her enemies when pressed.

Revelation 12:14
And to the woman were given two wings of a great eagle, that she might fly into the wilderness, into her place, where she is nourished for a time, and times, and half a time, from the face of the serpent.

When my mother was alive she would always say, "Nonye, take the high road!" And I would—sometimes. You would think that I would uphold her memory by always taking the high road now that she has passed, but that could not be further from the truth. I have had many moments of getting down in the muck and mire—and it would always be to my own detriment. If not ending in a complete and total debacle (thanks be to God that it never has) I would feel guilty about my decision to react, embarrassing both myself and my upbringing. Today I do my best to demonstrate the 747 Anointing in which I walk. Eagles are not unlike planes in their ability to avoid danger via ascension. Certain species of eagles can fly to an altitude of between 10,000 to 20,000 feet above sea level. Correspondingly, eagles will snatch their opponents from their habitats or the ground, and take them to an altitude where they cannot survive or even breathe. When pondering this, I like to bring to mind my favorite Michelle Obama quotable, "When they go low, we go high!" As such, the 747 woman has learned not to engage the enemy at their low level of vibration or immaturity. That is the enemy's territory and comfort zone—mudslinging, character besmirching, slander, gossip, physical threats, and the like. It is best for the 747 woman to rise to an altitude to which their enemy is ill-equipped spiritually, intellectually or emotionally to ascend to.

Proverbs 20:3
It is to one's honor to avoid strife, but every fool is quick to quarrel.

Proverbs 19:11 (NIV)
A person's wisdom yields patience; it is to one's glory to overlook an offense.

Galatians 5:22-23
But the fruit of the Spirit is love, joy, peace, longsuffering, gentleness, goodness, faith, Meekness, temperance: against such there is no law

Colossians 4:6

Let your speech be always with grace, seasoned with salt, that ye may know how ye ought to answer every man

TO THE VICTOR BELONG THE SPOILS

Another eagle characteristic that must be included is that bald eagles can be kleptoparasitic. Kleptoparasitic is a word derived from the word kleptomaniac which brings to most of our minds a negative depiction of a person with a serious pilfering habit. Yet in this sense, kleptoparasitic refers to the means by which the eagle will supplement its food intake with food they procure or pilfer from other birds. The 747 anointing is not suggesting that we are thieves in any way, but it does point to a promise in the bible that states his promise to allow His children—His servants to take, keep and benefit from the possessions of non-believers. This blessing is inherent in the Eagle anointing.

Isaiah 61:6

But you shall be named the priests of the LORD, They shall call you the servants of our God. You shall eat the riches of the Gentiles, And in their glory you shall boast.

Psalms 105:44 (NLT)

He gave his people the lands of pagan nations, and they harvested crops that others had planted

Judges 6:9

And I delivered you out of the hand of the Egyptians and out of the hand of all that oppressed you, and drave them out from before you, and gave you their land

Deuteronomy 6:10-12

When the LORD your God brings you into the land he swore to your fathers, to Abraham, Isaac and Jacob, to give you—a land with large, flourishing cities you did not build, houses filled with all kinds of good things you did not provide, wells you did not dig, and vineyards and olive groves you did not plant—then when you eat and are satisfied, be careful that you do not forget the LORD, who brought you out of Egypt, out of the land of slavery

THE LION ANOINTING

Quite like the eagle, the lion is referenced many times throughout the bible. The ferocious feline is used to convey power, protection, strength, merciless fierceness, and triumph in battle. You may be most familiar with its use in the bible as one of the personifications of the strength, valor and royalty of our Lord and Savior, Yeshua the Christ, by his crowning in Revelation 5:5 as the Lion of the Tribe of Judah. It is also used often as a warning to the believer to remain sober and vigilant watching for our enemy who, "as a roaring lion, walketh about, seeking whom he may devour" (1 Peter 5:8).

Yet, the Lion Anointing may not be as known. I do not believe it is as common in Christian circles as the Eagle Anointing. Yet, in Kindra Warner's *Embracing The Lion's Anointing*, she denotes the way it manifests in the life of the believer. Her book embodies components of the anointing and ways in which the lion's behaviors and instincts can serve as a blueprint for the Christian with this anointing. In the following section, I will share Warner's revelation about the anointing. I will end the section with a closer look at the Lion anointing as well as the behaviors and instincts of the animal, particularly, the lioness, and how they correspond to the 747 woman and her anointing.

Kindra Warner asserts that the Lion's Anointing includes:

1. <u>The Lion's Roar</u> – "…lions have the loudest roar of any cat. It's possible to hear one five miles away…God created you and me to have the loudest roar. We are created to demand attention of our Heavenly Father. We are created to be light in this world. We are created to be a voice to those who are too scared or weak to speak. There are many injustices going on in our own backyard. How do you know which one to roar at? Let God be your guide…The lion will roar to let others know the boundaries of

his territory and no enemy can trespass…it's the roar of the lion which acts as the first line of defense for his family." "The king's fury is like that of a roaring lion; to rouse his anger is to risk your life," Proverbs 20:2 (NLT)

2. <u>The Lion's Lens</u> – "Lions have special lenses in their eyes that absorb light and then reflect it. This causes them to have excellent vision in the dark. All it takes is a light source: the moon, stars, or even one star shining in the night. The light passes through their retina and reflects back through reflective cells in the back of their eyes (2 Corinthians 4:6 (NLT)…It's during our seasons of abundant light [when] we can do the most damage in the darkness. It's because you learned to see and reflect God's light on the one star nights that you get the full moons. To see the full moons, you have to worship God through your praise, pray, study His word, and speak God's Word into your darkness. Use your past times of darkness as motivation to speak light into other's lives. We can look out for others and warn them of dangers we see lurking."

3. <u>The Structure of the Pride</u> – "The male lion is the authority, protection and covering of the pride. As long as the lionesses and cubs don't' wander off, they will be under his protection [1 Kings 10:20]…While the primary job of a lion is protection, the primary job of the lioness is hunting and rearing the young…"

In the structure of the family, the older lioness will initiate the hunt with less experienced lionesses by her side. The older lionesses will teach the younger how to hunt… (Titus 2:4-5 (NLT)…We know that we are to train and teach our own children. Now, reach outside those borders and help teach and train someone else's children. Along the way, continue and remember your own training. Be the lioness that refused to give up on the younger one."

In addition, Warner contends that this anointing extends to the children as they are afforded protection by the anointing. "…lion cubs are born into a kingdom protected by a powerful family. Because they are born into their father's kingdom, they have rights to the kingdom and all it offers."

1. <u>The Lion's Destiny</u> – "…Lions go from being provided for and nurtured to having to fend [for] and protect themselves. The season for the lion changes…lions may spend several years as a nomad before finding and establishing their own pride. Yet without this time of being a nomad, the lion will never find his future pride. In order to fulfill the purpose he was created for, he has to do some work and some searching [Deuteronomy 2:3]
2. <u>Battle</u> – "…a lion generally has a major battle before he takes over a pride. Lions are designed for battles, and so are you and I. [For thus hath the LORD spoken unto me, Like as the lion and the young lion roaring on his prey, when a multitude of shepherds is called forth against him, he will not be afraid of their voice, nor abase himself for the noise of them: so shall the LORD of hosts come down to fight for mount Zion, and for the hill thereof. Isaiah 31:4]
3. <u>The Lion's Biggest Enemy</u>: "We cannot talk about battle without addressing our enemy. It didn't take long in studying lions before I was introduced to one of their biggest enemies. The thing that I found fascinating was their biggest enemy is a hyena. You see, "Hyenas have an inherent drive to kill its competitors"[1] Dear brothers and sisters in Christ, we are Satan's biggest competitors…Satan will try to take us out as early as possible. Even in the battle of lions and hyenas, hyenas do their best to kill lion cubs. If the hyena can get to the lion cub and kill it, this helps eliminate competition before the lion gets too big and strong to easily destroy." [1 Peter 5:8]
4. <u>Seasons</u> – "Seasonal transitions bring about changes. During the dry season, food is scarce. Just like when the season changes to a dry one in Africa and lions have to become more focused on what they eat, so must we. During the seasons of drought in our

life, we must be focused on the Word of God that we are taking in…" During seasons of rest, Warner asserts, "Some lions were just too exhausted to continue the hunt. They laid down to rest. Others from the pride continued the hunt into the daylight. It's important to note that the lions resting in the sun were not doing anything wrong…We can become judgmental when we see someone that is legitimately resting. Oftentimes we don't know what they have just come out of. Perhaps God has placed them in a season of rest. Many times when you are getting ready to give birth to something, God moves you to a place of rest. He keeps you to Himself for a brief period so that he can equip and speak to you."

Kindra Warner states that another season included in the Lion's Anointing is that of giving birth. She contends, "Just like the lioness giving birth alone, we oftentimes will give birth to our destiny in solitude. We need to nurture and grow our Godly dreams. This may mean researching, studying our Bible, and reading books written by those who are wise and have further insight. Like the lioness, you and I must take precaution and guard our new births from others until the time is right."

5. The Enemies Venom – "There are times we can take such a beating in our lives that the enemy's venom is slowly paralyzing us and causing us to not see clearly…How often we get attacked along with our dream. All too often our vision becomes impaired. But like the lioness, we just need to get to the living water! We need to get to our Heavenly Father and lay at his feet. We need to be refreshed and restored. We don't always see the immediate manifestation of this and I believe this is where many of us begin to give up the fight. It's important to remember that, like the lioness, sometimes the venom has been injected into our lives and it just has to run its course."

6. <u>Protection of Cubs</u> – "It is imperative that we train and teach our children in our home and scatter our love and knowledge to them...For us to embrace the lion's anointing for ourselves we must have our family life in order. We must submit ourselves to God and his authority." [Proverbs 22:6]

THE LIONESS ANOINTING: A CLOSER LOOK
THE LION'S ROAR

I believe Kindra Warner presents the importance of our ability to roar as Christians superbly. I would like to add though as 747 women, it is a very effective warring tactic against our enemies. When the 747 woman stands in faith and roars, the earth trembles, atmospheres shift, our enemies disassemble, head for cover and hope not to be run down. We are made in the image of our Lord and our roar is not unlike His!

Genesis 1:27
And God said, Let us make man in our image, after our likeness

Amos 3:8
The lion hath roared, who will not fear?

Isaiah 5:29
Their roaring shall be like a lion, they shall roar like young lions: yea, they shall roar, and lay hold of the prey, and shall carry it away safe, and none shall deliver it.

THE STRUCTURE OF THE PRIDE

Kindra Warner does an excellent job of illustrating the structure of the lion pride. I would like to take the role of the lioness a bit further by denoting how it manifests for the 747 woman. The lioness is the hunter for the pride and primarily responsible for the gathering of food. As such, the lioness anointing reflects the 747 woman's strong influence and involvement in ensuring her family's spiritual sustenance. You are the primary provider of the spiritual meals for those who are under your care, whether we are speaking of your husband, children, siblings, cousins, nieces, nephews, etc. When the family is in trouble, when there is a crisis and someone needs prayer, you are the one they are requesting to answer the main line. This is not to state that these family members are not actively walking with God, but it is to state that they understand you are the driving spiritual force in your family unit. You provide the meat their soul needs at critical times. Whether you are asking them to stand with you in agreement for an answer to a desired prayer or entering in a fast, you are their go-to prayer warrior.

John 4:34
"My food," said Jesus, "is to do the will of Him who sent me and to finish His work."

John 6:51
I am the living bread which came down from heaven: if any man eat of this bread, he shall live for ever: and the bread that I will give is my flesh which I will give for the life of the world

John 6:35
And Jesus said unto them, I am the bread of life: he that cometh to me shall never hunger; and he that believeth on me shall never thirst

Luke 22:19
And he took bread, and gave thanks, and brake it, and gave unto them, saying, This is my body which is given for you: this do in remembrance of me. Likewise He also took the cup after supper, saying, "This cup is the new covenant in My blood, which is shed for you."

Matthew 4:4
But he answered and said, it is written, Man shall not live by bread alone but by every word that proceedeth out of the mouth of God

I would like to make clear that I am not suggesting there are not Godly men in your home. Nor am I suggesting that men are not called to be the spiritual leaders in their home. Yet, when considering the 747 woman and her life's current season, she is the spiritual leader in her family and home.

In this same manner, I believe that as the lioness are the hunters of the pride, they are the front line and foremost brigade for spiritual battle. Kindra Warner asserts that the male lion defends the home base and kingdom territory. As such, I believe it is the lioness that tracks and launches attacks on the enemy. Accordingly, the 747 woman will not wait for spiritual attack. She does not wait to see what the enemy will do. She is acutely aware of her spiritual surroundings and knows when she, her loved ones or her mission is in danger. When she senses danger, perceives an intruder is lurking or an enemy is planning an attack, she will always launch a preemptive strike. When the bible references the lions sent to fight for the Lord, I believe it is speaking of an elite battalion of lionesses.

2 Kings 17:26 (NLT)
So a message was sent to the king of Assyria: "The people you have sent to live in the towns of Samaria do not know the religious customs of the God of the land. He has sent lions among them to destroy them because they have not worshipped him correctly."

Numbers 23:24 (NLT)
These people rise up like a lioness, like a majestic lion rousing itself. They refuse to rest until they have feasted on prey, drinking the blood of the slaughtered!"

Proverbs 30:30
A lion which is strongest among beasts, and turneth not away for any

Proverbs 28:1
The wicked flee though no one pursues, but the righteous are as bold as a lion

Upon delving deeper into the unique nature of prides and of the lioness, I discovered that prides are primarily matriarchal, and that lionesses build and operate in highly effective teams. For the 747 woman, this shows up in your life as the very small group of girlfriends—no more than two to three, with whom you have forged a secret, but highly impactful, spiritual combat unit. This is not to be confused with a church sponsored bible study group. Instead it is a unit, that organically forms over time between a small group of lionesses. They may not see each other or even talk to each other very often, yet the group exists for one common goal—to intercede and war in the spiritual realm against powers and principalities for loved ones and strangers alike in need of healing, repentance, financial breakthrough, forgiveness and whatever else that once defeated would serve as a victory for the kingdom and point more people to the Lord.

Matthew 18:20
For where two or three are gathered together in my name, there am I in the midst of them

Matthew 18:19
Again I say unto you, that if two of you shall agree on earth as touching a thing that they shall ask, it shall be done for them of my Father which is in heaven

Ecclesiastes 4:12 (NIV)
Though one may be overpowered, two can defend themselves. A cord of three strands is not quickly broken

THE LION'S DESTINY

I want to make clear the correlation between what Warner asserts is a lion's nomad stage and the long wilderness season I sojourned for several years as well as most 747 women. I do believe it points to the same season and component of the 747 anointing, and firmly believe that without it you will not arrive at your destiny or experience the full breadth of your anointing. It is a season of testing, faith-building, sanctification, preparation and God's provision. And just as Warner suggests the nomad phase is essential to the young lion's arrival to be the head of his own pride so the wilderness is a very necessary part of the 747 woman's journey and eventual arrival to her prophetic Goshen.

Jeremiah 31:12
How long will you go here and there, O faithless daughter? For the Lord has created a new thing in the earth

Psalm 107:4
They wandered in the wilderness in a desert region; they did not find a way to an inhabited city

Deuteronomy 2:7
For the Lord your God has blessed you in all that you have done; He has known your wanderings through the great wilderness. These forty years the Lord your God has been with you; you have not lacked a thing

Deuteronomy 32:10 (NKJV)
He found him in a desert land And in the wasteland, a howling wilderness; He encircled him, He instructed him, He kept him as the apple of His eye

THE BATTLE, THE ENEMY AND ITS VENOM

I want to bring your attention to these three components Kindra Warner mentioned as part of the Lioness anointing as they speak directly to what I have mentioned as part of the events that take place prior to the 747 woman's unveiling and promotion. I would also like to add that I had already started outlining and writing this book, and the Lioness anointing had already been imparted to me as part of the larger 747 Anointing's framework before I came across and purchased *Embracing the Lion's Anointing*. Yet Warner's inclusion of these components in her book serve as further confirmation for me that the Lioness anointing and the incidents the 747 woman experiences prior to full activation of her anointing is spiritually accurate and exactly what I was supposed to share.

In the previous sections entitled *Battle in The Spiritual Realm* and *Winning the Final Showdown against Your Enemy to Advance to Your Promise,* I present the notion that there are battles you must fight and win in order to advance into your anointing. Warner too asserts the idea of battles that those with the lion anointing must engage in order to be fully positioned in the anointing. David serves as a great biblical example of the battles that must be waged and won prior to the release of the anointing, but we tend to only think of his early battle with Goliath. However, David was a mighty warrior and fought many battles after his fight with Goliath. And prior to being named King over all of Israel, there was another that had been named king of Israel—Saul's son Ish-Bosheth. Just as I enumerated my experience with a counterfeit, and noted it as a very real experience for the 747 woman, David too had an experience with a counterfeit who was put in position to reign over Israel after Saul's death. Yet David, who was anointed by God would emerge as the true king just as you and I are the true followers of Christ, worshipping him in Spirit and Truth. As part of the battle experience, God will ensure that time reveals who is a counterfeit and who is not.

Correspondingly, God will reveal our enemies. If you recall, I drew attention to the many enemies the 747 woman faces during this time—one of which is the hyena. I introduced the spirit of the hyena as an enemy of God, a primary foe of a prophet and a supreme narcissist. Kindra Warner takes the characteristics of the hyena even further and although she does not make the correlation, the animal's characteristics are eerily akin to that of a narcissist. For example, Warner points out that the Kenyan Maasia tribe call hyenas 'doctors' because a of their unique ability to recognize the sick and weak amongst the livestock. It is experience that tells the hyena what animals to isolate..." Just as narcissists and Satan, "look for those who have moved beyond the confines of their protective 'pack' of other brothers and sisters in Christ." I am not stating any of you were wounded or sick before entering your battle season as you may find the use of those words offensive. Yet I am stating that you may have been in a season where you were healing or nursing wounds. Upon entering the relationship I referenced, I was still healing from the loss of my mother. It was a time during which I was emotionally fragile, extremely vulnerable and yearning for familial connection. As you continue your journey as a 747 woman, it is important to be acutely aware of the season you are in, and of all of the spirits I highlighted. Be especially alert around the hyena spirit as they are in direct opposition of your lioness anointing—and will be detrimental to your calling if given the chance.

Prepare For Landing: Your Final Destination

Another warning from Warner includes her identification of a secondary enemy. She shares that the hyena works along with the vulture to identify unwitting victims. The vulture spots the sick and wounded and encircle their location, which gives the hyena the drop on the location of their next meal. And once the hyenas are done feasting, the vultures -who desire the leftovers, particularly the dead animal's bones as they provide nutrients for their eggs- are able to feed. As such, the relationship is one of reciprocity. They work in tandem to eat.

Although the vulture was not an animal I identified, I would like to state that their behavior is akin to the flying monkeys the narcissist tends to recruit to cause instability, chaos and fear in their victim/the believer. Although flying monkeys typically do not signal a narcissist to a potential victim, once the victim is pointed out by the narcissist, the vultures come running to see or feed off the show which they believe will eventually involve the victim's (or in our case, the believer's) demise. That too is a reciprocal relationship because the narcissist feeds off the light and blessings of the believer and the vulture off the impending drama, humiliation and ostracization of the believer. These are additional hazards on the road to your higher calling—pitfalls that must be avoided. Yet, there are also signposts that should signal to you that you are on your way to higher ground, elevation, promotion and appointment if you remain connected to and led by the Holy Spirit.

AFTERWORD

I have been called to be a prophet. I am a recovering Jonah. I am most assuredly a prophetic scribe, a hearer and anointed. I have the ability to hear from the Lord and messengers from the Lord. The Lord speaks to me as He chooses and in ways He chooses, and many times it is through numbers. I am sometimes graced with the gift of sight, dream interpretation and prophecy. I now understand I am not only called, but I am qualified. I come from a matriarchal line of believers in Christ. My training includes attending parochial school from the third grade until my senior year in high school, the years I attended Brooklyn's Christian Cultural Center in Canarsie as a parishioner under the auspice of Pastor A.R. Bernard, the years I spent attending Marble Collegiate Church in New York City on Fifth Avenue (the church founded by Norman Vincent Peale, the author of the Power of Positive Thinking) as a parishioner under the auspice of Arthur Caliandro, and as a parishioner at the Word of Faith Family Cathedral in Austell, Georgia under the leadership of Bishop Dale C. Bronner. Whether you choose to agree or not, it is spiritual truth. You can try as you may to refute it, it is your right. But there is nothing you can do to change it. There is nothing I can do to change it for I have tried—to change it, avoid it and give it back (smh) yet my efforts have been futile. Unless and until Yeshua the Christ,

Afterword

Elohim Chayim, the Everlasting Father, the One and True living God of Israel changes it, it is so.

I would also like to state that as weird as it may sound, I do not believe my experience with having to confront my Goliath or severe witchcraft before walking into my anointing is uncommon for those who answer the call. It was a long, hard, drawn-out fight. Yet I believe it has met its end. As a matter of fact, I am certain that this past season—at least the warfare from it on the grand scale I experienced it on, is over. I believe I received my confirmation of its end just before closing this book. Upon walking outside of my home, in the midst of September, a yellow butterfly fluttered past me. I understand butterflies to symbolize transformation, and the color yellow in Christianity, according to Susan J Nelson, Christian Blogger, Author and Speaker, to symbolize "faith, the Glory of God," and "God's anointing." She further defines yellow as, "the glow or shining of something that is releasing energy." She adds, "The production of good works requires the release of energy [and that] the radiance of light production is represented by yellow. I do not know if you recall, but I stated in the introduction that upon looking up 747 in the online Hebrew Concordance, it was defined as "Beacon of Light." I am in no way stating that I am, but I believe this book will be just that for many.

I penned this book to be a roadmap for the Glory of God and for those who have been unable to clearly understand or accept their calling, position in the kingdom and identity in Christ with one hundred percent certainty. In recent years I have grown very accustomed and accepting of my choice to be meek, quietly humble and live in obscurity with extremely rare sightings. Yet I have been chosen in this season to write this book for a particular sect of believers. I have been chosen to instruct them of the Lord's edict to rise in their true identities and to activate their callings. This sect of believers to whom I have been sent are typically artists, musicians, writers and entrepreneurs, whether they are actively working in their giftings or not. However, the roadmap may serve any woman who is unclear of her identity in Christ. My hope is that my offering will be deemed acceptable to the Lord. I am no longer afforded the comfort of blending in the background in this season. My season of obscurity, unbeknownst to me was a season of separation for the purpose of preparation. Yet I have been called for such a time as this (Esther 4:14), and this book is a clarion call to the 747 woman, the 747 Elite, and it is just one sect of many that will rise in the seasons to come. Woman of God, Glory be to God as you have been called to a higher altitude!

Numbers 10:9
And if ye go to war in your land against the enemy that oppresseth you, then ye shall blow an alarm with the trumpets; and ye shall be remembered before the LORD your God, and ye shall be saved from your enemies.

Afterword

Isaiah 29:18-24

"And in that day shall the deaf hear the words of the book, and the eyes of the blind shall see out of obscurity, and out of darkness. The meek also shall increase their joy in the LORD, and the poor among men shall rejoice in the Holy One of Israel. For the terrible one is brought to nought, and the scorner is consumed, and all that watch for iniquity are cut off. That make a man an offender for a word, and lay a snare for him that reproveth in the gate, and turn aside the just for a thing of nought. Therefore thus saith the LORD, who redeemed Abraham, concerning the house of Jacob, Jacob shall not now be ashamed, neither shall his face now wax pale. But when he seeth his children, the work of mine hands, in the midst of him, they shall sanctify my name, and sanctify the Holy One of Jacob, and shall fear the God of Israel. They also that erred in spirit shall come to understanding, and they that murmured shall learn doctrine."

King James Version (KJV)

www.ingramcontent.com/pod-product-compliance
Lightning Source LLC
Chambersburg PA
CBHW071957070526
44583CB00015B/1226